DEVELOPMENT PROGRAMMES AND TRIBALS
Some Emerging Issues

DEVELOPMENT ROGRAMMES AND TRIBALS
Some Emerging Issues

Kakali Paul (Mitra)

Publications

KALPAZ PUBLICATIONS
Delhi-110052

Development Programmes and Tribals: Some Emerging Issues

Rs. 790

ISBN: 81-7835-306-7

Published in 2004 in India by
Kalpaz Publications,
C-30, Satyawati Nagar, Delhi-110052
E-mail : Kalpaz@hotmail.com

Laser Typesetting at : Shree Vaishnavi Creations, Delhi
Printed at : Mehra Offset Press, Delhi

To My Parents

Contents

List of Tables

Foreword

Dr. Kakali Paul's (Mitra) book, *Development Programmes and Tribals: Some Emerging Issues* is essentially an anthropological study of tribal transformations in modern India. Unlike most other studies of tribal transformation this book deals specifically with aspects of directed change among a group of tribal peoples. Dr. Paul elegantly discussed in her book the nature of change and development among them in both quantitative and qualitative terms.

The author reviewed the concept of 'tribe', discussed the statutory positions and privileges accorded to the various tribal groups in the Constitution of the decolonized new state of India and described the policies and programmes adopted from time to time for their development and integration to the mainstream of India's polity.

She selected four tribal groups living under one ITDP project area in West Bengal and made a critical evaluation of the impact of the development programmes on their life and society. She collected quantitative as well as qualitative information; she observed the beneficiaries' behaviour in their social and cultural contexts and asked about perceptions of their life and society. Her study reveals that despite some changes in the material aspects of their life most of the people seem to suffer from an ambivalence between individuality and collectivism, modernity and traditionalism. Although there is noticed, among some individuals, a growing sense of individual ownership and achievement orientation in the context of economic and political modernization the people do not seem to give up their traditional collective conscience. The author observes that the development programmes are mostly individual/family oriented but the tribal people, by tradition, are society-oriented. Individual households are socially and culturally tied to one another and there is a strong kinship bond among them. The people are afraid of losing individual positions in their traditional kin-based society in the context of our development programmes. They lack an appropriate arena for social and cultural communication in the larger society. The participation of the tribal peoples in the development programmes is thus more instrumental and intended for marginal material gain.

In the words of the author the people are 'consciously or unconsciously maintaining equilibrium between the tribal solidarity, morality and ultimately social obligations to the traditional society with the growing sense of ownership, privatization of modernization and a contradiction between them'.

The book I think, would be of much use to the students of anthropology and allied social sciences as well as those who are concerned with policy-making and development work for the tribal peoples in India.

Dr. Ashim Kumar Adhikary
Professor, Social Anthropology,
Former Head, Department of Social Studies and Rural Development;
And former Dean of the Institute of Rural Reconstruction,
Visva-Bharati, Sriniketan - 731236, West Bengal, India

Preface

The problems of tribals have attracted special attention of social reformers and political leaders since the attainment of independence of India. Therefore, planned efforts have been made and series of innovative plans, programmes, structure and institutions have been created with a view to bring about a desired change in the life of the tribal people. Tribal people constitute a different social group in view of their socio-cultural characteristics and varied geographical setting. The tribal people having their own spirit, world view and community feeling sometimes confused with the planned approaches of development programmes. Generally they are found to participate in the development programmes, avail the opportunities gladly but if they feel that the programme is going against the spirit of their society, it hurts their conscience and solidarity; they refuse to participate in the programme wholeheartedly. Tribal people are very much conscious about their group solidarity and always try to maintain it. They have their own perception about the programmes, about their own society and even some aspiration regarding their own development. In fact, ethics has a greater role to play for such a tradition bound society which is culturally and ideologically different from others. Planning a project for the tribals which involves directly some cultural changes; the planners have to find out what the normal and local channels of influence and infiltration are in population. It is extremely valuable when deciding how to introduce a programme of change for the tribals. Mystery of success of any programme for planned change is entrusted largely on whether the targeted population wants and likes to adopt the proposed programmes and to what extent the targeted population is aware or prepares to accept the benefits of the proposed change.

The present volume is the outcome of my Ph.D thesis submitted to Visva Bharati in the year 2000. The work was carried out by me after getting the award of Research Fellow from Ministry of Tribal Development, Govt. of India in the year 1995.

The present volume tries to give a thorough review of the history of administrative measures of Indian Constitution and series of plans and programmes through Five Year Plans for tribal development. Then it intended to depict with empirical evidences to what extent tribal development get its success and what is its nature. Do the tribals feel themselves integrated with the mainstream or still they are at the receiving end and nothing but the object of development. It also tries to make an endeavour to identify the emerging issues for further development from their own point of view and apprehension regarding the plans and programmes. Finally, an attempt has been made to illuminate the disparity between the proposed programme and the real need and perception of the tribal themselves.

It is really a great pleasure to me that I avail the opportunity to express my deep sense of gratitude to my esteemed teacher Prof. Ashim Kumar Adhikary, Department of Social Studies and Rural Development (Palli Charcha Kendra), Visva-Bharati. His constant guidance and encouragement have steered this work to completion.

I am grateful to the Ministry of Welfare (Tribal Welfare Division), Govt. of India. This work is made possible by their financial support. They provided the financial assistance in the form of a Doctoral Fellowship through the Cultural Research Institute, Backward Classes Welfare Department, Government of West Bengal. I express my deep sense of gratitude to Dr. M.K. Choudhury, Director, Cultural Research Institute, Backward Classes Welfare Department, Government of West Bengal from whom I have got valuable suggestions and encouragement through the entire study period.

Though it may be considered too formal yet it would be a great omission if I fail to express my deep sense of gratitude to my husband Dr. Sujit Kumar Paul. Without his constant inspiration, guidance and encouragement, successful completion of the work cannot be possible.

KAKALI PAUL (MITRA)

1
Introduction

The English term 'tribe' came from the Latin 'tribus', Umbrican 'trifu' or the equivalent Greek 'phule', linguistic terms designating Indo-European Institutions of great antiquity. From the outset these concepts were empirical ones and as a result, have taken on different meanings in the course of these peoples' history; in their most ancient form, however, they designated a particular kind of social and political organization existing in all these societies, before the appearance of the city state.

Anthropologists used the term 'tribe' to refer to two distinct, yet related realities, fields of facts – one, a 'type of society' and the other, a 'stage of evolution' (Godelier, 1977: 70). Almost everyone uses the term to distinguish a type of society from others, one specific mode of social organization from other modes of organization in society–'bands', 'states' etc. According to evolutionists' viewpoint, each stage of evolution is characterized by a specific mode of social organization and they use the term 'tribe' as a stage of evolution. Initially, Indian Anthropologists looked at the tribal people as an archaic base of development of Indian civilization; later on, they are found to show more interests in the nature and type of their society in relation to the caste-based Hindu society in India. The 'tribe' is, therefore, found to refer to a group of people who are characterized by a series of social and cultural features distinct from those of the caste society.

In India when the British gained control over the country they discovered that the people of this subcontinent lived mainly in numerous self-regulating villages, where various endogamous *Jati* (caste) groups lived pursuing their hereditary occupations. They observed that these *Jatis* were arranged in a rigid system of birth-ascribed status hierarchy with an ideal *Varna* order on the basis of ritual purity and pollution. Early British administrator-scholars also discovered that certain human groups remained outside this Brahmanic *Varna-Jati* hierarchy. They lived in hills and forests, or in the plains skirting the forests, in relative isolation from the caste-based peasant villages, as unstratified endogamous groups. Even when cultivating land with ploughs, they did some hunting and gathering of wild products of the forest. Many of them also practised slash and burn form of primitive farming and a few lived substantially on hunting and gathering. These essentially pre-literate groups, which were apparently outside the threshold of the Brahmanic hierarchic civilization, were labeled as 'tribes' by the British administrator-scholars in the analogy of similar groups they encountered in aboriginal America, Africa and Oceania. Gradually, tribes came to be recognized as a same category for the purpose of Census and administration in India. After independence, the Government of India has also accepted the term 'tribe' and used it for all administrative purposes.

The tribal people of India are differently termed as *Adivasi* (indigenous peoples), *Vanavasi* (forest dwellers), *Pahari* (hill dwellers), *Adimjati* (original communities), *Janajati* (folk people) and the like. It is significant that each of the terms either denotes their ecological, economic, historical or cultural characteristics. Of all these terms the most popular one is *Adivasi*, which connotate their aboriginality or indigenousness while the Constitutional term for them is *Anushuchi Janajati*, the scheduled tribe peoples (Vidyarthi, Rai, 1985). As many as 67, 758, 380 persons was enumerated in 1991 Census as scheduled tribe constituting 8.0 per cent of the total population of the country.

State and Union Territory-wise lists of Scheduled Tribe

peoples were in the first instance, notified by the President of India in 1950. Any amendment or modification of the notification is to be made by an Act of the Parliament. It is however, difficult to tell the exact number of scheduled tribe peoples simply from the lists. As the ethnic boundaries of various communities are not rigidly fixed and as they are constantly subjected to the processes of fission and fusion, it is left to ethnographers' judgment whether some of the names occurring in the lists of STs are to be treated as distinct entities or as synonymous to sub-castes/sub-tribes of the same or a different category. As a result the estimated number of Scheduled Tribes in India is varying from 250 to 593.

The tribal communities are distributed in most of the states of India. Three tribal zones were demarcated by Guha (1951, 1955). Dube (1960), has identified four geographical zones of the tribals, viz. the North and North-Eastern Zone, the Middle Zone, the South Zone and the West Zone. Atal (1965) too made a fourfold geographical classification of the tribes, viz. North and North-Eastern, West and North-Western, Middle and South Zone. Roy Burman (1971), has divided the tribal communities living in different regions into five territorial groups, taking into consideration of their historical, ethnic and socio-cultural saliences. These are; North-east India, Sub-Himalayan region of North and North-West India, Central and East India, South India and Western India. Taking into account of these classifications as well as ecological, social, economic, administrative, ethnic and racial factors Vidyarthi (1976) has classified into six regions; North-Eastern region, Himalayan region, Central India region, Western India region, Southern India region and Island region.

Indian tribals also may be classified in terms of their language, race, levels of integration and also in terms of their subsistence technology and economy. Vidyarthi (1966), further made an attempt to classify the tribal people in terms of their culture. He classified the tribal people into six culture types – (i) Forest hunting type, (ii) Primitive hill cultivation type, (iii) Plain agriculture type, (iv) The simple artisan type, (v) The pastoral and cattle-breeder type, and (vi) Urban industrial type. He considered five factors to identify these culture types. These are – their economy, their ecology, socio-cultural adaptation of the tribes to ecology and the economy, the religious beliefs, and emerging contemporary situation, influx of other groups of people.

The socio-economic and cultural life of the tribal groups of India varies from tribe to tribe and region to region. They belong to various ethnic stocks, have distinct pattern of economy, technology, and religious behaviour and speak a large number of languages and dialects. Though there is diversity in 'life style' and 'mode of life' of these communities, but there exists a good deal of similarity in their socio-cultural and psychological level. Till today the tribes are more or less trying to retain their separate social identity, customs and regulations. As a whole however, they can be regarded as comparatively isolated and backward.

Tribal Situation in Pre-British, Pre-Modern India

Tribals form an integral part of Indian civilization. The tribals contributed various elements in ancient civilization of India. It is believed that they were the earliest and original inhabitants of the country. In the ancient literature of India they are often referred to as *Nishadas, Savaras, Bhills* and *Kollas, Kiratas, Dasas, Dasyus, Sudras, Dramidas* and *Dravidas*. When the Aryan immigrants entered the country they called these non-Aryan people as *Dasyus* to denote the people other than themselves, i.e. the Aryans. The names of a number of *Dasyu* warriors and their Aryan opponents have been preserved in the *Rig-Veda.* The Dasyus of Vedic antiquity, the non-Aryans are mainly of two stocks, viz. the Kolarians and the Dravidians (Ragozin, 1961:287). The Mundas and the Santals of today are considered to be the descendents of the non-Aryan Kolarian stock. The major representatives of Dravidian tribes are the Gondhs and the Kondhs. The ancient Sanskrit work suggests that the

Mundas and other cognate tribes occupied northern India before the forefather of Aryan Hindus entered the country. There is, however, a suggestion in *Manu Sanhitas* (X4) that the tribes, which by loss of sacred rites become outcastes from the people of the recognized castes and sub-castes are the *Dasyus*.

The *Ramayana* also tells us about some tribal people. It assigned only two groups of people - the Aryans and the non-Aryans. Among the non-Aryans the most important groups were the Rakshas and the Vanaras, both being the aboriginal tribes of Deccan. The other tribes were the Nishadas, the Grdhrajs, the Savaras, the Yaksas and the Nagas (Vyas, 1967:24). The Rakshas are regarded by Vyas (1967:43) as the earliest inhabitants of southern India and Srilanka. Racially, they are perhaps identical of the Dasyus of *Rig-Veda*.

The *Mahabharata* also mentions a few tribes. In the accounts of the Great War in the epic Sanjay mentions the Mundas as one of the constituents of the allied army of the Kourava. The comparison of the Mundas to the Danavas in the Mahabharata (Drono Parva, 117,23) would seem to indicate that the reference was to an aboriginal people of the name of Mundas.

In the context of aboriginality of the Indian tribes different authorities have expressed different views. Elwin (1939)', called the Baigas "the original owners of the country" they inhabit. Thakkar Bapa (1941), considers the tribals to be the 'Adipraja', i.e., aboriginals of the country and the sons of Bharatbhumi, older than the Hindus. Ghurey (1963:12), opines that it is possible to contend that even if the tribes are not aboriginals of the exact area they now occupy, they are the autochthons of India and to that extent they may be called the aboriginal. However, the tribals fall in the line of ancestry of the Indian people and are a constituent of the admixture of Indian population.

In the early historical period of India, which coincides, with the Hindu period, the tribals either compromised with the Hindu neighbour or went further in the deep forest. All through the long centuries of Hindu rule the tribals find themselves assimilated into the neighbouring Hindu culture. Ghurey (1963:18), has discussed the matter in detail, and opines that "almost all the so-called aboriginal tribes of the region have a Hinduised section, small or large, that they have been in fairly intimate contact with the Hindus for a long time, and that they have common interest with the Hindus in matter of religion and gainful occupation". He also opines that they have shown a tendency to look upon themselves as Hindus or as people closely connected with the Hindus. For the section of tribals who have remained in the isolated mountain he (Ghurey, 1963:19), states that only very small section in the recesses of hills and the depths of forests, has not been more than touched by Hinduism and have retained much more tribal creeds and organisation than many of the Hindu society, yet they are in reality Backward Hindus. The observations of Bradley Birt (1903), Baine (1891), Risley (1901), O'Malley (1911), Shoobert (1931), and Elwin (1952), also suggest the assimilation of the tribals with the Hindu culture. It indicates that during the Hindu period of Indian history the tribal people had more or less good relations with Hindu neighbours and in the course of their interaction with the Hindu neighbours they emulated many socio-cultural elements of the Hindus.

During the long Hindu period there was, however, no assertive or stated policy for the tribal people, but they had more or less good mutual relations. It resulted in a slow but spontaneous tribal absorption into the major Hindu tradition. The tribals, however, seemed to have enjoyed autonomy and free life of their own.

The tribals enjoyed this autonomy until the beginning of the Medieval period. By the end of the 16th century the Mohammedan rulers harassed them in different way and gradually they lost their status. In this period various types of rent and cesses were imposed on the tribals, which was in cash and also in kind. The system of service - *jagir* grants was also introduced in this period. And this was the beginning of the agrarian troubles among the tribals. In some regions the tribal peoples felt disturbed due to large-scale conversion of the tribals to Islam. They were also attempted to rule the tribals. Sometimes under the oppressive rule of numerous Mohammedan chiefs and rebellions made them restless. In this way during the medieval period, the tribal people inhabiting different parts of India were again and again either disturbed by the then Mahammedan rulers or the regional rulers or by both.

Tribal Situation in British Period

During the British period the tribals had to face many conflicting situations as a good many neo-settlers like non-tribal moneylenders, usurers etc. gradually came in, and tried to exploit them in various ways. The forest contractors began to carry away a part of the forest produce. The land settlement policy of the Britishers affected the land tenure system of tribal peoples. Ultimately these led to a number of disturbances and uprisings. These were started in 1772 by the Malpaharias and there followed a series of disturbances in 1795, 1800, 1801, 1807, 1808, 1816, 1821, and the Chour or Paik rebellion in Bengal between 1787 and 1830. In 1831-1832 followed the great Kole Rising. After 1833 when regulation XIII was passed the rising was suppressed. Chhotanagpur was declared a non-regulating area. This was the beginning of the isolation policy of British Government. The Khond rising in 1846, the Santal rebellion in 1854, the unrest in Dhanbad in 1869-70, etc. extended the non-regulating system.

In 1874 the Scheduled District Act was passed under which the Executive was given wide powers. Still a few risings like Sardari Agitation in 1887, Birsha movement in 1895, Tana Bhagat movement in 1914 etc. were held. By then the tribals started taking part in the National Freedom Movement.

The tribals in different regions and pockets of the country were not satisfied with the rulers. Actually the

British rulers were then more interested to protect themselves rather than to protect the tribal. Hence, the policies, which were adopted by the British rulers, were to isolate the people from the general mass and separate the tribal areas, which as a result, tribals remained cut off from the rest of the population. A few roads that were constructed were for security purposes and to enable the contractors to exploit forest produce. A very small number of people were allowed in these isolated areas. They are some contractors, Government officials and a few businessmen. They grouped together and started business on their own terms. They interpreted the rules in their own way and their terms of business swept in purchase and sale of the goods and thus exploitation of an extreme degree pervaded.

In fact the area-wise isolation began with the enactment of the Government of India Act 1870 and a few tracts were specified as "Scheduled Tracts" viz. the Himalayan region, the then Assam, Darjeeling, Kumaon, and Garwal, the then Tarai Parganas, Jaunsar-Bawar, Lahaul, etc.

In 1874 the Scheduled District Act gave effect to the Government of India Act 1870. A number of Acts were enforced from time to time till 1919 when certain territories were declared Backward Tracts under the Government of India Act 1919. The areas were more or less the same as those of "scheduled tracts" and "scheduled districts" with certain additions and omissions. Actually the British Government was eager enough to show that something had been done to help the tribals through special administration in the areas concerned.

Again in 1936, the British declared some areas 'excluded' and some as 'partially excluded' under section 91 and 92 of the Government of India Act, 1935. The main features to distinguish an 'Excluded' area from 'Partially Excluded' area were : (i) the Governor functioned in his own discretion in an "excluded area" whereas he sought advice of the Ministers in a "partially excluded area"; (ii) the expenditure in regard to the former was non-votable while the demands in the later case were subject to vote of the legislature; (iii) the discussion of any matter regarding the excluded areas needed prior consent of the Governor. In 1939, Elwin advocated (1939:511-519) for the "establishment of a sort of National Park" of the tribals and advised that their contact with the outside world should be reduced to the minimum.

Thus, the British rulers approached the tribal people of India in quite a different way. The stated policies of the British government were for isolating the tribal people from the mainstream of the national life and consequently to grow a sense of separatism among them.

Other than administrative level, tribal people of India faced another encroachment in the form of conversion to Christianity by the Missionaries who accompanied the British rulers in the name of serving the tribals. And the means they applied are social service, education and medical aid. This helped the tribals but created factions among them in different regions who were now divided into two sections, i.e., traditional tribals and Christian tribals. In the north-eastern India the major portion of the tribal population was converted to Christianity. The conversion as well as Excluded Area Policy gave rise to a sense of separatism in the minds of the tribals of that region.

Tribal Situation in Post Independent Period

India got independence in the year 1947. The base of the Indian culture, i.e., "Unity in diversity" once again got its due importance. The social reformers, politicians, and the administrators were well known about the vast socio-economic gaps between the tribal groups on the one hand and rest of the Indian mass on the other. From the past experiences the administrators also realized that the solution to the problem of backward area and people lay into integration not in isolation. No doubt the policy and approach towards the tribals after independence was influenced by Pandit Nehru to a great extent. He strongly believed in the co-existence of numerous diverse cultures and thus felt that the tribal groups can become a part of integrated India like the non-tribal groups, who in spite of maintaining their distinct cultural identities are an integral part of Indian Nation. The approaches to the tribal problems and development, as conceived by Nehru, are clearly stated in his Foreward to Elwin's Philosophy of NEFA (2nd Ed.), which really formed the basis of the national policy towards tribal development (1959). He stated five fundamental principles, which are popularly known as "Panchsheel". The principles are :

(i) People should develop along the lines of their own genius and we should avoid imposing anything on them. We should try to encourage in every way their own traditional arts and culture.

(ii) Tribal rights to lands and forests should be respected.

(iii) We should try to train and build up a team of their own people to do the work of the administration and development. Some technical personnel from outside will no doubt, be needed, especially in the beginning. But we should avoid introducing too many outsiders into tribal territory.

(iv) We should not over-administer these areas or overwhelm them with a multiplicity of schemes. We should rather work through, and not in rivalry to their own socio-cultural institutions.

(v) We should judge results, not by statistics or the amount of money spent but by the quality of human character that evolved.

However, the strong desireness of the national leaders of India to help and uplift the tribals is reflected in the Constitution where tribals were given special care.

Constitution of India and the Tribals

The main objective of Indian Constitution regarding the tribal folk is not to disrupt the harmony of tribal life but to work for its advancement, not to impose anything on them but to work for their integration in the national democratic set up. In the new federal structure of Independent India, a special place was assigned to the tribal areas. The founding fathers of the nation appreciated their unique socio-economic situation which was simple and which may require a complete different dispensation during the period of transition.

Tribal development or administration of tribal areas was not formally assigned to the provisions made in the Constitution. But these areas were brought under two schedules (Fifth and Sixth), for which special provisions were made. The "excluded" areas were put under the Sixth Schedule. The "partially excluded" areas and some of the tribal area in the erstwhile Indian States were included in the Fifth Schedule. The Governor has been given almost unlimited power in the Fifth Schedule to make Regulations for the scheduled areas. This regulation can negate or modify any law passed by Parliament or State Legislature in its application to the entire Fifth Schedule area or a part thereof. Special regulations can also be made for these areas under the same provision. Under the Fifth Schedule the Constitution also provides for establishment of a Tribes Advisory Council who are consulted by the Governor in relation to his regulation-making power. It shall be the duty of Tribes Advisory Council to advise on such matter pertaining to the welfare and advancement of the Schduled Tribes in the State as may be referred to them by the Governor.

A number of articles of the Indian Constitution contain many provisions for the protection and welfare of the tribal population. The prohibition of the discrimination on grounds of religion, race, caste, sex, or place of birth (Article 15), equality of opportunity in matters of public employment (Article 16), abolition of untouchability (Article 17), prohibition of traffic in human beings and forced labour (Article 23), securing a social order for the promotion of welfare of the people (Article 38) and protection of interest of minorities (Article 29) are of general in nature. There are so many articles in the Constitution those are directly related to the tribal safeguards. Article 46 of the Constitution enjoined upon the State to promote with special care the educational and economic interest of the tribals to protect them from social injustice and all forms of exploitation. Another special provision was offered in Article 164, which makes it obligatory to appoint a Minister-in-charge of tribal welfare in the States of Bihar, Madhya Pradesh and Orissa. These three States are having the largest number of tribal population in our union followed by Maharashtra and Rajasthan respectively. Article 244 makes applicable the provisions of the Fifth Schedule to the administration and control of the Scheduled Areas and Scheduled Tribes in any State specified in Part A and Part B of the Fifth Schedule, other than the State of Assam. It also mentions that the provisions of the Sixth Schedule shall apply to the administration of the tribal areas in the State of Assam.

However, in the early period of independence, Government of India also adopted the policy of isolation but in a slightly modified form. The declaration of India Government a few particular areas of tribal concentration as "Scheduled Area" and "Tribal Area" is an example of isolation. The governmental machinery remains confined to the scheduled area. The tribal people outside the scheduled areas were not duly protected.

The origin of the term "Scheduled Tribe" itself is the result of our Constitution coming into force on January 26, 1950. However, the first serious attempt to list these communities as primitive tribes was made during the Census 1931. In the Government of India Act (1935) a reference was made to "Backward Tribes" and again the Thirteenth Schedule to the Government of India (Provincial Legislative Assembly) Order, 1936 specified certain tribes as backward in the then Provinces of Assam, Bihar, Orissa, Central Provinces, Barar, Madras and Bombay. In the 1941 Census these people were recorded as "Tribes" and separate totals were furnished for a few selected individual tribes.

Here, again the old British concept of "excluded area" was applied in a modified form where the ethnic groups were the basis rather than the area. The Constitutional safeguards and the inclusion of the tribes in the Fifth Schedule created again a Constitutional gap between general population and the tribal population.

Article 275(1) ensures grants of financial assistance to States for implementations of schemes for promoting the welfare of the Scheduled Tribes or raising the level of administration in the Scheduled areas to that of the administration of the rest of the areas in a State.

Article 330/331 of the Constitution makes special provision for reservation of seats for Scheduled Castes, Scheduled Tribes in the Lok Sabha and Legislative Assemblies of the States, except the Scheduled Tribes in the tribal areas of Assam and in the Autonomous District of Assam.

Article 335 seeks reservation of posts in public services of the Union and States for the Scheduled Caste/Scheduled Tribe population but this must be consistent with the maintenance of efficiency of administration.

Both the above Articles were initially meant for 10 years since the commencement of the Constitution but the provision has been amended after every 10 years extending the period of 10 years.

Article 338 provides special provision for the appointment of a special officer for the Scheduled Castes and Scheduled Tribes with view to ensuring the supervision and control of the Union Government. Article also specifies his duties as to investigate all matters relating to the safeguards provided to them. The President of India appoints this officer, who submits his reports before both Houses of Parliament. The Commission for Scheduled Castes and Scheduled Tribes has been functioning as per the provision of this Article and his scope includes States as well as Union Territories.

Article 339 outlines the control of the Union over the administration of the Scheduled Areas and welfare of Scheduled Tribes. Under the provisions of this Article President may appoint any time and shall at the expiration of 10 years from the commencement of this Constitution a commission to report on the administration of the Scheduled Areas and welfare of the Scheduled Tribes. A National Commission for Scheduled Castes and Scheduled Tribes has since been appointed. This Article also empowered the Union to give directions to any State in regard to drawing up and execution of schemes specified in the direction and essential for the welfare of the Scheduled Tribes in the State.

Thus, the Constitution enjoyed special responsibility on the Central Government as a whole and State Government in particular to make earnest endeavour for the development of the Scheduled Tribes and the areas inhabited by them. To sustain all the Constitutional safeguards Central Government and State Government launched various Plans and Programmes through the Departments specially set up for the purpose and different Ministries and agencies.

Five Year Plan Periods and the Tribal Development Programmes

The First Five Year Plan was started in 1951. Development Programme was started in 1952 as a Community Development Programme and 56 Community Development Projects were started. Various programmes were initiated with particular reference to health, communication and housing. The programme was very comprehensive and the concept was equally applicable to the tribal areas with rest of the country but very soon the government realized that the task to be accomplished in the tribal areas was much more difficult. As most of these areas comprise hilly and forest regions and sparsely populated with poor communication and little institutional infrastructure. Therefore, it was decided to supplement the Community Development Programme and accordingly 43

Special Multipurpose Tribal Development (TD) Blocks were started during 1954. Special emphasis was given to education in addition to health, agriculture, communication and housing programmes.

In the Third Plan (1961-66) the TD blocks numbered 458 and the coverage of population was 32.50 per cent. The major emphasis was given on economic development along with education, health, housing and communication. At the end of Third Plan it was reviewed and revealed that the programme did not have the desired impact. Therefore, it was decided to add a third phase of five years to Blocks and desist from establishing new ones. The Tribal Development Blocks covered all the areas having more than two-third tribal population. However, exceptions were made in case of West Bengal and Karnataka where TD blocks were not feasible due to their dispersed nature of tribal population.

Isolated tribal populations of Karnataka were covered by the adhoc tribal development projects and in case of West Bengal, TD blocks were established temporarily for two years in each area having sizable tribal population. The coverage of tribal population in these two States was lean. By the end of Fourth Five Year Plan (1969-74) 39.37 per cent of the total tribal population were covered in 504 Tribal Development Blocks. On the whole, the areas with more than two-third tribal population got the benefits of this development effort. Upto the end of Fourth Five Year Plan the remaining tribal population were derived benefits from the general development programme.

A series of programmes were introduced during the Fourth Plan period. Special attention was directed to individual families in addition to area based programmes. These programmes were: The Small Farmers Development Agencies (SFDA), Marginal Farmers Development Agencies, and Drought Prone Area Programme (DPAP). In the wake of establishment of these area specific and weaker group oriented projects, the programmes for tribal area were also intensified on a plot basis. Tribal Development Agencies

(TDAs) were established on the pattern of SFDA. Six TDAs were started during Fourth Plan and two more were added in the Fifth Plan. The purpose behind setting up of these agencies was for massive investment exclusively for tribal folk from central funds while making state outlays for development of both tribals and non-tribals.

For making the tribal development programme more effective and meaningful these were reviewed by special committees and commissions from time to time. Their experiences and insights enabled the planners and policy-makers to think in terms of formulating an integrated tribal development strategy with requisite intimate linkages with the national strategy of socio-economic development. A new phase of tribal development started since Fifth Five Year Plan and may be considered as a turning point in the history of tribal development. During this plan period the concept of Tribal Sub Plan (TSP) within the broad frame of State and Central Plan took concrete shape. The Fifth and Sixth Five year Plan periods are also remarkable as it was the first time when the anthropologists, development administrators and policy-makers joined together to review the earlier policies and programmes and devised way for launching the new one for the welfare of the tribals specifically.

Briefly, the concept consists of identification of development blocks within a State having more than 50 per cent tribal population launching of massive effort for tribal development in such areas called the Sub-Plan area. For the preparation of Tribal Sub-Plan the Planning Commission issued a set of guidelines to the States. The guidelines spelt out the long-term objectives of the Tribal Sub-Plan as :-

1. Narrowing the gap between the levels of development of tribals and other areas.
2. Speeding up the processes for social and economic development.
3. Building up the inner strength of the people.

4. Improving their organizational capabilities.

Thus, the guideline laid down the criteria for identification of the sub-plan areas, the approach and strategy for development and also the pattern of funding and formulation of programme in these areas. The guidelines also stated that the sub-plan areas in each State should comprise a number of viable projects. Such unit of planning is an Integrated Tribal Development Project (ITDP) in a State, comprising an aggregate of Development Blocks. The ITDP is being smaller than a district and bigger than a development Block. The lowest unit of performance of the programme is the Development Block. It has a development team with the Block Development Officer as its leader. Programmes have to be planned for an ITDP in the shape of a sub-plan for the tribal region of the State. Guidelines laid down that the planning should be based on the needs of the area and the people, and, hence, the process has to be commenced at the grass-root level, i.e., the Development Block and funneled upwards to the ITDP, State and National level.

There are altogether 191 ITDP areas spread over the country in 16 States and 2 Union Territories. Out of these, 33 are located in West Bengal and these are spread over 12 districts. These ITDP areas curbed out with a cluster of adjoining villages and in each village the proportion of tribal population appeared with 50 per cent or more. The twelve districts of ITDP areas of West Bengal are spread over north to south and east to west of the State. Considering the salient geographical characteristics these districts may brought under the certain distinct zones. The northern most zones represented by Darjeeling and Jalpaiguri districts fall in sub-Himalayan region. In this zone in all 5 ITDP areas are included. The immediate southern districts of West Dinajpur and Malda are within upper Gangetic Plain and form separate ecological zone. In these two districts there are 5 ITDP areas. Three other districts namely Birbhum, Burdwan and Midnapore fall under ecological zone of West Bengal plain. Altogether 11 ITDP areas are covered in these three districts. The two more districts of Bankura and Purulia come under the plateau region characterised by arid and dry zone. There are 9 ITDP areas (Bankura-3 and Purulia-6) in these districts. The remaining three districts of Murshidabad, Hoogly and 24 Parganas are in the lower Gangetic valley. Only three ITDP areas are identified in these three districts (Murshidabad -1, Hoogly-1, 24 Parganas - 1).

Problems and Approaches to Tribal Integration

Since Pre-British period the tribals are spontaneously absorbed and assimilated with larger Hindu tradition. During British period tribals have to face some assertive and stated policies and approached in quite a different way. Isolated tribals were becoming more isolated from the mainstream of national life and their sense of separatism was rising high. After independence the great desireness of the administrators and social reformers to integrate the tribals into mainstream is reflected in the Constitution, and then through the stated policies, plans and programmes during the Five Year Plans. The problem of the tribal is recognized in the Constitution which promises to promote the tribals and makes provisions for protecting them from social injustice and all forms of exploitation. But it is becoming debatable whether all the measures in operation and desireness of directed changes to integrate the tribal people with the mainstream have helped, solve or rather aggravated the problem. In this context a precise but adequate appraisals of few works of different scholars would be relevant and give us some new dimensions regarding the problems of the tribals in the Indian context.

Mathur (1972), thinks that are the 'tribal' people in India ethnically and culturally distinct from the rest of the population so as to deserve a distinct social category or is the gap between them and us a merely political gulf, which was created by the Imperial colonial power and which has widened in recent years after 1947? If they are found ethnically and culturally distinct from their non-tribal neighbours, their demands for distinctive treatment and even autonomy could be valid and would have to be sympathetically endorsed by the anthropologists.

Verrier Elwin (1942), makes a three-fold categorization of the tribal peoples of India. The first group consists of the tribal landlord and noble-man, the second group of Hinduized segments of the aborigines, the third group being formed by those tribe who keep up a vigorous tribal life in remote areas of forest and on the height of hills. The Hinduized aborigines according to Elwin 'suffer from a sense of frustration and dismay, a certain loss of nerve'. Elwin very emphatically made the point that the opening of tribal areas to the non-tribal outsiders had destroyed tribal religion, art and organisation. He observes that the tribals belonging to the third group living in forests and hill slopes did not experience any loss of nerve; they also maintain cultural identity and social solidarity. He believes that the tribal areas needed to be protected and suggests for an isolation of tribal peoples in certain extreme cases.

As a Chairman of the Committee on Special Multipurpose Tribal Block Elwin (1960), recommends the development of the people on the lines of their own tradition and genius. He opined that it is essential to make it absolutely clear that "we have no interest in any kind of artificial preservation of tribal customs or way of living, where they are good we should encourage them, where they are less good we should try carefully to help the people to develop from within into something better. We should recognise and honour their way of doing things not because it is old and picturesque but because it is theirs, and they have much right to their own culture and religion as any one else in India".

Ghurye is not worried if in the process of social change the tribals get, to an extent deprived of their pristine homogeneity and unity. He observes that so called aborigines in India share the culture and language of the non-aboriginal Hindu rural communities of the respective regions they live in. This view was also shared and supported by Majumdar (1950) and Aiyappan (1960). This implies a spontaneous integration of the people in the regional context.

Based on his observation on the process of structural formation of Hindu Society Nirmal Kumar Bose (1929), noted that the numerous tribal groups of the land, among other ethnic groups, were absorbed slowly into the techno-economic fold of the local Hindu polities. These tribal groups, though operated within the broader framework of the agrarian economic structure of the Hindu caste-peasants in the villages were able to maintain their cultural autonomy. What Bose was trying to note is that the tribal peoples chose by themselves the superior agrarian technology of the Hindu caste society without any political and administrative intervention from the Hindus.

Desai (1977), views the tribal problem essentially as an economic-political one. In respect of Hindus or other non-tribal sections of society, Desai stands for natural justice, without raising the issue of relativity of moral and starvation. The tribal problem should be approached keeping in view the fundamental issue of the establishment of a social order founded on equality of opportunities and the elimination of exploitation.

D.N. Majumdar (1950), views the problem of tribal integration in the context of the local needs of the tribals. There is no one solution to tribal problems, there is no one common platform to demand it. There are levels of cultural development and there are different patterns of life that the tribes own. In fact, the tribal problem has to be viewed in the light of its historical and social background. In various parts of India, changing economic environment has forced tribal and backward people to new moorings. The problems of tribal people, therefore, need to be viewed in the light of the tribal dynamics.

Christoph von Furer-Haimendorf (1960), does not consider the tribal distinctive way of life as special feature in the process of tribal integration. To him the tribal problems are springless from the existence of different styles of living and social patterns as such, than from a tendency on the part of India's economically and politically dominant population to impose their own curb of behaviour on the tribal neighbours.

Bailey's (1960), approach to tribal problem being structural in nature rests largely on the incorporation of the tribal people into the caste system. He envisages a situation in which a tribe integrates into a caste and the castes in the long run into the nation. In this process Bailey is hopeful that like the Konds of Orissa the tribals in general would retain their identity and maintain their independent economic status. For Bailey the tribal problem is essentially an economic and political problem. A region is bestowed with natural resources. All the groups compete for allocation of scare resources. Control over resources, which are of economic nature, depends on the political alignments made by different groups.

To Zaheer (1975), the proposition of Fifth Five Year Plan assumes two postulates; (i) the present quality of life of the tribal community is not satisfactory (ii) that the quality of our lives or that of those who are non-tribals is much more satisfactory. Therefore, he says that the planners, are in position to judge and also lay the standards of the improvements needed. He asks if any tribal considers the quality of his life inferior to that of his non-tribal neighbour. Is any tribal anywhere in India ever willing to accept this proposition? While a tribal can become a non-tribal the converse is not true. Similarly, the custodians and governors of tribals also assume that the tribal situation is a static one and not changing. Zaheer said, it is only a one way traffic.

S. Mahalingam (1988), has agreed with Zaheer. He thought, the problem of tribal development has reached critical stage and has assumed an added significance in the context of high priority accorded to social justice in the new planning effort. Therefore, to take a fresh look at the tribal situation in the hill tracts, review the strategy of development and define the total needed national effort with a view to making tribal communities equal partners in all sphere of national life.

In Indian context, B.D. Sharma (1992), considers the problem of tribal people as a sub-national issue and therefore should be tackled in the specific context of these groups. Sharma desires that the State to refrain from initiating and or supporting the entry of alien items into the tribal cultural milieu may, directly or indirectly, have the potential of becoming culturally catastrophic. Spontaneous change, however, is to be accepted; and change need to be initiated by numerous factors including education; and the people are to be allowed to conduct their affairs.

L.M. Prasad (1995), believes that ethics has greater role to play in Tribal Administration than in any other administration. This is because of the fact that tribals constitute a different social group in view of their socio-cultural characteristics and geographical setting. Evidently one has to be very careful in passing judgement on ethical behaviour in a society, which may be culturally, economically and ideologically different from others. Administrators should be aware of the general ethical standards of the different tribal groups.

Prescribing ethics for the public services of Papua New Guinea, Dwivedi (1981), suggests that the aim should be to illuminate the ethical situation of public administrators – rather than to prescribe a particular set up of public service values.

Though development is popularly regarded as an economic process, Belshaw (1972), believes that equal emphasis should be placed on the qualitative aspects of the human development. Development should be looked upon as an organized activity with the aim of satisfying certain basic needs and to psychologically orient the tribal to adopt new skills, attitudes, and life styles. From this point of view, Schneider, 1975, believes that development is a multi-dimensional process to progressively improve in social, cultural, economic, and human conditions of the people. Due emphasis should be paid to establish a meaningful link between the local and national levels of development and of the world at large.

Sanders (1958), envisages tribal development as a movement emphasising upon building up organizational structures, a programme emphasising on activities, a method emphasising certain achievable ends, a process emphasising upon what happens to people not only and economically and socially but also psychologically, and institutionalization of newly discovered skills and procedures leading to social change without completely breaking away from the past.

"The modernizer cannot compel but must persuade : to do this he must know what values the people already hold; how they see the world and society around them; in short he must know their cognitive maps. In this situation knowledge is a substitute for – one might say a kind of – power; with an adequate map – and adequate understanding of the traditional way of life - the modernizer can most economically and most effectively deploy his limited resources" (F.G. Bailey, 1966).

On another occasion, Bailey hopes to make similar analysis of the cognitive maps of the elite themselves: of politicians, administrators, merchants, entrepreneurs, students and (one might add) city mobs.

Bailey also believes that, both the uncertainty of peasant life and the fact that they explain failure by blaming people rather than by supporting a miscalculation or impersonal forces means that policy-making and planning are not part of their cognitive map of the world and human society. They do not reject the idea of planning as wicked; they simply do not have the category.

According to Prabhu Pradip (1993), sustainable tribal development must be based on self-determination and ethno-development within the framework of provisions in the Sixth Schedule of our Constitution. He thinks that it is high time to acknowledge that traditional tribal cultures and knowledge systems have much to offer to our imperilled planet and hence self-determination and ethno-development cannot be separated from the aspirations for human rights and the history of all human beings. It conveys that tribals will choose to confront the challenges posed by the modern world rooted in their traditional institutions and values. This is not a self-imposed isolation or political secession but redefining development and nation building on the basis of the legitimate aspirations of culturally distinct groups.

The tribal milieu is particularly happy in social context for the roots and growth of co-operatives since their life is characterised by co-operative ventures. A tribal may not be able to appreciate the official conventional co-operative structure, but its spirit permits his active life. Mahalingam (1984), says that, in fact, a package of integrated services offered by the co-operatives are the basic support for the tribals around which their economy tends to grow.

T. Nogbri (1989), said that although, by and large tribes have existed within their own economic and political framework, their varied cultures and distinctive styles of life lend colour and richness to India's cultural heritage. However, the process of acculturation and modernisation has taken their toll of our vast tribal culture.

T. Nogbri has also opined that we need to re-examine the theories of tribal development in the Indian context, while tribes have existed for centuries outside the framework of the Indian caste system. To be sure, tribes and castes have existed side by side through millennia, which has given rise to active acculturation processes between them. But to equate tribes with castes and incorporate them within the umbrellas of Hinduism is to ignore the rich ethnographic evidence existing at the periphery, which shows wide distinctions between the two.

It is precisely this kind of cultural colonialism perpetuated by the intellectual mainstream that has facilitated the state to adopt a casteist approach to the problems of tribes. The policy of protective discrimination, which identifies tribes with the Harijans have also inadvertently equated their status ambiguous position but have also inadvertently equated their status with that of the latter.

According to Bailey (1966), the policy-maker sees a future, which is different from the present not just because it is separated from the present by a week or a year, but because life then will be of a different kind from what it is now. Let us separate these two kinds of thought about the future by calling the first 'the round of time' and the second 'time's arrow' (Bourdieu, 1963). Each resource is seen against a round of time. Whereas, those who make Five-Year Plans are thinking of time as an arrow. The work has a beginning and an end : there is a target to be reached. The end is a state of affairs quite different from the beginning, and itself is a starting point for further ventures. We have no difficulties with this notion. To plan a future state of affairs, which is radically different from the present is to us quite rational. But those who think in terms of the round of time see such changes as coming from mystical forces like fate, or luck, or witchcraft or acts of God, and to plan for such events makes nonsense. The politician who promises a good life in store for everyone, if they help to implement the plan, is heard by the peasants as we would hear a man promising everyone a first dividend on the pools every week.

From the above description it is observed that the scholars viewed the problems of tribal integration to the mainstream of Indian national life from different angles. Some have viewed the problem as economic and political one. They think that it should be approached keeping in view of two fundamental issues - equality of opportunities and elimination of exploitation. The problem is also viewed in the light of historical and social background of the people.

The changing economic environment has forced the tribal people to new moorings. Thus, problem is the result of the imposition of middle class and high caste norms and values on them. Its solution is concealed on the growth of a spirit of cultural tolerance and the acceptance of tribal value system as legitimate alternatives to the value system of traditional Hindu Society.

The scholars have raised a number of pertinent issues for preparing development plans for the tribal areas and the peoples. The tribal society is culturally, economically and ideologically different from others. They are always trying to maintain their cultural identity and their social solidarity. Thus, some scholars have raised the ethical issues for the tribal administration. Administrators should have to know the ethical standards of different tribal groups and they must have the ability to relate their practical experience to the ethical reasoning. Development Programme should be an organized activity with the aim of satisfying the basic needs of the people and orienting them psychologically to adopt the new skills.

Administrators and modernizers should have the knowledge about the 'cognitive map' of the peoples, that is, about the values the people already hold and the way and the manner, they see the world and society in and around which they live.

Another important factor raised by some scholars in achieving success in development is - involvement of the people. The participation of the people in the formulation and implementation of development programme must be genuine and meaningful. The tribal peoples are in fact, animated by two powerful, interdependent yet distinct motives – one, to maintain and perpetuate a distinct self identity, and the other, participate with dignity in the wider society in its process of nation building. Considering these perspectives, appropriate policy arrangements may be made so that the people can participate in the process of development meaningfully.

Some other scholars opined that the planning should be decentralized, because the nature of economic and social problems enormously differs from one tribal region to another. Planning however, should be area specific and need based. For this, it is necessary to identify the local problems, potentials and priorities, and decentralized the plans and programme implementation. Planning also needs the mobilization of local resources to the maximum possible extent.

The Problem

From the above point of view it is necessary to evaluate the tribal development programmes in the micro level for identifying the emerging issues, problems and changes after its long run implementation for the upliftment of the tribal people to integrate them in the mainstream. It is however, essential to know the economic, social and cultural needs of the peoples' own, to fill up the gaps between their actual needs and incentives offered by the Government. It is, therefore, felt essential to study the people's perception of their own self and society in a specific area and prepare them through appropriate intervention for making our development programmes more effective.

In the course of tribal development approaches in the post-independent India the Fifth Five Year Plan may be mentioned as the turning point for the launching of Integrated Tribal Development Programme (ITDP). ITDP was launched in the year 1972. It was initiated as an area development programme. During Sixth Plan emphasis was placed more on family oriented programmes than on infrastructure development. Thus, from the Sixth Plan period it was becoming a target group approach where individual families were to benefit specifically from the programme. During the Seventh Plan Tribal Development with ITDP pattern was continued without any basic changes in the approach, pattern or structure. In this plan period first thirty lakh tribal families were assisted to build up their economic base. The Eighth Five Year Plan gave emphasis on development of essential infrastructure facilities to achieve the objective of assisting the targeted number of tribal families to cross the poverty line and to increase their access to health, education and employment opportunities. These families were selected on the basis of their absolute economic status, the poorest being given the first preference. Any tribal individual inhabitant of an ITDP Mouza whose age is not below 18 and whose family income is below 11,000 per annum may take loans from these family benefit schemes.

In Birbhum District ITDP was introduced in the year 1983. If the number of beneficiaries in the study area is considered, it is found that 30.53 per cent of the total tribal population are under these schemes upto 1997.

Various kinds of schemes are introduced for the tribal people. Some of the schemes are meant for agriculture; some are employment and income generating schemes. In the present study however, the researcher is intrigued to study empirically the extent and nature of adoption of the schemes by the tribal people of the study area.

From the primary field investigation it was noticed that some beneficiaries are conducting the schemes successfully and in some cases schemes are become failure. However, there remain some factors for non-feasibility of the loans.

From the very beginning of tribal development it was realized that no developmental activities could be of benefit to the tribal population unless their exploitation was prevented and an integrated credit-cum-marketing services developed in the sub-plan areas. Hence, elimination of exploitation was given to marketing and credit priority in the objectives of Tribal Sub Plan. Priority was also given to do away with middlemen and the moneylender. But elimination of exploitation has limited success. In spite of financial assistance through ITDP loans, private sources are also being used by the tribal people side by side. Private sources are still standing between the development agencies and the beneficiaries as an alternative. In the present study an attempt has also been made to find out the contexts in which the tribal people are compelled to take loans from these alternative sources.

After getting some financial assistance from Government there have occurred many socio-economic and socio-cultural changes in their social organization and cultural activities. The study is intended to evaluate the various developmental schemes and to note the extent to which the programme has succeeded in improving economic and social status of the tribal beneficiaries in the study area.

No significant study is available for West Bengal in general and Birbhum in particular; to assess the implementation of ITDP and its impact on the beneficiaries to judge whether or not, and to what extent the programme has succeeded in raising the family incomes of its beneficiaries and helping them to raise above the poverty line. However, the present study is an attempt to evaluate the programme in Birbhum district of West Bengal where ITDP has been running for about 15 years. The problem is approached in terms of following objectives.

Major Objectives of the Study

1. To enumerate the socio-economic status of the ITDP beneficiaries in the study area.
2. To evaluate the utilization of the ITDP loans by the beneficiary households.
3. To identify the other sources of borrowings beside ITDP loans prevalent in the study area.
4. To observe the extent and nature of socio-economic and socio-cultural changes taken place among the beneficiary households by obtaining ITDP loans.

5. To assess the attitude and perceptions of the beneficiaries regarding the ITDP loans.
6. To identify the constraints or obstacles which are hindering the successful implementation of the programme.
7. To assess the impact of the programme on the beneficiary households.
8. To recommend some policy measure to revitalize the scheme to set its fullest potential.

2

Tribal Development : Policies, Plans and Programmes

During the first two decades of planned development in the country no special development strategy was adopted for identified tribal areas and their inhabitants. As a strategy of comprehensive development of the rural areas of the country a programme of Community Development (C.D.) was launched in 1952 in the First Five Year Plan. All facets of community life was envisaged as the main task of the programme. The programmes in C.D. Blocks covered a wide spectrum of activities in agriculture, animal husbandry, education, health, communication, social services, rural industries, panchayets and so on. Blocks Advisory Committees and District Advisory Committees were constituted for constant consultation with the people and pragmatic review of the programme. This programme which applied equally to the tribal areas covered the entire country. But from the very beginning it was clear that the tribal areas needed special treatment. Most of the tribal areas are hilly with meagre communication and very little institutional infrastructure. For bridging up these areas with the rest of the country higher financial investment; personal attention and the extension workers were needed. It was, therefore, decided to supplement the programme of Community Development in these areas. Hence, the existing efforts were sought to be strengthening in 1954 by launching 43 Multipurpose Tribal Development Projects as a part of the Community Development Projects. Only 5.73 per cent of the total tribal population was covered by the development projects. The norm for the establishment of a Tribal Development Block was considerably smaller both in terms of population and area coverage, compared to a C.D. Block. The following criteria were adopted for the creation of development Blocks: (i) its total population should be at least 25,000, (ii) minimum tribal concentration of 62-63 per cent in the area, (iii) area should be 150 to 200 square miles, (iv) viability of the area to function as normal administrative unit.

Special Multipurpose Tribal Development Block was renamed as Tribal Development Block in the Third Five Year Plan. It was multiplied and numbered 458 and the coverage of tribal population was 32.50 per cent. However, in the beginning the Tribal Development Blocks were taken up in areas having highest tribal concentration. At the end of the Third Five Year Plan the programme was reviewed and it revealed that the programme did not have the desired impact. It was felt that the gain so far made required to be consolidated. Though the tribal development programme at the original plan was designed for a period of 10 years, comprising two phases of five years each but now it was decided to add a third phase of five years to the Blocks already started and desist from establishing new ones. But exceptions were made in the cases of West Bengal and Karnataka where TD Blocks were not feasible due to the dispersed nature of their tribal population. Isolated tribal inhabitants were covered by adhoc tribal development projects in Karnataka. In case of West Bengal TD Blocks were established temporarily for two years in each area having sizable tribal population. On the whole it was true that the areas with more than two-third tribal population only got the benefit of these development efforts up to the end of Fourth Five Year Plan. The total number of TD Blocks upto this period was 504, which covered 39.37 per cent of the total tribal population.

The Community Development approach and the Tribal Development Block approach both were multi-sectoral in nature; both were developmental in outlook. But the projects were deficient in relevance to tribal needs. Their management was weak and the non-tribal population of the concerned Blocks tended to grab most of the development opportunities and benefits. Exploitative practices resulting in alienation of tribal owned lands increasingly in favour of moneyed non-tribals, despite some legal protection, tended to inhibit economic improvement of highly depressed tribals. In the beginning of the decade of seventies, during the Fourth Five Year Plan, it was decided by the Government to set up Special Tribal Development Agencies in certain States. These were to accelerate promotion of agriculture and allied sectors, social services and arterial roads with emphasis upon flow of benefits to the tribals. The purpose behind setting up these agencies was for massive investment exclusively for tribal folk from central funds while making of state outlays for development of both tribals and non-tribals. They were also to take appropriate measures to counter the exploitative practices of some non-tribal elements to take over the land of the tribals and also extract bonded labours, in lieu of loans advanced to the tribals at very exorbitant interest. Six Tribal Development Agencies were in operation in some areas with tribal population in Andhra Pradesh, Bihar, Madhya Pradesh and Orissa. Another two agencies were introduced in the beginning of Fifth Plan.

The pilot experiment with the Tribal Development Agencies was not a cent per cent success as the agencies confined themselves in practice mostly to agricultural programmes and development of arterial roads; however, they provided valuable insight into deficiencies in planning and administration, both organizational and financial.

To make the tribal development programme effective more and more the Government formed several committees and commissions. The Elwin Committee made the first review of Special Multipurpose Tribal Development Block. Another commission was appointed under the chairmanship of U.N. Dhebar who submitted a detail report in the year 1961. This report critically examined and assessed the tribal situation prevailing after 10 years of planned development and made several practical suggestions and recommendations. The major findings of the commission may be summarized as follows:

1. Slow pace of development and meagre investment in the tribal areas.
2. The protective measures were sporadic and inadequate which could resist exploitation and injustice.
3. Simple administrative system for these areas.

The commission under the chairmanship of Shilu Ao in 1969 set up another study team. Some of the main drawbacks pointed out by the committee were:

1. A tribal development Block was too small to function effectively as a basic unit for planning and implementation.
2. The indebtedness, land alienation, educational backwardness and inadequacy of communication were identified as the basic problem of the tribal communities and these did not receive adequate attention in the frame of tribal development Block.
3. The tribal development Block failed to get any significant support from the general development programmes including the CD programme.
4. The committee suggested vigorous action to implement the recommendations of the Dhebar Commission as these remained unattended till that time.
5. The team also suggested for preparing comprehensive tribal development programme with larger resources commensurate with the size of the problem and the overall national development effort.

On the eve of Fifth Five Year Plan, in the year 1972, the Planning Commission constituted another Working Group for the tribal areas under the chairmanship of Shri H.N. Haldipur. Several other groups and teams were to go into problems of tribal area, cooperatives, rural indebtedness, land alienation, excise policy, etc. The experience and insights enabled the planners and policy-makers to think in terms of formulating an integrated tribal development strategy with requisite intimate linkages with national strategy of socio-economic development.

The result of these deliberations was the birth of a new strategy of Tribal Sub-Plan (TSP) within the broad framework of State and Central plans. This is to achieve a balanced development comprising economic development, educational advancement, infrastructural expansion and improvement and protective measures against tribal exploitation. The tribal areas in the country were classified by the committee under three broad categories:

(i) States and Union Territories having majority of scheduled tribe population;

(ii) States and Union Territories having substantial tribal population but majority tribal population in particular administrative units, such as Blocks and Tehsils;

(iii) States and Union Territories have dispersed tribal population.

In the light of above demographic situation, it was decided that tribal majority States like Arunachal Pradesh, Meghalaya, Mizoram, Nagaland, Lakshadweep, Dadra and Nagar Haveli may not need a Tribal Sub-plan as the entire plan of these States/Union Territories was primarily meant for ST. population constituting the majority. For the second category of States and UTs Tribal Sub-Plan approach was adopted after delineating areas of tribal concentration. A similar approach was adopted in the case of States and UTs having dispersed population by paying special attention to patches of tribal concentration, keeping in view of their tenor of dispersal. To handle the tribal population coming within the new TSP strategy in a coordinated manner, Integrated Tribal Development Project (ITDP) for the substantial tribal areas, Modified Area Development Approach (MADA) for pockets having a total population of 10,000 and ST components of 50 per cent or more and special projects for primitive tribal group (Micro Projects) were conceived and adopted.

The seventeen States namely, Andhra Pradesh, Assam, Bihar, Gujarat, Himachal Pradesh, Karnataka, Kerala, Madhya Pradesh, Maharashtra, Manipur, Orissa, Rajasthan, Sikkim, Tamil Nadu, Tripura, Uttar Pradesh and West Bengal and two UTs viz. Andaman and Nicober Islands and Goa, Daman and Diu are implementing the Tribal Sub-Plan through the approach of ITDP. 5 per cent tribal population was covered till the end of Fifth Five Year Plan. A new approach of MADA in sixth plan and micro project for primitive tribes have helped in bringing the coverage of tribal population about 75 per cent.

The Tribal Sub-plan Strategy Comprises:

(a) identification of tribal majority areas in a State/ UTs and launching there integrated tribal development projects having thrust both in socio-economic development of the areas and on betterment of the highly depressed tribal families (employment, income, education etc.);

(b) earmarking of appropriate funds for the TSP and ensuring regular flow into it from state outlay and also from the outlays as well as credit from financial institutions for backing up some of the schemes launched under ITDP;

(c) creations of appropriate administrative structure with appropriate personnel for implementation of ITDPs.

Integrated Tribal Development Project

A tribal development Block has been taken up as the smallest unit for inclusion in the new programme. A group of Blocks which generally comprises a tehsil, has been taken as the basic unit for planning and development of the new tribal development programme. The unit is known as Integrated Tribal Development Project.

The qualifying minimum size of the compact tribal majority area inclusion in the TSPs was reviewed with reference to the degree of tribal concentration obtaining in different States. A minimum population threshold of 20,000 was accepted as the smallest unit in Maharashtra, Andhra Pradesh and Assam. This norm was further relaxed to 10,000 in Tamil Nadu, Kerala and Uttar Pradesh. In case of West Bengal and Tripura it was necessary to go down further and identify groups of villages for special development programmes. In Karnataka and Daman, it was not possible even to identify sizable villages of tribal concentration. The new programme in their cases therefore was designed entirely for dispersed tribals.

The delineation of the areas of tribal concentration was taken up in the beginning of the Fifth Plan and completed by the end of 1976. Although the ITDP was conceived as comprising a group of Blocks, the actual size varied from State to State depending on the demographic structure of the tribal community in that region. The total numbers of ITDP established by the beginning of 1978 was 180. An ITDP with more than one Block is termed as Meso Project and ITDP comprising only one Block or less than one Block can be termed as Micro Project. Out of 180 ITDPs, 121 are Meso units and remaining micro-units. The Sub-Plans and ITDPs do not include the tribal majority States and UTs and whose cases the plans of the States or UTs, as the case may be, have been taken as plans for tribal development.

Since, an Integrated Tribal Development Project has been accepted as the unit of planning and implementation at the micro level, it was also desired that the administrative boundaries should not be changed unless considering essential for the preparation of TSP, the Planning Commission issued a set of guidelines to the States. The guidelines spelt out the long-term objectives of the TSP as :

(1) narrowing the gap between the levels of development at the tribals and other areas;

(2) improving their quality of life.

The immediate objectives were :

(1) elimination of exploitation in all forms

(2) speeding up the processes of social and economic development

(3) building up the inner strength of the people

(4) improving their organizational capabilities.

However, the guidelines laid down the principles for identification of sub-plan areas, the approach and strategy for their development and also the pattern of funding and formulation of programmes in these areas. The guidelines also stated that the sub-plan areas in each state should comprise a number of viable projects. For each such ITDP, an inregrated area development plan focussing specific attention on the specific problems of the area and the tribal people was to be formulated. The sub-plan areas in each state thus comprise a number of viable projects.

The unit of planning an ITDP in a state, comprised an aggregate of Development Blocks. The ITDP area being smaller than a district and bigger than a Development Block appears more feasible for planning. The lowest unit of execution of the programme is the Development Block. It has development team with a Block Development Officer as its leader. The programmes have to be planned for an ITDP in the shape of a sub-plan for the tribal region of the state. Guidelines lay down that planning should be based on the needs of the area and the people, and hence, the process has to be commenced at the grass root level; i.e., the Development Blocks, and funneled upwards to the ITDP, state and national level.

Administrative Structure

The administrative structure set up for TSP varies

across the States concerned.. Basically it comprises four levels, the Block, ITDP, district and state administration. The Block administration is being reconstructed to remove existing deficiencies and improve its capacity to shoulder increasing responsibility for implementing the various schemes of tribal development handed over to it by ITDP. The Block Development Officer (BDO), the subject specialists and various field workers at the village level diploid in Block administration are being reoriented and professionally improved to play their respective roles completely and cooperatively.

The administration of ITDP, has its place within the district administration. It can play an effective part in formulation of integrated area projects and then in its coordinated implementation largely through the Block administration. The ITDP administration and its multi-disciplinary team of officers have thus a deliberative, advisory and supervisory role to play. There is a project implementation and Review Committee with Deputy Commissioner as a Chairman, project administrators as secretary, MPs and MLAs (mostly tribals) and various district officers concerned as members. The body approves the various schemes to put into operation under ITDP and coordinates and reviews the implementations of the schemes.

The department of Tribal Welfare, headed by a Tribal Development Commissioner is functioning at the state level. The Welfare Department supports and directs the ITDPs. Besides this, it has the responsibility of supervising and coordinating the implementation of various policy decisions the state regarding the tribal matters. At the state level there is a high powered Committee under the chairmanship of either the Chief Minister or the Chief Secretary. Committee provides overall guidance, direction and support to implement the policies and programmes in regard to tribal welfare and development.

Financial Structure

The Tribal Sub-Plan is being implemented through the

resources drawn from; (a) State Plan, (b) Special Central Assistance from Ministry of Home Affairs, (c) Flow from Central Sector/Centrally Sponsored Schemes and (d) Institutional Finance. To ensure resource mobilisation for meeting the requirement of Tribal Sub-Plan, the State Plan outlay, sectoral outlays of Central Ministries and Institutional finance were specifically identified as the source of finance for implementation of programmes by the tribal area administration. From the year 1983-84, in addition of new scheme of Special Central Assistance to be administered by the Ministry of Home Affairs in the interest of tribal area development programmes was instituted as a additive to State Plan efforts. Special Central Assistance has been used in some cases State Government on the schemes of infrastructure development not having any bearing on the family oriented schemes and poverty amelioration. While infrastructure development in tribal areas is extremely important the Commission suggests that Special Central Assistance be used mainly for family oriented programmes and incidental infrastructure (Report of the Commission for Scheduled Castes and Scheduled Tribes 1983-84).

The norms for Special Central Assistance is as follows:

The share of the three programmes under the broad strategy of Tribal Sub-Plan, namely, TSP (ITDP), MADA (Pockets) and primitive tribes from the total outlay of Special Central Assistance (SCA) is calculated in proportion to the Scheduled Tribe population covered under each programme. The Inter-State allocation of SCA for these programmes is made as follows:

For allocation of SCA to ITDPs, the States are grouped in three categories viz. A, B and C. Category A consists of States with substantial areas predominantly inhabited by the tribals such as:

(i) Andhra Pradesh

(ii) Bihar

(iii) Gujarat

(iv) Himachal Pradesh

(v) Madhya Pradesh

(vi) Maharashtra

(vii) Manipur

(viii) Orissa

(ix) Rajasthan and

(x) Sikkim.

Category B consists of States having dispersed tribal population with some area of tribal concentration;

(i) Assam,

(ii) West Bengal and

(iii) Tripura.

Category C consists of the States / UTs where tribal population is by and large dispersed with very small areas of concentration, such as:

(i) Karnataka

(ii) Kerala

(iii) Tamil Nadu

(iv) Uttar Pradesh

(v) Andaman and Nicobar Islands and

(vi) Goa

(vii) Daman and Diu.

The total outlay of SCA for the tribal sub-plan is allocated to the three categories on the basis of tribal population of the States or UTs included in each group. The funds allocated to category 'A' are distributed to the States on the basis of three criteria:

(i) 50 per cent on the basis of Scheduled Tribe population in the TSP area

(ii) 30 per cent on the basis of the TSP area of the State and

(iii) 20 per cent in inverse proportion to per capita Net State Domestic Production (NSDP) of the States with weightage to tribal population within the TSP area.

For category B and C States, the share of individual States/UTs is worked out on the basis of two criteria, i.e., 70 per cent according to ST population of the TSP and 30 per cent in inverse proportion to per capita NSDP of the States/UTs with weightage to tribal population within the area (Roy Burman,1995).

Sub-Plan During the Sixth Plan Period

Since the Fifth Five Year Plan a CD/TD Block was adopted as the smallest unit for inclusion in the Tribal Sub-Plan, substantial portion of the dispersed tribal population could not get the benefits of the area approach. The draft Sixth Plan, therefore, provided for extension of sub-plan approach to additional areas of 10,000 population with a tribal concentration of 50 per cent and above. It was estimated that the additional 10 per cent of the country's tribal population would be covered by the extension of the sub-plan strategy. The long-term objective of the Sixth Plan continued to be the same as the Fifth Plan. The strategy of development has given emphasis on consolidation of the gains of protective measures, programmes of full employment, education, and health services. To remove the present inadequacies in implementation, the programmes under different sectors of development have a requirement of intensified and suitable modifications.

The approach in the Sixth Plan for the development of backward areas in general was to rely, to a greater extent, on the development of agriculture, village and small-scale industries, subsidiary occupations and related services and also the Maximum Need Programmes and area development programmes. As the tribal regions fall in different agro-climatic regions, a clear strategy for agricultural development of each region have to be worked out. It has been considered most essential to improve the economic status of the tribal by taking up the suitable programmes of horticulture, cattle development, poultry and piggery, etc. In respect of these economic programmes, the role of marketing and credit organisation such as LAMPs has been reemphasised. This would help to eliminate the middleman and the moneylenders and thereby give economic benefits direct to tribal population.

After the Fifth Plan the planning process received a set back due to a change in the Government at the Centre. The Janata Party came to power and formulated its Sixth Plan for 1978-83 which laid stress on the Minimum Need Programme.

After the defeat of the Janata party the Congress Party came to power and introduced a new Sixth Plan (1980-81 to 1984-85) which took into account the shortcoming of the previous plan. The total size of the tribal sub-plan during the period was estimated to be of Rs. 5,000 crores. The outlay and expenditure on the socio-economic programmes for the Scheduled Tribes during the Sixth Plan has been shown in the following Table.

Table 2.1

Sixth Plan Outlays on Socio-Economic Programmes for the Scheduled Tribe

(Rs. in crores)

Sl.No.	*Fund From*	*Sixth Plan outlays*	*Sixth Plan expenditure*
1.	States allocations for Tribal Sub-Plan	3521	3409
2.	Special Central Assistance*	485	485
3.	Institutional Finance	NA	800

* Funds from special component Plan to ensure a higher degree of devolution of funds.

Source : Tribal Administration and development, S.G.Deogaonkar, 1994.

During the Sixth Plan Period emphasis was placed more on family-oriented programmes than on infrastructure development. Special Component Plans (SCPs) had a Special Central Assistance counterpart by way of addition to the States Plan Programme. It was proposed to assist 50 per cent of the Scheduled Tribe Families to cross over the poverty line and as against a target of 2.70 million ST families to be brought above the poverty line. 3.46 million ST families received this assistance though it was not certain whether they had actually crossed the poverty line or required further assistance (Deogaonkar, 1994:59).

Sub-Plan During Seventh Five Year Plan

The objectives of the development strategy during the Seventh Plan period remained two-fold :

(i) Socio-economic development of the scheduled tribes;

(ii) Protection of tribals against exploitation.

However, the programme of tribal development with ITDP pattern was continued without any basic or major changes in the approach, pattern or structure, but better coordination was sought between various agencies, and social services were given priority. It was admitted that the planning process in the tribal areas had to be a judicious mixture of beneficiary-oriented programmes, human resource development and infrastructure development and during the Seventh Plan, the first 30 lakh tribal families in the TSP were to be assisted to build up their economic base. Socio-economic development of the tribal areas as well as of the tribal families was to continue.

During the Seventh Plan period, the Tribal Sub-Plan strategy benefits were extended to all the tribals including the dispersed tribals who were not covered by the ITDPs, MADA, clusture groups and primitive groups. Family-oriented programmes were extended to them. By the end of Seventh Plan the position was as under :

		ST population covered
ITDPs	191	303.41 lakhs
MADAs	268	45.82 lakhs
Clusture areas	74	3.43 lakhs

All these are in 19 TSP States and Union Territories.

Tribal Sub-Plan During Eighth Plan Period

The Eighth Five Year Plan was started late, i.e., from 1992. Government of India approach to the Eighth Plan, Planning Commission takes note of the following:

1. The resource base and the socio-cultural heritage of our Scheduled Tribe population are getting eroded through a combination of development intervention, commercial exploitation and ineffective legal and administrative system.

2. Projects for irrigation, power, transport, etc., often disrupt the life and environment of a large number of Scheduled Tribe families, while benefits accrue mainly to population on the plains. Measures for relief and rehabilitation in such cases have been neither imaginatively did not conceive nor whole-heartedly need to be shown to this diminution.

3. Programmes need to be devised with the involvement of the Scheduled Tribes themselves in the light of their own order of priorities to remove economic, educational and social disparities. The line of action should include, besides access to minimum social services, assistance in scientific resource conservation, construction of small water-harvesting and storage systems, restoration of their traditional rights in the forest produce and direct link with market and strengthening of their traditional community organisations (Government of India Approach to the Eighth Five Year Plan, Planning Commission, 1990).

The main objectives of tribal development envisaged during the Eighth Plan were :

(a) effective tackling of exploitative practices in tribal

areas in matters related to alienation of land, right to collection of forest produce, payment of proper wages for their labour, remunerative prices for their produce to ensure sustained flow and full utilization of benefits of the Plan programme;

(b) ensure full rehabilitation of displaced tribals due to establishment of projects;

(c) emphasis on development of essential infrastructure facilities to achieve objective of assisting the targeted number of tribal families to cross the poverty line and increasing their access to health, education and employment opportunities;

(d) full implementation of projects for integrated development of identified primitive tribal group;

(e) restructuring and defining the TSP strategy to ensure adequate qualification for TSP adoption of schemes to suit the needs of tribal people, adequate per tribal family assistance and participation of tribal beneficiaries;

(f) special focus on programmes to deal with the education and health needs of tribal women;

(g) emphasis on monitoring and evaluation of programmes;

(h) there are some Tribal Sub-Plan districts in the country which have more than 50 per cent Scheduled Tribes and which are also specified as Scheduled Areas under the Fifth Schedule to the Constitution. In these districts, relevant area-based and family-oriented Schemes on need-based criteria, backed by an effective administrative set-up supported by provisions under Fifth Schedule to the Constitution, were to be effectively taken up. It was felt that such an innovation in the TSP approach might yield better results.

An experimental measures is taken up that the full district numbering about 26 in different States under the

TSP were to be brought under a unified administrative structure (DRDAs and ITDPs) and all financial and administrative powers for socio-economic development of tribals were to be vested in an officer of the rank of District Collector.

Financial Allocation for the Tribal People in Various Plan Periods

For an overall development of the tribals the Community Development Programmes in general was introduced. Through these Development Blocks monitory help was injected and many kinds of assistance were given. Efforts were made from time to time to improve the tribal life. Since 1957, 43 Multi-purpose Tribal Blocks on the lines of Community Development Block have been opened throughout the country, each with a special and heavy allotment of Rs. 27 lakhs for five years. Larger amount was made available for irrigation, soil conservation, communications etc. But result achieved was meagre.

In the Third Plan 300 Tribal Development Blocks were set with an allotment of Rs. 22 lakhs. On these Tribal Development Blocks the Union Government has spent Rs. 15.83 crores and Rs. 20.04 crores in the Third Plan and the three Annual Plans, i.e., 1966-69. The Fourth Plan outlay shows steep rise in the expenditure which goes to the extent of Rs. 32.50 crores.

Table 2.2
Plan Expenditure and the Backward Classes

(Rs. in Crores)

	First Plan	*Second Plan*	*Third Plan*	*Annual Plan*	*Fourth Plan*	*Fifth Plan*
Scheduled Tribe	17.00	41.00	53.00	34.64	75.00	105.00
Denotified Tribes	1.00	2.00	4.00	-	4.39	N.A
Total for Backward Classes	26.00	78.00	102.00	68.49	166.34	255.00
Special allocation for hilly and tribal areas						500.00

Source: Tribal Culture in India, L.P.Vidyarthi (1985).

Till the beginning of the Fourth Five Year Plan sum of Rs. 375 crores had been spent by the State and Union Government on the welfare of backward classes. The State Governments, contributed nearly 100 crores from their own resources during this period. Here the economic programmes include reclamation of lands, minor irrigation works, loans for cottage industries, distribution of *charkas*, opening of grain-golas, reservation of certain percentage of jobs, etc.

The expenditure incurred exclusively for the Scheduled Tribes as compared to the total expenditure and per capita expenditure under the various plans gives rise to the fact that the progress is very slow. The launching of the Tribal Sub-Plan in the Fifth Plan period led to a marked uprising in the financial investment. The Plan-wise investment was as follows.

Table 2.3
Planwise Investment in Development Programmes

Plan Period	*Total Plan Outlay (Rs. in Crores)*	*Tribal Development Programmes (Rs. in Crores)*	*Percentage*
First Five Year Plan	1,960	19.93	1.0
Second Five Year Plan	4,672	42.92	0.9
Third Five Year Plan	8,577	50.53	0.6
Annual Plan	6,756	32.32	0.5
Fourth Five Year Plan	15,902	75.00	0.5
Fifth Five Year Plan	39,322	1,067.27	2.71
Sixth Five Year Plan	97,500	5,535.50	5.47
Seventh Five Year Plan	1,80,000	13,000.00	7.22

Source : Report of the Commission for Scheduled Tribes [April 1985-March 1986], Eighth Report.

The table shows a progressive increase in plan outlay for the tribal people. Total plan outlay increased 49 fold as against 277 fold in the case of tribal development programmes from First Plan to the Sixth Plan.From the First to Fourth Plans the investment in the tribal areas was meagre to made up properly of allotment for special programmes. The percentage of investment in the total First Plan outlay was 1.0 which declined to 0.9 in the Second Plan, 0.6 in the Third Plan and further to 0.5 for Annual Plan (1966-67) and Fourth Plan (1969-74). During the Fifth Plan and Sixth Plan, uprising in the financial investment is remarkable. It rose to 2.71 in the Fifth Plan and 5.47 per cent in the Sixth Plan. Outlay during Seventh Plan (7.22 per cent of the total outlay) almost corresponds to the percentage of the tribal population of 7.76 (1981 Census) of the country.

Table 2.4

Per Capita Expenditure on Tribal Development

Plan period	*Per Capita Expenditure (In Rs.)*	*Total Expenditure (Rs. in lakhs)*
First Plan Period	15.05	118.77
Second Plan Period	18.89	250.25
Third Plan Period	13.56	178.77
Fourth Plan Period	59.00	977.77
Fifth Plan Period	266.00	4,879.85
Sixth Plan Period	750.47	13,598.00
Seventh Plan Period (1985-89)	1,827.00	732.13

Source: Socio-economic and Ecological Development, Ed. by Buddhadev Choudhury, 1992.

Tribal Sub-Plan in West Bengal

In the Fifth Plan, the State Government of West Bengal after discussion with the Planning Commission identified areas of tribal concentration at the village level where the tribal population was at least 50 per cent of the total village population. The villages were grouped together and thirty three Integrated Tribal Development Project (ITDP) areas were formed with those villages, which are located in twelve districts of the State (excluding the districts of Nadia, Howrah and Cooch Behar). From the year 1997, district Nadia has been included.

The sub-plan will be financed from various sources comprising State Plan outlays in the Central Ministries for the tribal areas; Special Central Assistance and Institutional Finance. The outlays for sectoral development have fixed mainly for Agriculture (including land reforms), Irrigation, Animal Husbandry and Veterinary Services, Forests, Co-operations, Power, Village Industries, Roads, Education, Health, Rural Water Supply, Housing, Nutrition, Backward Classes Welfare, Industries and Administration.

The Scheduled Tribes and Scheduled Castes Welfare Department plays a role of coordinator and monitoring agency. Under the Tribal Sub-Plan inputs of various sectors are intensified and channelised in particular areas mainly for the concerned population. The economic sector comprising agriculture, irrigation, cooperation, forest, animal husbandry, and village industries have been given an edge over Fifth Plan position during Sixth Plan period and the infrastructural developmental sector and Social Services sector have been given proportionately less priority.

Agriculture sector includes different schemes like distribution of seeds, fertilizer, minikit etc. minor irrigation, soil and water conservation, area development in D.P.A. Irrigation sector also covers small and minor irrigational schemes. Major programmes of land and land reforms sectors are: (i) updating of land records of tribal people in the district of Purulia and Islampur Sub-division of West Dinajpur district, (ii) restoration of tribal lands, (iii) free legal aids to the tribals, apart from 'Operation Barga' and distribution of vested land among the weaker sections of the community.

Establishment of Large-size Multipurpose Cooperative Society (LAMP) covers different schemes like; (i) facilities of short-term, medium-term loan and consumption loan, (ii) supply of seeds and fertilizer, (iii) collection and marketing of *sal* seeds and *kendu* leaves, (iv) consumer stores (v) distribution of livestock, etc.

Animal Husbandry and veterinary sector include mainly schemes on (i) Distribution and supply of livestock and poultry like House Dairy, Sheep and goat rearing and pig keeping, (ii) Distribution of Stud Bull, (iii) Fodder demonstration plots, (iv) A.I. Centres and (v) Ambulatory Clinic Van, etc.

To bring more Scheduled Tribe people in occupation relating to Cottage and Small Scale Industries; concerned sector given more emphasis on (i) Development of Lac industry, (ii) Sericulture (iii) Stone-mining and ballast production unit, (iv) Ghooting lime manufacture, (v) Training-cum-production centres (vi) Marketing facilities, etc.

The sector Fishery includes number of developmental schemes of following types: (i) Subsidy for fishing nets and fishery requisites, (ii) Intensive development of tank fisheries, (iii) Demonstration centre for composite pisiculture (iv) Development of air breathing fishes, prawn culture, etc.

Health and Rural Water Supply sector cover schemes like (i) Establishment of Primary and Subsidiary Health Centres, (ii) Rural dispensaries, (iii) Establishment of Leprosy and V.D. clinics, (iv) Supply of drinking water and conversion of dry latrines to sanitary latrines.

Major thrust of education sector is on establishment of primary school, construction of building, textbooks, school dress, attendance scholarship and Ashram Hostels.

Outlays for Tribal Development in West Bengal

Sectorwise break up of supplemental outlays for tribal development in different Plan Periods reveals substantive portion of money was meant for "Economic uplift" then in order came "Education" and "Health Housing", etc. receiving least consideration upto the end of Fourth Plan. The following Table will present a clear picture in this respect.

Table 2.5
Sectorwise Supplemental Outlays for Tribal Development in West Bengal

(Rs. in Crores)

Plan Period	*Education*	*Economic Uplift*	*Health Housing*	*Total*
First Plan	5.10	8.46	3.81	17.37
Second Plan	8.05	22.70	9.76	40.51
Third Plan	13.23	30.72	7.10	51.05
1966-69	9.32	24.07	1.93	35.32
Fourth Plan	31.50	42.25	10.45	84.20

In the Fifth Plan period (1974-79) the total plan outlay was Rs. 39.322 crores of which 3.01 per cent was for the Tribal Development Programmes. The detail outlay and expenditure of the TSP during 1974-79 is given below:

Table 2.6
Outlay and Expenditure of Tribal Sub-Plan During Fifth Five Year Plan in West Bengal

(Rs. in Crores)

Year	*State Plan*			*Special Central Assistance*		
	Outlay	*Expenditure*	*% Utilization*	*Outlay*	*Expenditure*	*% Utilization*
1974-75	23	25	109	4.03	3.08	72
1975-76	72	60	83	20.00	14.59	73
1976-77	181	154	85	40.00	30.99	77
1977-78	248	223	90	55.00	51.49	94
1978-79	332	290	87	67.00	64.96	97
Total	856	752	88	186.30	165.1	189

Table shows that in the Fifth Plan both State Plan and the SCA outlay and expenditure increasing yearly but the percentage of utilization is decreasing. Following statement showing Special Central Assistance received from Government of India, outlays, expenditure, for TSP in the Sixth Plan, Seventh Plan and Eighth Plan Period.

Table 2.7

Outlay and Expenditure of the Tribal Sub-Plan in West Bengal During Sixth Plan Period

(Rs. in Lakhs)

Year	*Total State Plan Outlay*	*S.C.A Received from Govt. of India*		*Expenditure*	
		S.C.P.	*T.S.P.*	*S.C.P.*	*T.S.P.*
1980-81	58,036.41	1002.00	364.58	1043.18	366.16
1981-82	63,850.00	944.00	366.00	943.20	370.89
1982-83	49,910.25	1093.00	421.00	928.76	418.17
1983-84	54,300.75	1170.80	500.00	1224.36	527.46
1984-85	74,800.00	1418.21	524.60	1418.11	531.15
Total	3,50,000.00	5628.01	2176.18	5557.61	2213.83

Following statement showing State Plan outlays, flow to T.S.P. and expenditure made thereof during Seventh Five Year Plan and onwards.

Table 2.8

Outlay and Expenditure of the Tribal Sub-Plan in West Bengal During Seventh Plan Period

(Rs. in Lakhs)

Year	*Total State Plan Outlay*	*Flow to Tribal Sub-Plan*	*Expenditure*
1985-86	67,500.00	2492.72 (3.69%)	2423.28
1986-87	77,600.00	2983.96 (3.98%)	2386.546
1987-88	86,200.00	3266.89 (3.79%)	2771.831
1988-89	95,088.90	3652.265 (3.84%)	2971.85
1989-90	1,11,500.00	3785.97 (3.39%)	4571.075
1990-91	1,32,822.30	5306.40 (3.99%)	6158.65 (Anticipated)
1991-92	1,48,600.00	6062.56 (4.08%)	

The concept of family oriented schemes or beneficiary oriented schemes has been introduced in tribal development programmes since Sixth Five Year Plan. The main purpose is to raise the Scheduled Tribe families above the poverty line.

Table 2.9
Outlay and Expenditure of the Tribal Sub-Plan in West Bengal During Eighth Plan Period

(Rs. in Lakhs)

Year	*Total State Plan Outlay*	*Flow to Tribal Sub-Plan*	*Percentage*
1992-93	1,50,100.00	6,866.90	4.56
1993-94	1,55,000.00	7,533.535	4.86
1994-95	1,70,600.00	6,422.156	3.76
1995-96	2,20,730.00	12,546.00	5.68
1996-97	3,08,094.40	5,485.58 (Budgeted)	1.78
Total	10,04,524.40	38,854.171	3.86

Table 2.10
Outlay and Expenditure of Special Component Plan During Eighth Plan in West Bengal

Year	*SCP Released by Govt. of India (Rs. in Lakh)*	*to*	*TSP Expenditure (Rs. in Lakh)*
1992-93	1,171,67		1,64,33
1993-94	1,319,06		940,37
1994-95	1,335,83		1,335,83
1995-96	1,763,21		1,763,21
1996-97	1,381,42		1,381,42
Total	6,971,19		7,067,16

It was estimated by the Ministry of Home Affairs that an account of Rs. 800 Crores approximately was invested towards family benefiting schemes from the State Plan and Central Assistance during Sixth Plan. Such schemes mainly come under agriculture, horticulture, animal husbandry, minor irrigation, fishery, cooperation, and small industries. During Sixth Plan 2,28,267 lakh families were programmed to be assisted during the plan period. The total family assisted during Sixth Plan may be around 2,77,618 lakhs. The report of the Working Group reveals that, of these families about 10 per cent of the total coverage of tribal families under economic assistance have crossed the poverty line, while the rest were assisted economically to a certain degree. Further it has been seen that majority of tribal families were still left to be economically assisted to cross the poverty line. During Seventh Plan the investment towards this sector has to be substantially increased both in the State Plan and Central Assistance.

3
Research Setting

3.1. Methods and Techniques Adopted in the Study

In pursuance of the objectives, full information on Integrated Tribal Development Programme under operation within the jurisdiction of the selected District as well as Block was acquired at first. In the matter of implementation of the programme official records were consulted for securing the primary information regarding different schemes in operation and the beneficiaries under them. To obtain a concrete list of beneficiaries all the official records of ITDP section of District Scheduled Castes and Scheduled Tribe Welfare Corporation, District Rural Development Agencies (DRDA), District Land and Land Reforms Office (DLLRO), Block Development Office (BDO), Panchayats, Large Sized Multipurpose Co-operative Society (LAMPs) and all the related Commercial and Gramin Banks were consulted.

To collect the primary data survey method was followed. Complete enumeration of the beneficiary households has been conducted. Each and every beneficiary household of the study area has been approached personally. The conventional anthropo-logical techniques like interview, both structured and unstructured, as well as participant observation have been used for collection of data. The concerned beneficiaries were interviewed about the schemes adopted by them. Other members of the households who also interviewed, and the respondents were asked about the benefits of the schemes. Reactions of tribal individuals to some welfare projects and programmes have been examined and their views about the operating schemes or projects were obtained. Their ideas about the viability, feasibility, implementation procedures etc. were carefully examined. Case studies have also been recorded during the field work. Attempts have been made to analyze and interpret the impact of the schemes on the beneficiary households in the traditional and the changing socio-cultural context of the tribal groups.

Finally, all the collected sets of information have been recorded, collated and scanned. Then to satisfy the objectives tabular and percentage analysis have been followed for quantitative and qualitative judgements.

3.2. The Study Area

There are altogether 191 ITDP areas spread over 16 States and 2 Union Territories in India. In the Fifth Plan, after discussion with the Planning Commission, the State Government of West Bengal identified areas of tribal concentration at the village level where the tribal population was at least 50 per cent of the total village population. The villages were grouped together and 33 ITDP areas were formed. Twelve, out of seventeen districts of West Bengal have been selected for this project after determining the numerical strength of the tribal population.

Name of the District	*No. of ITDP Areas*
Purulia	6
Bankura	3
Birbhum	4
Malda	2
Darjeeling	1
Jalpaiguri	4
West Dinajpur	3
Midnapur	5
Murshidabad	1
Burdwan	2
24 Parganas	1
Hooghly	1

Out of these twelve ITDP districts of West Bengal, Birbhum district is selected purposively for the study. The programme has been operating in this district since 1983.

The district consists of four ITDP areas covering 7 Police Stations and comprising 232 Mouzas. Out of 19 Blocks, eight Blocks are under these ITDP areas. These Project Areas are; - Rajnagar (10), Sainthia, Suri I and II (11), Bolpur, Labhpur (12) and Mahammadbazar, Rampurhat (13). From these Project Areas, Bolpur-Labhpur Project Area (12) has been selected due to its highest concentration of ITDP Mouzas. This Project Area consists of two Blocks namely Bolpur-Sriniketan Block and Labhpur Block. Total fifty-five mouzas are under this project area. Lists of the mouzas are given below.

List of ITDP Mouzas of Bolpur Sriniketan Block

Sl.No.	*Name of the Mouza*	*J.L.No.*	*Name of the Gram Panchayat*
1.	Damodarpur	17	Kasba
2.	Gopalnagar	18	Kasba
3.	Kandarpapur	20	Kasba
4.	Danbaripur	22	Sarpalehana Albandha
5.	Gobindapala	25	Sarpalehana Albandha
6.	Damdama	27	Sarpalehana Albandha
7.	Naodangal	28	Sarpalehana Albandha
8.	Kalaharpur	30	Sarpalehana Albandha
9.	Sarbanandapur	31	Sarpalehana Albandha
10.	Uttar Gopinathpur	32	Sarpalehana Albandha
11.	Sehalai	33	Kasba
12.	Bidhyadharpur	34	Kasba
13.	Kahanjanpur	35	Kasba
14.	Faridpur	46	Sattor
15.	Chakpali	49	Ruppur
16.	Vinodpur	50	Ruppur
17.	Dakshin Harirampur	51	Ruppur
18.	Bishnubati	58	Sattor
19.	Asadullapur	59	Sattor
20.	Uttar Chandipur	60	Kasba
21.	Kamalakantapur	61	Kasba
22.	Mandarpur	62	Sattor

Contd.

Sl.No.	Name of the Mouza	J.L.No.	Name of the Gram Panchayat
23.	Ballavpur	63	Ruppur
24.	Boiradihi	66	Singi
25.	Mahisdal	70	Sarpalehana Albandha
26.	Donaipur	72	Kankalitala
27.	Bengutia	73	Kankalitala
28.	Karpatikuri	75	Kankalitala
29.	Keudaha	81	Sarpalehana Albandha
30.	Dholtikuri	86	Kankalitala
31.	Amdahara	89	Kankalitala
32.	Patharghata	91	Kankalitala
33.	Khoskadampur	95	Kankalitala
34.	Kalikapur	98	Sian
35.	Chandanpur	110	Raipur-Supur
36.	Rashulganjhat	114	Raipur-Supur
37.	Gheropara	118	Raipur-Supur
38.	Mahuli	119	Sian
39.	Dakshin Narayanpur	120	Raipur-Supur
40.	Goyeshpur	122	Sian
41.	Tatarpur	124	Sian
42.	Uparkhara	149	Bahiri
43.	Jahanabad	169	Singi

List of Mouzas of Labhpur Block

Sl.No.	Name of the Mouza	J.L.No.	Name of the Gram Panchayat
1.	Sundripur	20	Chowhatta-Mohodori I
2.	Faridpur	21	Chowhatta-Mohodori I
3.	Rajarampur	22	Chowhatta-Mohodori I
4.	Srikrishnapur	23	Chowhatta-Mohodori II
5.	Babna	25	Chowhatta-Mohodori II
6.	Tushkunda	27	Chowhatta-Mohodori II
7.	Penchagange	28	Chowhatta-Mohodori II
8.	Tatinapara	40	Chowhatta-Mohodori II
9.	Mastali	83	Labhpur I
10.	Sekhampur	84	Chowhatta-Mohodori I
11.	Sarparajpur	102	Labhpur I
12.	Ekut	37	Chowhatta-Mohodori II

From the above list of Mouzas of Bolpur- Labhpur Project Area consisting of Bolpur-Sriniketan Block and Labhpur

SAMPLING DESIGN FOR THE STUDY

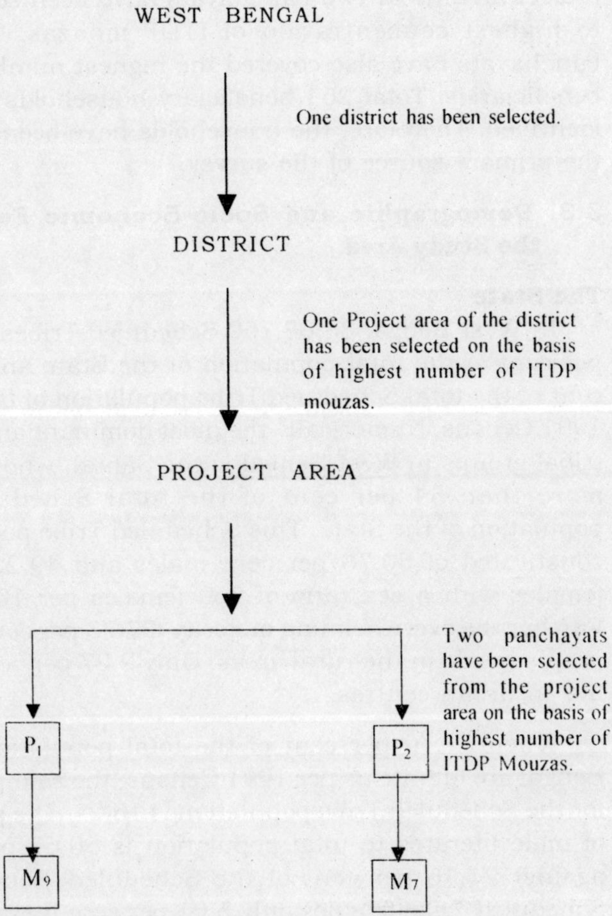

P_1 = Sarpalehana – Albandha Gram Panchayat

P_2 = Kankali Gram Panchayat

M_9 = Nine Mouzas of Sarpalehana Gram Panchayat

M_7 = Seven Mouzas of Kankali Gram Panchayat

Total No. of households = 264

(Primary unit of the study)

Block, it is found that the highest number of ITDP mouzas are located in the Sarpalehana-Albandha Gram Panchayat. It covers 9 ITDP mouzas. The second highest number of ITDP mouzas are located in the Kankali Gram Panchayat. It consists 7 ITDP mouzas. However, from the Bolpur Labhpur Project area these two Panchayats have been selected due to highest concentration of ITDP mouzas. These two Panchayats have also covered the highest number of ITDP beneficiaries. Total 264 beneficiary households have been identified. Therefore, the households have been treated as the primary source of the survey.

3.3. Demographic and Socio-Economic Features of the Study Area

The State

In West Bengal 38,08,760 Scheduled Tribes form 5.59 per cent of the total population of the State and 6.16 per cent of the total Scheduled Tribe population of India as per 1991 Census. Numerically the most dominant among these tribal groups in West Bengal is the Santal, who constitute more than 54 per cent of the total Scheduled Tribe population of the State. This Scheduled Tribe population is constituted of 50.78 per cent males and 49.22 per cent females with a sex ratio of 969 females per 1000 males. Further the overwhelming majority (97.73 per cent) of these people reside in the rural areas. Only 2.27 per cent of them live in urban centres.

When 57.70 per cent of the total population of West Bengal are literate as per 1991 Census, the said percentage for the Scheduled Tribe population is 16.21. The percentage of male literates to total population is 50.67 per cent as against 21.16 per cent of the Scheduled Tribes. Of the Scheduled Tribe females only 5.01 per cent literate against 30.25 per cent of the total population.

A diagrammatic representation of selection procedure of the study area is given below :

On an examination of the occupation pattern of the Scheduled Tribes population, it is found that 41.45 per cent of the total Scheduled Tribe population of this State are workers. This working force is obviously much higher in number that the same among the total population of this State (28.47 per cent). Of the total Scheduled Tribe workers highest number of them (48.73 per cent) are employed as agricultural labourers. The next highest number of Scheduled Tribe workers (31.04 per cent) are found to remain involved in cultivation. Of the remaining 20.23 per cent workers, 1.05 per cent are engaged in household industry etc. and other workers constitute 19.18 per cent. In the case of general population 30.64 per cent are cultivators, 24.82 per cent are agricultural labourers, 4.12 per cent are engaged in household Industry etc. and the remaining 40.42 per cent are other workers.

In the West Bengal the tribal peoples numbering 30,70,672 are spread all over the State. But the most important feature is that, nowhere in this State they are found to form a concentrated tribal zone as is found in some other States like Madhya Pradesh, Bihar, Orissa. These tribal peoples as per 1981 Census have come from 38 tribal groups. Since 1950 the number of Scheduled Tribes have been increased from 7 to 38. The number of Scheduled Tribes were 7 in 1950, become 19 in 1956, but finally increased to 41 in the same year with the reorganization of the States and ultimately amended to 38 in 1976.

These Scheduled Tribes of West Bengal may be classified into three distinct categories. Tribals like Oraon, Munda, Santal, Mahali, Malpaharia, Bhumij, Kheria, Ho, Kora and others who seem to have migrated from Bihar are distributed throughout the State including the tea-estates of Darjeeling and Jalpaiguri district. Secondly, tribes like Rabha, Garo, Mech, Hajong and Chakma who have come from Assam, Tripura and Bangladesh are mainly found in Tarai and foothills areas (Jalpaiguri and Cooch Behar districts) and the third category includes tribes like Bhutia and Lepcha who possibly have come from Bhutan and Sikkim and have ultimately settled in Darjeeling district.

Of the total tribal population of West Bengal, nine communities shared a little of over 90 per cent during 1971. These nine communities were the Santal (54.35per cent), Oraon (11.49 per cent), Munda (7.85 per cent), Bhumij (6.69 per cent), Kora (3.69 per cent), Mahali (1.87 per cent), Lodha/ Kheria (1.81 per cent), Bhutia (1.33 per cent) and Malpaharia (1.22 per cent). It is interesting to note that the first five ethnic groups alone contributed 84.07 per cent of the total Schedule Tribe population of the State in 1971. That means the rest of the tribes covered only 15.93 per cent.

The District

The district of Birbhum lies between 23°32'30" and 24°35'00" north latitudes. The easternmost extremity of this district is marked by 88°01'40" east longitude and the western most extremity by 87°05'25" east longitude. The Santal Parganas of Bihar bound it on western side and by the districts of Murshidabad and Burdwan on the east. The river Ajoy forms the southern boundary of the district separating it from Burdwan. The district is a part of the tract known as "Rahr".

The soil of the district is mostly covered with lateratic nodules. Granite veins are also observed to traverse the district at places running up on the surface for hundreds of acres, in Block barren plateaus. 82 per cent of the soil of the district is acidic.

The climate of the district is warm and dry. The Summer begins from March and continues well upto June. The minimum temperature is 10°C in January and the maximum is 41°C in May. Monsoon starts from June and continues upto September. The average annual rainfall is about 1423 mm.

The district is well drained by a number of rivers and rivulets running in nearly every case from west to east with a slight southernly inclination in the Suri Sub-division and north-eastern inclination in the eastern half of Rampurhat Sub-division.

The rivers of the district are Ajoy, Mayurakshi, Kopai, Bakreswar, Hinglow in the south and Dwarka, Brahmani, Barsloi and Paghla in the North. Agriculture is the chief occupation of the people of the district. The majority of the working populations of the district are cultivators and agricultural labourers. According to 1991 Census, 76.37 per cent of the total workers of the district are either engaged in cultivation or in agricultural labourers.

The district is composed of nineteen development blocks or Panchayat Samities. Each of these blocks comprises a several numbers of Gram Panchayats. There are 169 Gram Panchayats in the district. The district is characterized by 2461 villages of which 2229 are inhabited. Although there are 2229 inhabited villages in the district, the Schedule Tribe population are found only in 927 villages, i.e., 41.59 per cent of the inhabited villages only. There are seven towns in the district, out of which the Municipal Board of Commissioner administers Bolpur, Dubrajpur, Rampurhat and Suri and the Notified Area Authority controls Sainthia. The remaining towns namely Bakreswar tourist centre township and Nalhati are non-municipal census town.

There is no regulated market in the district, for which producers have to depend upon middlemen. There are four A-Class marketing centres in the district, i.e., Suri, Sainthia, Rampurhat and Bolpur. Besides, there are Seven B-Class and a few C-Class 'hats'. Principal commodities transacted are paddy, potato, wheat and vegetables. There are three cattle market at Sainthia, Rampurhat and Illambazar. Besides 17 rural godowns under Thana Marketing Societies, there are few rural godowns under PACS. 55 grain 'golas' and 10 cold storages.

The Block

The Bolpur-Sriniketan Block, one of the nineteen Blocks of Birbhum District, is located in the extreme southern part of Birbhum District, between 23°33' and 23°46' North latitudes and 87°34' and 87°50' East longitudes. It is bounded on the north by the Sainthia Block, on the West by the Illambazar, on the East by the Labhpur and Nanoor Block and on the south by the river Ajoy and Burdwan District.

The Block consists of nine Gram Panchayats, out of total 169 Gram Panchayats of Birbhum District. The Block has a total area of 331.30 square kilometres and a total population of 1,23,321 according to 1991 Census. This gives a density of 500 persons per square kilometres. The majority of its present population (76.88 per cent) still live in rural areas. Bolpur is the only urban centre, having a population of 38,386 according to 1991 Census. The Block is dominated by small sized villages. Out of 156 inhabited villages in the Block 67 villages have population of less than 500, 49 villages have less than 1,000. There are only 10 villages whose population is found to be above 2,000. This feature presents very dispersed settlement and petty peasant economy.

Bolpur-Sriniketan Block presents a varied landscape. Its landforms show a transitional character between the deltaic plain in the east and the plateau fringe in the west. Much of its present surface contains alluvial terraces of pleistocene age, partly laterised and considerably eroded. Such a landscape, where it is flat, is intensively cultivated with rice, while uplands, which were once forested now presented a bare lateratic face. Six, out of nine Gram Panchayats are plainlands and the remaining three are moderately undulating. The ground rises towards the west and slopes to the south-east. The watershed of the Block corresponds generally to a high ground in the central part on which the Kopai South Main Canal is laid. The streams or *Kandars* to the south of this watershed flow into the river Ajoy and those to the north join the river Kopai. The area is well drained. The Ajoy and Kopai are the two principal rivers and has been the mainstay of water supply for agriculture in the region.

Soil of the Block is on the whole sandy and is not very rich in mineral nutrients. In general soil quality of the Block improves progressively form red lateratic to the sandy loam and then sandy loam to clayey loam to from higher to lower areas. Sandy loam is the most common type. There are two major types of soil in the Block - the red and laterite and the old alluvium. Red and laterite soil is the most extensive soil formation in the Block, occupying 60 per cent of the total geographical area. It occupies higher grounds of the Block. Texturally it is sandy and gravelly and hence it is locally named as *Kankar* soil. This soil is acidic, poor in lime and magnesia and deficient in nitrogen and organic matter.

The Block has hot and dry summer, high humidity and well-distributed rainfall during the monsoon. In this Block, rainfall is derived mainly from the South-West Monsoon. It receives on an average 1410 millimetre rainfall much of it going waste. The minimum temperature is 10° Celsius in January and the maximum temperature is 41° Celsius in May. Monsoon rain starts from Mid June and continues upto September.

Farming forms the principal occupation of the people. Nearly 74 per cent of the total geographical area of the Block are under cultivation. Out of 33,360 hectares of land as much as 24,700 hectares (74.04 per cent) are at present under cultivation. Forest occupies 450 hectares (1.35 per cent) and the remaining 8,210 hectares (24.61 per cent) are not available for cultivation. Rice ranks first amongst food crops, taking up about 95.4 per cent of the total kharif area. Wheat on the other hand occupies about 66.7 per cent of the Rabi area. The other crops grown include potato, sugarcane, pulses and oilseeds having very little acreage. In Bolpur-Sriniketan Block canals, tanks, tube wells, river lift etc., form the bulk of irrigation.

Industrial development in the Block has not made rapid headway. Rice-milling, brick-kilns, oil-processing, saw-milling etc., are the principal industries. The household industries of the Block include weaving, leather works, brass and metal works, potteries, etc. Most of the household industries of the Block are, at present, in a moribund condition, resulting in a stagnant village economy where very meagre employment opportunities exist.

Communication is not well organized in the Block. Roads and railways are the principal means of communication but its level of development is rather poor. The Block has good external connection but its internal road development remains poor. Most of the roads in the Block originate and terminate at Bolpur town, indicating it to be the needlepoint of economic activity of the area. From the foregoing account it can be said that the social and economic infrastructural facilities of the Block are very weak. Roads, schools, health, communications, industry and marketing facilities etc. in the Block are so weakly developed that it seems productive forces have not been harnessed at a high level of efficiency.

The economy of the Bolpur-Sriniketan Block principally stands on agriculture. Nearly 74 per cent of the total geographical area of the Block are under cultivation and 68 per cent of the total working force are engaged in agriculture. This shows a predominant role of agriculture in the economic activities of the people. In this Block, the percentage of agricultural labourers is overwhelmingly high (40.15 per cent according to 1991 Census) in comparison to the land owning cultivators (27.74 per cent). Scheduled Castes and Scheduled Tribes form the bulk of the labour force amounting to 42 per cent of the total labour force engaged in agriculture. Because of too much dependence on agriculture, low level of productivity of land and labour, the magnitude of poverty in rural areas is high. On average they are employed for 150 days per year.

Besides agricultural labourers, the problem of small farmers is also manifold. In Bolpur-Sriniketan Block, the majority of the farmers are marginal farmers. Over 75 per cent of the agricultural holdings are of less than 2.5 acres. These holdings are uneconomic and these do not allow the farmers to earn adequate income to support their family in reasonable comfort after paying necessary expenses for agriculture.

In the Block, agriculture and industrial employment are not adequate in relation to the requirement of the people. These, coupled with the incidence of drought and flood, which occur once in every three or four year, make life very hard. The economy of the Block is geared to agriculture with rice, wheat, potatos, pulses, oilseeds as principal crops per hectare yield of major crops is not high and double cropping is negligible. Recently, adaptations of new technology in agriculture have brought about some changes in the lifestyle of the people of Bolpur-Sriniketan Block.

3.4. The People: Aspects of Their Traditional Economy, Society and Culture

Four tribal communities namely, the Santal, the Mahali, the Kora and the Oraons are living in the study area. Here, an attempt has been made to introduce these people with special reference to their traditional structure of socio-economic organization and cultural pattern.

Santal

The Santal is the third largest tribal community of India with a population of 4,260,842. They are distributed in the States of Bihar, West Bengal, Orissa, tea plantation areas of Assam, Meghalaya and Tripura and the southern part of Nepal, the North Western part of Bangladesh and the southern part of Bhutan. In West Bengal the Santal constitutes the single largest tribal group. They are found in almost all the districts of West Bengal. Specially, they are concentrated in the districts of Midnapur, Bankura, Purulia, Birbhum and Malda.

According to known history, their traditional homeland was Chhotanagpur plateau and the surrounding plains of south of the river Damodar. The highest concentration is found in Santal Parganas located in the eastern extremity of Chhotanagpur and regarded as the nucleus of the tribe.

The Santal call themselves as 'Hor', that is man and others as 'Diku' or alien. Dalton in his book, *Descriptive Ethnology of Bengal* depicted the fact of originality of Santals. He says that the Santals are originally a Mundari speaking people. They probably took its name from a geographical area known as Saont or Samanta Bhum where they settled after their split from their mother stock. The affix "a l" in the sense of son has been added to the word Saont to form the complete word "Saontal" or "Santal" meaning the inhabitants of the region of Saont or "Samanta Bhumi". Chatna in Bankura district is held to be the Saont or Samanta land of old days.

The Santal migration started after the famine of AD 1770 into Birbhum and Santal Pargana, their present homeland. Their highest concentration is in the Rajmahal hills of Bihar and in the neighbouring areas.

The Santals of Birbhum, according to the District Gazetteer 1975, came to inhabit this area after the enactment of the permanent Land Settlement Act of 1793. They migrated to this region through the Chhotanagpur belt.

The Santals are a Mundari speaking people, included in the Austro-Asiatic sub-family of the great Austric flank. Their language Santali is one of the oldest dialect of India.

While the primary occupation of the Santal is agriculture; hunting, fishing and collecting form their subsidiary economic activities. Actually, Santals are expert hunters and they hunt any game, big or small, that comes their way. Hunting probably formed as considerable part of their subsistence effort in the past but deforestation, excepting in the reserved forest, has led them to lay more stress on agriculture.

Fishing is another form of subsidiary economic activity of the Santals. They fish in rivers, tanks, ponds and other water logged places with the help of their nets, traps, bows and arrows.

The people also know animal husbandry but it plays a minor role in maintaining their food supply.

Besides agriculture, hunting, fishing, rearing animals, collection of a wide variety of plants, fruits, flowers, roots etc. constituted a major part of the Santal economy. Nowadays many of them are employed elsewhere in services, in mines and quarries.

The traditional social structure of the Santals like most other Mundari groups of tribals in the central-east India is traditionally characterised by segmentary system based on territorial and kin groups. The ideal typical territorial organization is based on village-*pargana-Dishum*.

Every household of the Santal villages operates more or less as an independent production and consumption unit. But it is highly embedded within the social and cultural matrix of the village (*ato*) and as such many of their economic decisions and activities are subject to the approval and sanctions of the village society. Different phases of productive activities of the Santal households are always accompanied by some rituals and ceremonies that are held communally in the village. They perform rituals and ceremonies at first in each case communally and then the households of the village are permitted to perpetuate their independent productive activities. This kind of ritual sanction, in fact, act as a moral force in binding the households of village into a corporate productive organization and stands in the way of complete nuclearization or individualization of the family households, their primary productive unit.

In the Santal community it was very commonly found to set up an authority to deal with inter-village relationships. The Santals have, in historic times, applied the term '*pargana*' to the collection of villages accepting the authority of an inter-village council and to the council itself. In the later stages they organized their villages into *pargana* groups and developed *pargana* council. The *pargana* council was made up of groups of elders; each group, with its headman represented one of the villages in the *pargana*.

The term *disum* literally means the country. It is closely associated with the life and culture of the Santals. Unlike the other territorial groups, village and *Pargana* it has no secular chief or head. But to the Santals it is more than its territory infested area specifically the area located in the Jungle Mahal. It is an institution of great importance emphasizing the solidarity of their entire ethnic group.

The Santal society is characterized by the segmentary social system based on kin groups - lineage and clans. Lineage is the simplest type of unilateral grouping, which consists of all the descendants in one line of a particular person through a determinate number of generations.

The Santals have a notion of another kin group larger than the lineage. This is the sub-clan. It consists of several lineages agnatically related to one another. Sub-clan in fact, is indicative of the specific clan affiliation. The Santals are divided into twelve patrilineal exogamous clans. The members of a clan are believed to have descended from a common ancestor. The Santal distinguish themselves as *hor* from all other people who are broadly categorised as *diku* or the alien. A Santal attains his horhood by conforming to necessary socio-cultural rituals and this confirms his or her Santalhood or his status as *hor*.

Mahalis

Mahalis are supposed to have lived originally in the Chhotanagpur plateau of Bihar. From there they migrated to West Bengal in the districts of Birbhum, Bankura, Burdwan, Midnapore, Malda, 24-parganas, West Dinajpur, Jalpaiguri, Darjeeling and several other districts. The population of the Mahali in West Bengal is 10,827 according to 1981 Census.

According to Risley (1891), Mahali is Dravidian caste of labourers, palanquin-bearers and workers in bamboo. They are divided into five sub-castes - *Bansphor Mahali*, who make baskets and do all kinds of bamboo work; *Patar Mahali*, basket makers and cultivators; *Sulunkhi Mahali*, who are cultivators and labourers; *Tati Mahali*, who carry palanquins; and *Mahali Munda*, a small outlying sub-caste.

Mahalis form an artisan group of the Santali speaking peoples. After a comparison of the totemic sections of the Mahali, Risley says the main body of the Mahali community is merely a branch of the Santals separated at a comparatively recent date from the parent stock. Their language and social customs reveal traits of their Santali origin.

Risley has mentioned different section of the Mahali Community profess different types of occupations. But he also mentioned that they believe that their original occupation is basket making and generally bamboo work. For marketing purposes of their commodities in towns and villages, they have to come with the close contact of Bengali society and thereby they have adopted many Bengali practices in their social life and Bengali terms in their language. In Birbhum, the Mahalis in addition to their occupation of basket making are also employed as agricultural labourers by the land owning agriculturists.

The Religion of the Mahalis is at present a mixture of the half-forgotten animism and Hinduism. They perform various religious Hindu festivals like *Haripuja*, *Manasapuja*, *Gram Thakur Puja*, *Karampuja*, *Kali* and *Goal* or *Gareya puja*, etc.

In the study area Uttargopinathpur is a multiethnic Mouza, situated in the Sarpalehana-Albandha Gram Panchayat of Bolpur-Sriniketan Block of Birbhum. The Mouza consists of three hamlets viz. Gopinathpur, Ampukurdanga and Dighidanga. Gopinathpur only is inhabited by the caste community and other two hamlets inhabited by the two tribal communities Mahalis and the Santals.

Koras

The Koras are a little known community of West Bengal. Risley (1891), states the Koras are a Dravidian Caste of earth workers and cultivators in Chhotanagpur, Western and Central Bengal, probably an offshoot from the Munda tribe. On the other hand the Koras of Santal Parganas claim to have come from Nagpur. S.C. Roy (1915), while writing about the Oraons stated "A number of Oraons now living in the eastern parts of the Ranchi District and in the adjoining district of Manbhum are known as Modis and sometimes as Koras. The name Modi like the name Kora - has reference to their skill in working in earth such as raising embankments, Mud walls etc." Grierson (1931), states that the Koras use the surname 'modi' and their language is derived from Mundari.

It has been observed that the mother tongue of these Koras also differs from area to area in different parts of West Bengal. In Purulia district they speak a dialect which is akin to *Kurukh* (Oraon) language. In Midnapore district Kora dialect is very much akin to Santali language. In Burdwan it is reported to be a variant of Bengali. In case of Murshidabad district it is akin to Mundari.

In West Bengal the Koras are numbering 96,835 according to the Census 1981. The biggest concentration of these 'Koras' is in the district of Burdwan and they are found mostly in the colliery areas. Next in order comes the Midnapore district. Out of sixteen districts in West Bengal about 88 per cent of the Koras are found in seven districts (Burdwan, Midnapore, Bankura, Purulia, Jalpaiguri, Birbhum and Hooghly) and the remaining are scattered in varied numbers in the rest of the districts.

From the distribution pattern of the Koras it reveals that they are mostly concentrated in those districts of West Bengal, which are adjacent to Southern Bihar which may be taken as the original homeland of the Koras. In other words it may be said that they are gradually infiltrated into this State from the neighbouring area obviously due to economic hardship in their original homeland.

In matters of religion Risley states that Koras affect to be orthodox Hindus, worshipping the regular gods and calling themselves *Saktas* or *Vaishnavas*, accordingly as they incline to the cult of *Kali*, *Durga* and *Manasa* or that of *Radha* and *Krishna*. Their village and household deities are *Bhairab Thakur*, *Gram Deoti*, and *Kudra*, to whom goats, fowls, pigeons, rice, sugar, and plantain are offered on no fixed dates and divided between the worshippers and the *Deogharia* Brahmans, who serve them as priests and keep in order the shrines (*Kudrasthan* and *Bhairabsthan*) of the village gods.

About the social position of Koras Risley states that, "The social position of Koras in very low, and they are usually classed with Bagdis, Bauris, Bunas and other dwellers on the confines of Hinduism. Risley has mentioned that their own practice in the matter of diet varies in different parts of the country. In Chhotanagpur they eat beaf, pork, and fowls, and all manners of fish, whether scaly or scaleless, but refrain from eating field-rats, snakes, lizards and animals which have died natural deaths. Further east they are more particular. No Kora will touch beaf and some members abstain from fowls and from strong drink, in the belief that by doing so they acquire some sort of social distinction (Risley, 1891).

The traditional occupations of these Koras were digging of wells, road making etc. i.e., they were a group of people of earth-workers. In the present day they earn their livelihood as cultivators, agricultural labourers, sharecroppers and also as diggers of tanks, wells and as construction workers.

In the district of Birbhum, Koras are mostly concentrated in Bolpur-Sriniketan, Murarai, and Mayureswar. In the study area of Bolpur-Sriniketan Block, a small numbers of Koras inhabit in a village viz. Naodangal in the Sarpalehana-Albandha Gram Panchayat.

Oraon

In the study area of Birbhum district Oraons are found in the village viz. Dholtikuri of Kankali Gram Panchayat of Bolpur-Sriniketan Block. The Oraons of this area call themselves as Sardar and believe that they migrated from the Ranchi area. When they asked about their original home every one speaks of Chhotanagpur, but none can give out the exact position of his origin and tradition.

The Oraons form a community of settled agriculturists. They call themselves as *Kurukh.* According to S.C. Roy (1915), they probably owe their name *Kurukh* to their hero king *Karakh.* The Oraons are supposed to have lived originally in the land called Kurusha, south-west of Ganga. Dalton also has the opinion that the tradition of the Oraons connect them with the western coast of India either with Gujarat or with Konkan, the lowland strip along the western portion of the Bombay Presidency (the present Maharashtra) lying between the range of the Western Ghats and the sea as their cradleland.

The people best known in many parts of India as 'Dhangars'. This word derived from *dang* or *dhang*, means a hill. However, 'Dhangars' may mean any hillmen, but amongst several tribes of the southern Tributary Mahals, the term *Dhangar* and *Dhangarin* mean the youth of the two sexes both in highland and lowland village and it cannot be considered as the national designation of any particular tribe.

Due to pressure from various forces, they have wandered eastward along the central range of hills. "There, with their newly acquired knowledge of agriculture, they gradually settled down on the fertile valleys of some great rivers like the Narmada," (S.C. Roy. 1915). During the Mahammedan invasion they were forced out from this settled habitat and split up into two divisions and to have moved in two different paths - one settled at the Rajmahal hills and the other took possession of the north-east portion of the plateau of Chhotanagpur. After reaching here they found that the Mundas already occupied the territory. For a period of time they lived in tolerable amity with the Mundas but with their comparatively superior equipment, better intelligence, better knowledge of agriculture the Oraons become gradually predominant in the north-western and central parts of the plateau (Roy : 1915).

After leading a settled life for a good length of time, some of them started migrating seasonally and/or permanently to different urbanised, industrialised or tea-plantation areas of Bihar, West Bengal, Orissa and Madhya Pradesh as labourers, due to economic hardships and other socio-political reasons. Oraons are, however, predominantly agriculturists in the plain lands. Some of them also work as daily labourers. Occupations such as hunting, fishing, cattle rearing are subsidiary to agriculture.

In West Bengal the Oraons are distributed in the

districts of Jalpaiguri, Midnapur, 24 Parganas, Bankura, Birbhum, Burdwan, Cooch Behar, Malda, Murshidabad, Nadia, etc. According to 1981 Census their total population in West Bengal is 4,37,574.

Oraons practice a mixed religion of Hinduism and Animism. They consider *Dharam* or *Bhagwan* as their Supreme Deity. They also worship *Devi Mai, Gaodeoti, Jnakraburia, Kali, Manasa, Sitala, Mahadev, Hari* and other.

In the study area they have been residing in comparatively small numbers surrounded by dominating Hindu Caste people. Not only that other dominating tribal community of the district the Santals have been residing in the same village but in a separate hamlet at a distance. Oraon hamlet is locally called as *Sardar Para* and the Santal hamlet is locally called as *Saontal Para* or *Manjhi Para.* Oraons of this area call themselves as Sardar and all of them use 'Sardar' as their surname. They also introduce them as *Dhangor.* They speak a language of their own which linguistically belongs to the Dravidian family of languages. They speak Bengali for inter-group communication. They use the Bengali script. The Young generation prefers to speak in Bengali than their original language. Oraons here practise agriculture as their main occupation. They also work as daily labourers.

The Oraon constitute an endogamous tribe. This tribe is divided into a number of exogamous clans of totemic nature. Their clan names are taken from birds, fish, animals, vegetables, plants or minerals. The Oraons do not believe that they have actually descended from the totem. They consider that the totem helped, protected and gave some services to their ancestors in crisis.

Each clan is divided into a number of exogamous lineages. It embraces all the agnatic male descendents, their wives and their unmarried children. A lineage is divided into a number of families.

The authority of the regional council, *parha* panchayat administers the Oraons. A *parha* or region is defined as a territorial unit consisting of a number of adjoining villages. This regional group has a particular territory where it owns and defends its rights in agricultural land, village sites, forest tracts, grazing land, water supplies and fishing pools. One of the regional groups is called the *raja* (chief) village, another *dewan* (prime minister) village, a third the *kotwn* (orderly) village, and the remaining villages the *praja* (subject) villages. The headman or the *mahato* of the *raja* village acts as the chairman of the *parha* council.

The authority of the *pahan* (village priest) and the *mahato* (secular headman) administer the Oraon village community. The *pahan* acts as the mediator between the people and the mystical powers by propitiations and prayers. He tries to maintain a good relationship between the people on the one hand and the super-natural powers on the other. The *mahato* is responsible for the protection of the village community from external threats. Naturally, he is to maintain a satisfactory relationship with the external world. They have no right to tax, tribute or service. Also, they have no power of enforcing their decisions in settling disputes without the consent of the village panchayat. The village panchayat being composed of the elders of all the lineages exercises greater influence on the affairs of the village community.

In the traditional Oraon society there are two separate institutions; one is the youth dormitory or *dhumkuria* and the other is the maiden's dormitory *pelerpa*. The membership of the dormitory is compulsory. Both boys and girls of the dormitory are to perform many social duties.

To sum up, it may be mentioned here that all the tribal groups of the study area live in the multiethnic villages. Each of the groups has, however, a habitation of its own well demarcated and distinct from the habitation of the other ethnic groups. Often they identify their habitation as a separate village, and maintain a distinct socio-cultural boundary. Every household of the tribal village operates more or less as an independent production consumption unit. The production and the consumption activities of the households are, however, largely controlled by the social and cultural norms of the ethnic group at the village level. Every household is in fact, embedded within the larger social and cultural matrix of the village. The tribal village, as a community always is trying to persist its solidarity and the distinct socio-cultural pattern of its own. It is reflected in every sphere of their life; their economic decisions, production, consumption and distribution, ritual processes, behaviour pattern during different village festivals etc.

Traditionally the tribal economy is of subsistence type. The mode of production of tribal economy is often designated as familial or domestic that is they produce only what they need. But a careful probe into the production, consumption and distribution activities of the people in contexts would reveal that the participation of the entire community at the village level is the norm of the household production of the tribals. Generally, the profit motive in their economic dealings is quite absent. Though the tribal people in the area has since long been exposed to the forms of market economy of the larger society, they are found to maintain to a great extent, their traditional mode of reciprocal exchange. A careful probe into the situation would reveal the presence of multiple spheres of exchange that are institutionalized and morally sanctioned.

The tribal society is a kin-based society. In their day to day interaction the relationship based on descent or affinity or proximal relationships are given more importance than their individual gain, benefit or wealth formation. In fact, their concept of 'good life' in economic spheres can hardly be separated from their general outlook towards life; their personal expectations and desires for material provision are thus, greatly influenced by their ideas of community life.

4
ITDP and the Tribals

4.1. Beneficiary Households and Their Socio-Economic Status

Four tribal groups are present in the study area. They are the Santal, the Mahali, the Kora and the Sardar. Total 264 beneficiary households have been surveyed. Out of 264 beneficiary households, 223 households (84.47 per cent) are the Santals. Eighteen households are the Mahalis (6.82 per cent). Eighteen households are Orans who call themselves as Sardars. Only five households are the Koras, i.e., 1.89 per cent (Table: 4.1.1).

Table 4.1.1
Tribewise Distribution of Beneficiary Households

Name of the Tribe	*No.*	*Percentage*
SANTAL	223	84.47
MAHALI	18	6.82
KORA	5	1.89
SARDAR	18	6.82
TOTAL	264	100.00

Total population of 264 beneficiary households is 1474, of which 772 (52.37 per cent) are male and 702 (47.63 per cent) are female (Table: 4.1.2). The total population of Santal beneficiary households is 1249. It is highest among the four communities of the study area. Of the sixteen mouzas studied the Santals occupy thirteen. Among the other three mouzas they share with Mahalis in one and Sardars in another. Another one inhabited by the Koras but they are few in numbers.

Table 4.1.2
Tribewise Population Distribution of Beneficiary Households

Name of the Tribe	M	(%)	F	(%)	Total
SANTAL	653	52.28	596	47.72	1249
MAHALI	43	49.43	44	50.57	87
KORA	11	44.00	14	56.00	25
SARDAR	65	57.52	48	42.48	113
TOTAL	772	52.37	702	47.63	1474

Land Holding

The most important asset of the rural people is land. Average operational holding of the Santal beneficiary households is 1.72 acres. Average own land of the Santal is 0.73 acres and they leased in average 0.99 acre. Mahalis have average 0.71 acre own land and leased in 1.14 acres. Their average operational holding is 1.85 acres. In case of the Koras, average operational holding is 1.12 acres. Their average own land is 0.59 acres and leased in land is 0.53 acre. Average operational holding of the Sardar community is highest and it is 2.06 acres. They have average 1.03 acres own land and their average leased in land is 1.03 acres. (Table: 4.1.3).

Table 4.1.3
Average Operational Holding of the Beneficiary Households

(In Acre)

Name of the Tribe	Own Land	Leased In Land	Leased Out Land	Total Operational Holding
SANTAL	.73	.99	-	1.72
MAHALI	.71	1.14	-	1.85
KORA	.59	.53	-	1.12
SARDAR	1.03	1.03	-	2.06

Generally, these tribal people leased in land from the neighbouring Hindu Caste people and are known as sharecroppers (*Bhagchasi*). In these cases the tribals either have'some land or no land but have their own plough and cattle. Total 148 beneficiaries, i.e., 67.77 per cent of the landholders are sharecroppers. The other category is the *Kisan*, who have neither land nor plough, mostly work as the annual contract labourers in the land of the neighbouring Hindu caste people. Fifteen beneficiaries identified as *kisan*. Sharing of production between landlord and sharecropper is according to the sharing of inputted costs of cultivation. Hundred sharecroppers, i.e., 67.57 per cent, share their production with their landlord by 75:25 ratio. Thirty one beneficiaries, i.e., 24.94 per cent sharecropper used to share the production with their landlord by 50:50. Seventeen sharecropper beneficiaries are also identified who shared the production during rainy season in the ratio of 75:25, while during summer season they shared by 50:50 or 60:40. Though the sharing depends on inputted costs but it is nothing but a mutual understanding between the landlord and the sharecroppers. According to the condition of sharing the sharecropper have to convey all the costs of labour and of irrigation. Costs of labour do not make a problem to a tribal household as all the members of a household engaged themselves in cultivation and also get the co-operation from their kins and neighbours. But their problem is to convey the extravagant cost of irrigation. However, the landlords are conveying the total costs of irrigation or share with the sharecroppers. All the inputted costs of cultivation when equally shared by the landlord and sharecroppers, they shared their production also equally, i.e., the ratio of sharing is 50:50. When all the inputted costs are for the sharecropper then the ratio of sharing of crops between sharecropper and landlord is 75:25. Both the cases all the expenses for the labour costs are for the sharecropper. The ratio of sharing between the landlord and the *Kisan* is 60:40. In these cases, it is inevitable that all the costs of cultivation are bearing by the landlords.

Out of 264 beneficiary households, thirty-nine beneficiaries (14.77 per cent) are landless. Thirty-four landless are Santals; Mahalis and Koras each have one landless beneficiary and three among the Sardar beneficiaries are landless. For each of the tribal category most of the beneficiaries are marginal farmers (whose land size is 0.1- 2.50 acre). One hundred fifty three households, i.e., 57.95 per cent of the total beneficiary households are marginal farmers. Next among the beneficiary households are small farmers. Sixty-three, i.e., 23.86 per cent of the beneficiary households are small farmers whose average land size is 2.51-5.00 acres. Only six beneficiary households have the land size of 5.01-7.50 acre, may call the medium farmers. All of them are the Santals. Only three (1.14 per cent) households have above 7.50 acres of land, may call the large farmers. Two of them are Santal households and one of them is Sardar. (Table : 4.1.4).

Table 4.1.4
Tribewise Distribution of Beneficiary Households by Landsize

Land Size (Acre)	*Santal No.*	*(%)*	*Mahali No.*	*(%)*	*Kora No.*	*(%)*	*Sardar No.*	*(%)*	*Total No.*	*(%)*
Land Less	34	15.25	1	5.56	1	20.00	3	16.67	39	14.77
0.1 -2.50	125	56.05	14	77.78	3	60.00	11	61.11	153	57.95
2.51 -5.00	56	25.11	3	16.67	1	20.00	3	16.67	63	23.86
5.01 -7.50	6	2.69	-	-	-	-	-	-	6	2.28
Above 7.50	2	.90	-	-	-	-	1	5.56	3	1.14
Total	223	100.00	18	100.00	5	100.00	18	100.00	264	100.00

Primary Occupational Pattern

Most of the members of the beneficiary households are found to engage in cultivation and then as agricultural labourers. The most important point was felt regarding the occupational pattern of the tribal people in the study area is that, in so many cases each members of a tribal household engaged in various types of occupations to earn more for better livelihood. As for example, one household comprising six members have one acre of land. Parents are engaged in cultivation in their own land and rest of the time as agricultural labourers. One of their sons engaged most of the time as a mason helper and at the season time help his parents in cultivating their own land. On the other hand, sons' wife engaged most the time in the brickfield as a labour and then she also works in their own field or as agricultural labourer at the season time. This kind of diversification of occupation is prominently observed in case of the Santal households (Table : 4.1.5).

Three hundred and seventy-one (41.87 per cent) members of the total population are engaged in cultivation and three hundred sixty nine (41.65 per cent) are engaged as agricultural labourers primarily to earn their livelihood. Three hundred and twelve Santal individuals are engaged primarily in cultivation of which 61.54 per cent are male and 38.46 per cent are female. Another large number of Santal individuals are engaged most of their time as agricultural labourers of which 60.45 per cent are female and 39.55 per cent are male (Table: 4.1.5). That is, females are primarily engaged more as agricultural labourers than the males. Seven Santal males are found to work as Mason in the area of Bolpur and Santiniketan. Initially they were working as a mason helper. After a long-time experience they have becoming Mason themselves. Ten Santal male and eight females are working as mason helper. Three Santal males engage as shawmill labour primarily. Six male individuals and six female individuals are working as labour in the Rice Mill located at Bolpur, the nearest town of the study area. Thirty-six individuals earn their livelihood primarily from the brick kiln those are grown in some part of the study area at the side of the river Kopai. Besides these, Santal males are also engaged as labour of Lorry, as a labour for repairing rail line, as Rickshaw pooler and in carpentry. Not only that six Santal businessman also found in the study area. There are three Santal males and two females working as regular employee in the government concerns. Females are mainly the unskilled labourers of Visva-Bharati, the Central University established by Rabindra Nath Tagore. Among three male service holders, one is a teacher of a Higher Secondary School and the other two are the employee of Visva Bharati. Four Santal females are found to engage as maidservant in the households of

Table 4.1.5

Primary Occupational Pattern of Beneficiary Households

Name of the Tribe		Cultivation		Agricultural labour		Mason		Mason Helper		Shawmill Labour		Rice Mill Labour		Labour of lorry		Labour in brick field		Labour for repairing rail line	
		No.	%	No.	%	No.	%	No.	%	No.	%	No.	%	No.	%	No.	%	No.	%
	M	192	61.54	123	39.55	7	100.00	10	55.56	3	100.00	6	50.00	3	100.00	10	27.78	1	100.00
SANTAL	F	120	38.46	188	60.45	-	-	8	44.44	-	-	6	50.00	-	-	26	72.22	-	-
	T	312	100.00	311	100.00	7	100.00	18	100.00	3	100.00	12	100.00	3	100.00	36	100.0	1	100.00
	M	18	72.00	3	16.67	-	-	1	100.00	-	-	-	-	-	-	-	-	-	-
MAHALI	F	7	28.00	15	83.33	-	-	-	-	-	-	-	-	-	-	-	-	-	-
	T	25	100.00	18	100.00	-	-	1	100.00	-	-	-	-	-	-	-	-	-	-
	M	3	50.00	5	45.45	-	-	-	-	-	-	-	-	-	-	-	-	-	-
KORA	F	3	50.00	6	54.55	-	-	-	-	-	-	-	-	-	-	-	-	-	-
	T	6	100.00	11	100.00	-	-	-	-	-	-	-	-	-	-	-	-	-	-
	M	18	64.29	16	55.17	-	-	-	-	-	-	-	-	-	-	-	-	-	-
SARDAR	F	10	35.71	13	44.83	-	-	-	-	-	-	-	-	-	-	-	-	-	-
	T	28	100.00	29	100.00	-	-	-	-	-	-	-	-	-	-	-	-	-	-
TOTAL		371	41.87	369	41.65	7	0.79	19	2.14	3	Neg-ligi-ble	12	1.35	3	Neg ligi-ble	36	4.06	1	Neg ligi-ble

Contd......

Contd......

Name of the Tribe		Carpentry		Craft		Service		Business		Rickshaw Pooler		Maid Servant		Bagali		Others		Total	
		No.	%	No.	%	No.	%	No.	%	No.	%	No.	%	No.	%	No.	%	No.	%
	M	2	100.00	-	-	3	60.00	6	100.00	7	100.00	-	-	12	66.67	1	50.00	386	51.67
SANTAL	F	-	-	-	-	2	40.00	-	-	-	-	4	100.00	6	33.33	1	50.00	361	48.33
	T	2	100.00	-	-	5	100.00	6	100.00	7	100.00	4	100.00	18	100.00	2	100.0	747	100.00
	M	-	-	7	46.67	1	100.00	-	-	-	-	-	-	-	-	-	-	30	50.00
MAHALI	F	-	-	8	53.33	-	-	-	-	-	-	-	-	-	-	-	-	30	50.00
	T	-	-	15	100.00	1	100.00	-	-	-	-	-	-	-	-	-	-	60	100.00
	M	-	-	-	-	-	-	-	-	-	-	-	-	-	-	-	-	8	47.06
KORA	F	-	-	-	-	-	-	-	-	-	-	-	-	-	-	-	-	9	52.94
	T	-	-	-	-	-	-	-	-	-	-	-	-	-	-	-	-	17	100.00
	M	-	-	-	-	-	-	-	-	-	-	-	-	3	100.00	1	100.0	38	61.29
SARDAR	F	-	-	-	-	-	-	-	-	-	-	1	-	-	-	-	-	24	38.71
	T	-	-	-	-	-	-	-	-	-	-	1	-	3	100.00	1	100.0	62	100.00
TOTAL		2	Negligible	15	1.69	6	0.68	6	0.68	7	0.79	5	0.56	21	2.37	3	Negligible	886	100.00

neighbouring Hindu caste people. They work as agricultural labourer in their land at the time of cultivation and do the domestic works and look after of the cattles also. They get a fixed amount as a maidservant and payment for agricultural labour separately.

Exceptions are noticed in few cases among the traditional basket maker, the Mahalis (Table 4.1.5). One Mahali male individual is found to work as a Mason Helper and another male individual is a service holder. He is an employee of Visva Bharati working as a clerk in the account section of the central office of the University.

Secondary Occupational Pattern

In which occupation one individual engaged after his or her engagement in the primary occupation is considered as a secondary occupation. Most of the cases whose primary occupation is cultivation engaged as a agricultural labourer in the rest of the period that means when he has no work in his own land. Cultivation became a secondary occupation to those individuals whose land size is very small and obviously they primarily engaged as agricultural labourers or in any other occupation for the maintenance of their livelihood. One hundred and ninety-seven tribal individuals of the beneficiary households in the study area engaged in cultivation secondarily. Two hundred and ninety-eight individuals, i.e., 50.85 per cent of the total working population are engaged as agricultural labourer as their secondary occupation. In case of secondary occupation diversification is also noticed among the Santal community (Table 4.1.6). After cultivation and agricultural labourer they also engaged secondarily as a mason, mason helper, in carpentry and a large number of Santal individuals work as labour in the brickfield. Exception is noticed in few cases only among the Mahalis. The basket maker Mahalis try to continue their traditional occupation besides their primary occupation (Table 4.1.6).

Income Pattern

Though the tribal individuals of the beneficiary households are found to engage in different types of

Table 4.1.6

Secondary Occupational Pattern of Beneficiary Households

Name of the Tribe		Cultivation		Agricultural labour		Mason		Mason Helper		Shawmill Labour		Rice Mill Labour		Labour of lorry		Labour in brick field		Labour for repairing rail line	
		No.	%	No.	%	No.	%	No.	%	No.	%	No.	%	No.	%	No.	%	No.	%
	M	64	39.02	154	62.10	1	100.00	7	63.64	-	-	-	-	-	-	14	42.42	-	-
SANTAL	F	100	60.98	94	37.90	-	-	4	36.36	-	-	-	-	-	-	19	57.58	-	-
	T	164	100.00	248	100.00	1	100.00	11	100.00	-	-	-	-	-	-	33	100.00	-	-
	M	6	50.00	12	60.00	-	-	1	100.00	-	-	-	-	-	-	-	-	-	-
MAHALI	F	6	50.00	8	40.00	-	-	-	-	-	-	-	-	-	-	-	-	-	-
	T	12	100.00	20	100.00	-	-	1	100.00	-	-	-	-	-	-	-	-	-	-
	M	3	50.00	2	50.00	-	-	-	-	-	-	-	-	-	-	-	-	-	-
KORA	F	3	50.00	2	50.00	-	-	-	-	-	-	-	-	-	-	-	-	-	-
	T	6	100.00	4	100.00	-	-	-	-	-	-	-	-	-	-	-	-	-	-
	M	8	53.33	18	69.23	-	-	-	-	-	-	-	-	-	-	-	-	-	-
SARDAR	F	7	46.67	8	30.77	-	-	-	-	-	-	-	-	-	-	-	-	-	-
	T	15	100.00	26	100.00	-	-	-	-	-	-	-	-	-	-	-	-	-	-
TOTAL		197	33.62	298	5 0.80	1	0.17	12	2.05	-	-	-	-	-	-	33	5.63	-	-

Contd.

Contd.

Name of the Tribe		Carpentry		Craft		Service		Business		Bagali		Total	
		No.	%	No.	%	No.	%	No.	%	No.	%	No.	%
	M	2	100.00	-	-	-	-	-	-	4	66.67	246	52.90
SANTAL	F	-	-	-	-	-	-	-	-	2	33.33	219	47.10
	T	2	100.00	-	-	-	-	-	-	6	100.00	465	100 00
	M	-	-	17	45.95	-	-	-	-	-	-	36	51.43
MAHALI	F	-	-	20	54.05	-	-	-	-	-	-	34	48.57
	T	-	-	37	100.00	-	-	-	-	-	-	70	100.00
	M	-	-	-	-	-	-	-	-	-	-	5	50.00
KORA	F	-	-	-	-	-	-	-	-	-	-	5	50.00
	T	-	-	-	-	-	-	-	-	-	-	10	100.00
	M	-	-	-	-	-	-	-	-	-	-	26	63.41
SARDAR	F	-	-	-	-	-	-	-	-	-	-	15	36.59
	T	-	-	-	-	-	-	-	-	-	-	41	100.00
TOTAL		2	0.34	37	6.31	-	-	-	-	6	1.02	586	100.00

occupations but it is noticed for the every community that the major source of income is cultivation and then from agricultural labourer (Table 4.1.7). For every tribal community more than fifty per cent income is from cultivation. An exception is the Mahalis. In this case 49 per cent (Rs. 9,058/-) of the average annual income per household (Rs. 18,483/-) is from cultivation. In case of the Santal 54 per cent (Rs. 9,341) of the average annual income (Rs. 17,276/-) is from cultivation. On the other hand, in case of the Koras and the Sardars above 60 per cent of the average annual income come from cultivation. It is because of the fact that these two communities, Koras and the Sardars are not engaged in any other occupations beside cultivation and agricultural labourers. Their average annual income is also lesser than the Santal and the Mahalis. It is Rs. 14,121/- for the Koras and Rs. 14,433/- for the Sardars. More than thirty per cent annual income of the beneficiary households come from the agricultural labourers. Here also exception is noticed among the Mahalis (27.77 per cent of the total annual income). Actually, their most preferable engagement is basket making. In the rest of the period when they have no work in the land prefer to engage themselves in basket making than any kind of labour work specially the aged persons. Though they are conscious that they may earn more by working as labourers than from the basket making. About 9 per cent of the annual income come from the basket making, which is mentioned in the Table 4.1.7 as others. Only some Santal individuals are found to engage as non-agricultural labourer like labour in the rice mill or shawmill or labour in the brick field. Some Santal males are also found to engag as labour of repairing railway and labour of lorry. On an average it was calculated that Rs. 968/-, i.e., 6 per cent of the average annual gross income per Santal household (Rs. 17,276/-) come from working as non-agricultural labourers. Only five Santal individuals are serviceholders. Only Rs. 211/- (1.22 per cent) is the average annual income of the total Santal population, which come from service. It is Rs. 2,675/- (14.47 per cent)

Table 4.1.7

Average Annual Gross Income per Household from Various Occupations

(In Rs.)

Name of the Tribe	Cultivation	Agricultural Labour	Non-Agri- Labour	Service cutural	Small Trader	Others	Total
SANTAL	9341(54.07)	5754(33.31)	968(5.60)	211(1.22)	28(0.16)	974(5.64)	17276
MAHALI	9058(49.01)	5132(27.77)	-	2675(14.47)	-	1618(8.75)	18483
KORA	8904(63.06)	5217(36.94)	-		-	-	14121
SARDAR	9162(63.48)	4614(31.97)	-		-	657(4.55)	14433

in case of the Mahalis because of the fact that Mahalis are only eighteen households. Some Santals are also engaged in business. They are found to run grocery shop successfully. Some are engaged in running business of repairing bi-cycles. Average Rs.28/-, which is only 0.16 per cent of the total average annual income come from business and Rs. 974 (5.64 per cent) come from other sources like carpentry, Rickshaw pooling and so on.

In the target group approach of government development planning and programme the individual families are selected for getting benefit specifically from the programme. The target group is constituted at the panchayat level on the basis of the families' absolute economic status, the poorest being given the first preference. Here, poverty line has been taken as Rs. 11,000/- per annum for a household of five members. Out of 264 beneficiary households ninety-two households are below the poverty line (34.85% of the total beneficiary households). Twenty-nine of these below poverty beneficiary households are landless, which is 74 per cent of the total landless beneficiaries. Other sixty-three beneficiaries of below poverty line are marginal farmers, which is forty one per cent of the total marginal farmers. Another eight landless beneficiaries and eighteen marginal farmers are at the level of income just above the poverty line (Rs. 11,001 to Rs. 15,000) and two landless and twenty-seven marginal farmers are at the level of income of Rs. 15,001/- to Rs. 20,000/-. Forty-one beneficiaries are at the income level of Rs. 20,001/- to Rs. 25,000/-, of which thirty-seven are marginal farmers and four are small farmers. In the next the income level of Rs. 25,001/- to Rs. 30,000/- where five are marginal farmers and eighteen are small farmers. And in this way with the increasing land size of the beneficiary households income level is also proportionately increased, which is clearly depicted in the Table 4.1.8.

For most of the landless tribals only important source of the income is working as an agricultural labourer in

Table 4.1.8
Average Annual Income of the Beneficiary Households According to the Land Size

Land Size (in Acre)	*Land Less*		*0.1 - 2.50*		*2.51 - 5.00*		*5.01 - 7.50*		*Above 7.50*		*Total*	
Amount (in Rs.)	*No.*	*(%)*	*No.*	*(%)*	*No.*	*(%)*	*No.*	*(%)*	*No.*	*(%)*	*No.*	*(%)*
Below 11,000	29	74.36	63	41.18	-	-	-	-	-	-	92	34.85
11,001 - 15,000	8	20.51	18	11.76	-	-	-	-	-	-	26	9.85
15,001 - 20,000	2	5.13	27	17.65	-	-	-	-	-	-	29	10.98
20,001 - 25,000	-	-	37	24.18	4	6.35	-	-	-	-	41	15.54
25,001 - 30,000	-	-	5	3.27	18	28.57	-	-	-	-	23	8.71
30,001 - 35,000	-	-	2	1.31	5	7.94	-	-	-	-	7	2.65
35,001 - 40,000	-	-	-	-	15	23.81	-	-	-	-	15	5.68
40,001 - 45,000	-	-	1	0.65	4	6.35	-	-	-	-	5	1.89
45,001 - 50,000	-	-	-	-	14	22.22	1	16.67	-	-	15	5.68
Above 50,000	-	-	-	-	3	4.76	5	83.33	3	100.00	11	4.17
TOTAL	39	100.00	153	100.00	63	100.00	6	100.00	3	100.00	264	100.00

the lands of their neighbouring Hindu caste people. Wage rate of the agricultural labourer in this area is around Rs. 35/- per day. Though in so many cases the land of their landlord are becoming double cropped or multi-cropped, after the introduction of various modern agricultural equipments and irrigation facilities but mandays of any agricultural labourer can not exceed 120 - 150 days in a year. Not only that in so many cases it was noticed that they are engaged themselves in other occupation and also getting some financial assistance from government to substantiate their livelihood but in spite of that they are lying below the poverty line. It is also true for those marginal farmers having a very small amount of land. After cultivation of their own land they are depending on the source of income as agricultural labourers or any other types of daily labour. As a result, a remarkable percentage of the marginal farmers are belonging below the poverty line or just above the poverty line. Whereas, the small farmers and then the medium farmers and large farmers have some own land and engaged in cultivation. They have however, a scope to increase their income on the basis of their land. They are trying to convert their mono-cropped land to double or multi-cropped land by using some modern agricultural equipment and irrigation facilities. As a result, their income is becoming increased. In some cases they have the ability of hiring labourers and giving scope of education to their children. It is noticed in Table: 4.1.12 that only few high achievers in education are belonging to the income level of Rs. 45,001/- to Rs. 50,000/- and above Rs. 50,000. By getting government reservation policy they have got the scope of service and their income level have increased then.

Literacy Status

Out of total 264 beneficiaries 103, i.e., only 39 per cent are literate whereas 161, i.e., 61 per cent beneficiaries are illiterate. Illiteracy is highly prevalent among the beneficiaries (Table 4.1.9).

Table 4.1.9

Literacy Status of the Beneficiaries

	No.	Percentage (%)
Literate	103	39.02
Illiterate	161	60.98
Total	264	100.00

If literacy status of beneficiary households observed among the four tribal communities in the study area, it is found that for each of the category male literacy rate is higher than the female (Table 4.1.10). Literacy rate is higher among the Sardar community. On the other hand percentage of female illiteracy is highest among the Mahalis.

Table 4.1.10

Literacy Status of Beneficiary Households (Tribal Groupwise)

Name of the Tribe		Literate		Illiterate		
		No.	(%) to Total	No.	(%) to Total	Total
SANTAL	Male	356	61.91	219	38.09	575
	Female	172	32.70	354	67.30	526
	Total	528	47.96	573	52.40	1101
KORA	Male	6	54.55	5	45.45	11
	Female	4	36.36	7	63.64	11
	Total	10	45.45	12	54.55	22
MAHALI	Male	20	51.28	19	48.72	39
	Female	11	28.21	28	71.79	39
	Total	31	39.74	47	60.26	78
SARDAR	Male	39	66.10	20	33.90	59
	Female	19	44.19	24	55.81	43
	Total	58	56.86	44	43.14	102

Table 4.1.11 depicts the education level of beneficiary households of the study area. Among the Santals twenty-six per cent male and twenty-four per cent female are just literate. Forty-nine per cent male and sixty per cent female are at primary level. Whereas, only twenty per cent Santal male and

Table 4.1.11

Education Level of Beneficiary Households (Tribal Groupwise)

Name of the tribe		Just literate (%)	I -IV (%)	V -VIII (%)	IX-X (%)	H.S. (%)	Graduate (%)	Post-Graduate (%)
SANTAL	Male	25.84	48.87	19.94	4.21	0.89	-	0.28
	Female	23.84	60.47	14.53	1.16	-	-	-
MAHALI	Male	25.00	35.00	25.00	10.00	-	5.00	-
	Female	18.19	45.45	36.36	-	-	-	-
KORA	Male	33.33	33.33	16.67	16.67	-	-	-
	Female	25.00	25.00	50.00	-	-	-	-
SARDAR	Male	15.39	46.15	28.21	10.25	-	-	-
	Female	26.32	52.63	15.79	5.26	-	-	--

fourteen per cent Santal female are at the junior high (V - VIII) level. At the level of class IX – X the percentage is decreased rapidly to only four per cent in case of Santal male and one per cent for the Santal female. Only 0.89 per cent Santal male are at the level of Higher Secondary and only 0.28 per cent Santal male are found to go upto the highest level that is the post graduation level.

In case of Mahalis, 35 per cent male and forty-five per cent female are at the primary level. Then at the junior high level the percentage is decreased to twenty-five per cent for the male and thirty-six per cent for the female. At the level of class IX - X only ten per cent Mahali male could continue the study. No Mahali female is remained after junior high level. Only five per cent Mahali male go as high as graduation level. Among the Koras and Sardars it is also found that the percentage of both male and female is high at the primary level. But just after the primary level it is continuously decreased. A large number of them dropped out during or after the primary level. After the level of Madhyamik no one can retain.

Table 4.1.12
Educational Level of the Beneficiary Households by Income Group

Education Level

Income Level (Rs.)	*Illiterate*		*Literate*		*I - IV*		*V - VIII*		*IX - X*		*H.S.*		*Graduate*		*Post Graduate*	
	No.	*%*	*No.*	*%*	*No.*	*%*	*No.*	*%*	*No.*	*%*	*No.*	*%*	*No.*	*%*	*No.*	*%*
BELOW 11000	296	43.79	38	13.97	53	25.12	12	10.53	-	-	-	-	-	-	-	-
11001 - 20000	159	23.52	61	22.43	31	14.69	13	11.40	-	-	-	-	-	-	-	-
20001 - 30000	147	21.75	79	29.04	47	22.27	29	25.44	5	20.00	-	-	-	-	-	-
30001 - 40000	39	5.77	37	13.60	36	17.06	24	21.05	6	24.00	1	33.33	-	-	-	-
40001 - 50000	21	3.10	34	12.50	32	15.16	21	18.42	11	44.00	1	33.33	1	100.00	1	100.00
ABOVE 50000	14	2.07	23	8.46	12	5.69	15	13.16	3	12.00	1	33.33	-	-	-	-
TOTAL	676	100.00	272	100.00	211	100.00	114	100.00	25	100.00	3	100.00	1	100.00	1	100.00

There are so many facilities for the Scheduled Tribe people upto the highest level of education from the initial stage. It is revealed here that though most of the parents are illiterate but almost every parents are trying to impart education to their children by sending them to the school at the age of six years without any discrimination of male or female child. They are conscious about the utility of education for their children and interested to get all the financial support of government for the betterment of their children's education. But there is a contradiction also playing among them. The family, in their economy, is a unit of production. All the members of a family whether husband or wife, parents or children together form the production unit. By sending a child to the school the family losses his or her contribution to its economic activities. For this familial requirement parents are becoming disinterested. Ultimately it results in high dropout. In case of the female child it was felt that in absence of their parents the duty to look after of their younger brothers or sisters and other domestic works are devolved to them. And most of the cases it becomes the main cause of their early dropout. Early marriage is also another important reason behind it.

Another most important matter was noticed that the educational level of a tribal household is directly proportionate to the economic condition of the household. Those tribals who are at the level of below the poverty line and just above the poverty line, can not able to continue their education. Because they have to engage themselves earlier for earning to support their family income. It is very clearly noticed in the Table 4.1.12. Those who belong to the income level of below Rs. 11,000/ - and Rs.11,001/- to Rs.20,000/- all are dropped out at the secondary level (V-VIII). Those who are at income level of Rs. 20,001/- to Rs. 30,000/- and Rs.30,001/- to Rs.40,000/- found to go upto the level of class IX–X. Three members of the beneficiary households who are found to go upto the Higher Secondary level are from minimum of the income level of above Rs.30,000/- per annum. One from the income level Rs.

30,001/- to Rs. 40,000/-, one from Rs. 40,001/- to Rs. 50,000/- and the other from above Rs. 50,000/-. Only two high achievers; one graduate and one postgraduate are the members of those households whose income level is Rs. 40,001/- to Rs.50,000/-. Parents of higher income level are trying to appoint a private tutor for the betterment of their children's education. They have the ability of hiring one or two labours. They are however, ready to sacrifice the contribution of their children. It was also observed that they are trying to encourage their children (specially their sons) for getting the scope of government's reservation policy. Whereas to a landless or to a marginal farmer it was also observed that the parents treat the financial support of government as a source of income and spent all the money for family consumption.

Another important reason of dropout was observed in the study area was that after the primary level children have to go for another school which in most of the cases lying at a distance from their village. As a result, a large number of parents were becoming disinterested specially for the female child.

4.2. Development Schemes - Acceptance and Utilisation

So many family benefit schemes are running under the Integrated Tribal Development Project in this project area of Birbhum. The appropriate combination of schemes for different blocks was formulated with the help of block profile highlighting their characteristics in terms of present economic activities, existing facilities, needs, growth trends in different factors etc. Of course before arriving at the final list of schemes for any block, detailed discussions were held with district level and block level government officials and representatives of Panchayats and all the official schemes supposed to be implemented in the block were included. In order to ascertain the bankers views on different discussions were held with the branch-managers and field officers of different banks who also gave some idea about their capability to finance under different schemes.

The schemes those are listed for this area are targeted

for poverty alleviation and employment generation and thereby to improve the quality of life of this weaker section of the population. These schemes are designed for their economic protection and economic upliftment. Inputs of various sectors are intensified and channalized through those schemes among the tribal families.

Total sixteen different schemes are running in this study area. These are distributed among the beneficiaries either individually or two different schemes at a time as an integrated scheme and considered as a single scheme. Here, it is noticed that there are some schemes those are directly related to agricultural practices. Those are Bullock with cart, Shallow Tube well and Pump set and crop loan. Crop loan scheme provides adequate credit for seasonal agricultural operation and includes distribution of seed, fertilizer, minikit, and pesticides. There are some schemes for rearing animals and poultry birds. This animal husbandry or veterinary sector includes schemes on distribution and supply of livestock and poultry birds - like milch cow for house dairy, calf and heifer dairy and pig keeping, sheep and goat rearing. The idea of these schemes is to provide the farmers a subsidiary occupation. All these schemes are specially mean for landless, marginal and small farmers.

There are schemes for business. These are specially for generating employment as well as income for the landless labourers and marginal farmers. The schemes are of grocery, vegetable vending and different other types of business like tailoring, repairing bicycles and for clothing. Rice processing is another scheme of small-scale industry.

Rickshaw and Rickshaw-van schemes are two employment generating scheme for the landless.

The bamboo work is a scheme introduced in this area specially for the Mahalis. Traditional occupation of the Mahalis is basket making and they are popularly known as the basket makers.

Identification of Beneficiary

Every Panchayat has its own list of tribal individuals

under poverty line. This list is prepared through a survey by the village level workers of the panchayats. Preparation of the list is carried out according to the principle of the target group approach of Integrated Tribal Development Programme where the individual family is to get benefit from the programme on the basis of their economic status. The families with an income of less than Rs.11,000/- per annum are identified as members of the target group. They are enlisted and ranked in terms of their annual income. In a financial year selection of beneficiary is carried out according to this survey list. Allotment of loans for one financial year for a panchayat is limited. Hence, all enlisted households do not get the scope of assistance simultaneously. Here, the poorest is being given the first preference.

Financing

The beneficiaries are assisted through the viable bankable projects (Table 4.2.1 and 4.2.2) which are financed partly by subsidy and partly by bank loans. The major part of the project cost comprising the loan portion has to come through institutional credit. Therefore, it is a credit linked programmed and its success depends on the availability of credit from banking institution for the beneficiaries. Commercial Regional Rural and Co-operative Bank are making credit for the programme available. Two categories of schemes are there. One is the crop loan. This loan is given for a short-term, generally for six months. Short-term crop loans are primarily for seasonal agricultural operation. It is given to the beneficiaries in five consecutive terms. For this scheme no subsidy is given but exception is for those tribal farmers whose land size is up to 1 acre. Besides short-term crop loan all others are medium-term loans and financed partly by subsidy and partly by bank loans and margin money. The capital cost of the assets are subsidised by 50 per cent but it is restricted up to Rs. 6000/- whether the project cost is above Rs. 12000/-. Twenty per cent of the project cost is margin money, which is a share of State Government. The beneficiary should return it with interest. If it returned within the due time of 3 to 5 years 4 per cent interest is to be given but when the due period of 5 years is crossed the rate of interest increased to 10 per cent. Rest 30 per cent of the capital cost is bank loan financed by the Commercial Gramin Banks and should be returned with 12 per cent interest within the stipulated period of 3 to 5 years.

Distribution Procedure

According to the budgetary allotment for the State, allotment for the District is restricted. Now, from the year 1997, 6 per cent of the total budget of the State should be for the Tribal sub-plan. According to the budgetary allotment of one financial year for a district, its target group is prepared. At the district level, an autonomous agency called the District Rural Development Agency (DRDA) is responsible for planning, implementing, co-ordinating, supervising and monitoring the Integrated Tribal Development Projects. The DRDA is constituted under the Societies Registration Act, Public Trust Act and is chaired by the District Development Officer. The Governing Body of the DRDA consists of the local MP and MLAs, Chairman of Zilla Parishad or his representatives, district level heads of technical departments and the representatives of concerned co-operative and commercial banks.

Co-ordination with financing institutions is achieved through a district level consultative committee, which is chaired by the District Magistrate. This Committee reviews and monitors the progress of institutional credit support to programme beneficiaries. According to this review budget, target group and the schemes are allotted for the next financial year.

Block is the basic unit for the implementation of the programme and wholly dealt with by the Block Development Officer (BDO). Budgetary allotment for the District is distributed among the Blocks and then it is distributed at the Panchayat level. Panchayat Pradhan inform all the panchayat members about the allotment of schemes of that particular financial year and asked them for sending a list

TABLE 4.2.1

Acceptance Pattern of Schemes According to the Land Size

Land Size (in Acre)

	Name of the Scheme	Land Less	0.1 - 2.50	2.51 - 5.00	5.01 - 7.50	Above 7.50	Total
1.	Bullock with cart	-	20 (13.07)	14 (22.22)	-	-	34 (12.87)
2.	Calf rearing	4 (10.26)	16 (10.46)	3 (4.76)	1 (16.67)	-	24 (9.09)
3.	STW with pumpset	-	4 (2.61)	10 (15.87)	1 (16.67)	2 (66.67)	17 (6.43)
4.	Duckary	-	1 (0.65)	-	-	-	1 (0.37)
5.	Heifer rearing	2 (5.13)	10 (6.54)	-	-	-	12 (4.55)
6.	Rickshaw	1 (2.56)	2 (1.31)	-	-	-	3 (1.14)
7.	Piggery	-	1 (0.65)	-	-	-	1 (0.37)
8.	Goatary	-	2 (1.31)	-	-	-	2 (0.75)
9.	Rice processing	1 (2.56)	2 (1.31)	1 (1.59)	-	-	4 (1.52)
10.	Milch cow	2 (5.13)	11 (7.19)	-	-	-	13 (4.92)
11.	Carpentry	-	4 (2.61)	1 (1.59)	1 (16.67)	-	6 (2.27)
12.	Fishery	-	1 (0.65)	-	-	-	1 (0.37)
13.	Bamboo work	-	3 (1.96)	-	-	-	3 (1.34)
14.	Business	2 (5.13)	2 (1.31)	-	-	-	4 (1.52)
15.	Grocery	1 (2.56)	10 (6.54)	2 (3.17)	-	-	13 (4.92)
16.	Short term Agriculture	-	12 (7.84)	12 (19.05)	1 (16.67)	1 (33.33)	26 (9.84)
17.	More than one	26 (66.67)	52 (33.99)	20 (31.75)	2 (33.33)	-	100 (37.88)*
	Total	39 (100.00)	153 (100.00)	63 (100.00)	6 (100.00)	3 (100.00)	264

* Details breakup shown in separate table.

(Figure is parenthesis indicate percentage).

TABLE 4.2.2
Acceptance Pattern of Schemes According to the Land Size
(MORE THAN ONE SCHEMES)

Land Size (in Acre)

	Name of the Scheme	Land Less	0.1 - 2.50	2.51 - 5.00	5.01 - 7.50	Above 7.50	Total
1.	Calf rearing + Goatary	13 (50.00)	26 (50.00)	1 (5.00)	1 (50.00)	-	41 (41.00)
2.	Calf rearing + Sheep	4 (15.38)	1 (01.92)	2 (10.00)	-	-	7 (7.00)
3.	Calf rearing + Rice Processing	3 (11.54)	6 (11.54)	2 (10.00)	-	-	11 (11.00)
4.	Rickshaw + Rice Processing	1 (03.85)	-	-	-	-	1 (1.00)
5.	Veg. Vending + Calf rearing	2 (07.69)	2 (03.85)	-	-	-	4 (4.00)
6.	Duckary + Calf rearing	1 (03.85)	1 (01.92)	-	-	-	2 (2.00)
7.	Rickshaw + Calf rearing	-	1 (01.92)	-	-	-	1 (1.00)
8.	Van + Calf rearing	1 (03.85)	1 (01.92)	-	-	-	2 (2.00)
9.	Bullock Cart + Short term	-	3 (05.78)	11 (55.00)	-	-	14 (14.00)

Contd.

Contd.Table 4.2.2

Name of the Scheme	*Land Less*	*0.1 - 2.50*	*2.51 - 5.00*	*5.01 - 7.50*	*Above 7.50*	*Total*
10. Calf rearing + Milch cow	-	1 (01.92)	-	-	-	1 (1.00)
11. Calf rearing + Short term	-	-	1 (5.00)	-	-	1 (1.00)
12. Bullock cart + Bamboo work	-	1 (01.92)	-	-	-	1 (1.00)
13. Short term Agriculture+ Bamboo work	-	1 (01.92)	-	-	-	1 (1.00)
14. Grocery + Calf rearing	1 (03.85)	4 (07.69)	-	-	-	5 (5.00)
15. STW Pump set + Short term	-	-	1 (5.00)	-	-	1 (1.00)
16. Bamboo work + Calf rearing	-	3 (05.78)	-	-	-	3 (3.00)
17. Bullock cart + Duckary	-	1 (01.92)	2 (10.00)	1 (50.00)	-	4 (4.00)
Total	26 (100.00)	52 (100.00)	20 (100.00)	2 (100.00)	-	100(100.00)

of tribal individuals who need the financial support. Panchayat send the list to the associated Cooperative or Commercial Bank. Then Bank fixed up a date and calls all the candidates according to the list. With the presence of the Panchayat Pradhan, Members of the Panchayat, Manager and Field Officer of the Bank, the willing candidate is interviewed to assess the candidate's capabilities for effective implementation of the scheme. Sometimes, the Bank Manager and field officers may go to the house of the applicant with the local Panchayat member for some quarries, observe the actual situation of the candidate and as well as for an estimation about the eligibility of the candidate for running the scheme viably. If all the criteria are fulfilled he will be selected as eligible candidate. Then they fill-up the proper application form and submitted it to the Panchayat. Panchayat send the application form to the Block Office. Block office sends it to the District Rural Development Agency (DRDA) which is located at Suri of Birbhum district. DRDA sanctions the margin money and subsidy and send it to the associated Commercial Bank or Co-operative Bank (If it is distributed through Co-operative). Bank gives an information to the Panchayat and fixed up a date for the distribution of the loans. Panchayat informs the borrowers through the related panchayat members. On the due date, borrowers with the presence of the related Panchayat Pradhan, make an account in the Bank. Then the schemes are distributed among the beneficiaries according the list sanctioned by DRDA. Almost in every cases the schemes are given in kind not in cash. In case of rice processing, veg vending, grocery schemes the beneficiaries are given the amount in cash. For the other schemes the bank calls the wholesellers and they give the tenders. Regarding the purchase of animal husbandry schemes, the beneficiaries have the right to choose the animals according to his sanctioned scheme. But this purchase should be processed in front of a Veterinary Doctor, Field Officer, and Managing Committee members of the Co-operative, Panchayat staff and Manager of the Bank. After the disbursement of the scheme instalment of repayment are fixed up according to their schemes. After two years of acceptance Bank will send the first notice to the borrower for the payment of first instalment and it will be continued for the next three years. After a consultation with the borrower duration of the instalment is fixed up. It may be monthly, quarterly, half-yearly or yearly.

In case of a short-term agricultural loan the amount of loan is related to the amount of the borrowers operational land holding. When the loan is sanctioned the beneficiaries have to submit their documents of his own or 'barga' land. Other procedures are same like the mid-term schemes.

However, it is to be said that for getting a financial support from government one tribal individual has to be go through a long-term official procedures and formalities.

Acceptance Pattern of Schemes

Out of 39 landless beneficiaries, only 4 have taken the scheme of calf rearing, 2 for heifer rearing, 1 for rickshaw, 1 for rice processing, 2 for milch cow, 2 for business, 1 for grocery and the other 26 members have taken more than one scheme (Table 4.2.1). Among these 26 landless beneficiaries, 13 have taken the schemes of calf rearing and goatary, 4 for calf rearing and sheep, 1 for rickshaw and rice processing, 2 for vegetable vending and calf rearing, 1 for duckary and calf rearing. Among the other 2 members, one has taken van and calf rearing and the another one for grocery and calf rearing. However, it may be said that there are two categories of schemes for them. One is animal husbandry scheme and the other is trading like grocery, vegetable vending or other kinds of business by which they can get an alternative and continuous source of income. But from the acceptance pattern of the schemes it seems to be clear that the beneficiaries prefer schemes of animal husbandry to others because all of these tribal groups have traditional skill of animal rearing.

Most of the beneficiary households are marginal farmers. Out of two hundred sixty-four beneficiary households they are one hundred and fifty-three. It was found that among them twenty have taken the scheme of bullock with cart, sixteen have taken calf rearing scheme. Twelve of them have taken short-term loan for agriculture and fifty-two (33.79 per cent) for more than one scheme. For the remaining marginal farmers it was found that four of them have taken loan for shallow tubewell with pump set, one for duckary, one for piggery, two for goatary, two for rice processing, eleven for milch cow, four for carpentry, one for fishery, three for bamboo work, two for business and ten for grocery scheme. However, the marginal farmers have accepted almost all types of schemes. But their most preferable scheme is the animal husbandry scheme as preferred by the landless. The same pattern of acceptance is noticed among marginal farmers who have taken more than one scheme. Out of fifty-two, twenty-six marginal farmers are found to take the schemes of calf rearing and goatary. Another large number of marginal farmers are also found to take the calf rearing scheme associated with either any scheme of veterinary sector or any scheme of other sector like sheep, milch cow, rice processing, vegetable vending, rickshaw, rickshaw Van, grocery or bamboo work (Table 4.2.1). Besides these three marginal farmers are found to take bullock with cart and short term crop loan, one for bullock with cart and bamboo work, one for short-term agriculture loan with bamboo work, another one for bullock with cart with duckary scheme.

Thus, it reveals here that a considerable number of marginal farmers have accepted the schemes of agriculture. Most of the marginal farmers have negligible land and obviously can not afford to invest money for purchasing bullock with cart or a pump set but it is very much essential for cultivation. Hence, they have taken the opportunity of getting it without any investment. On the other hand, almost all the produced crops of a marginal farmer are utilized for consumption purposes. They don't have any surplus production, which they can sell in the market and buy the HYV seeds, chemical fertilizers, pestisides etc. for the better production. By taking of the short term crop loan they can afford to utilize those.

The small farmers are 63 in number among the beneficiary households. From Table 4.2.1 it is noticed that fourteen small farmers have taken the scheme of bullock with cart, twelve for short-term agriculture loan and then ten for the scheme of shallow tubewell with pump set. Only three of them have taken calf rearing scheme, one for rice processing, one for carpentry, two for grocery and other twenty for more than one scheme. Out of these twenty beneficiaries, eleven have taken the scheme for bullock with cart and as well as for short-term crop loan, one for calf rearing with short-term crop loan, one for shallow tubewell with pump set and short-term crop loan and another two for bullock with cart with duckary scheme. On the other hand only two small farmers are found to take the scheme of calf rearing with sheep and another two for calf rearing with rice processing.

Out of six medium farmers one have taken the calf rearing scheme, one for shallow tubewell with pump set, one for milch cow and one for short term crop loan. Rest of the two, one have taken calf rearing with goatary scheme and another one for bullock cart with duckary scheme.

Out of two hundred sixty-four beneficiaries only three are the large farmers. Among these three large farmers two are found to take the scheme of shallow tubewell with pump set and one for short-term agriculture loan. However, though a mixed type of acceptance is observed among the medium farmers but from the over all acceptance pattern it seems that the small, medium or large farmers, i.e., who have some land obviously tried to take the scope of financial assistance of government loan for agriculturally related schemes. Here also, it is to be said that the farmers have tried to take the opportunity of getting an agricultural asset without any own investment. Another thing is noticed here that the small farmers have taken all types of agriculturally related schemes more or less equally whereas the large farmers have given the preference for the scheme shallow tubewell with pump set. That is, the tribal individual who is belonging to the category of small farmers but land holding is lower have a necessity of support for more or less in every part of agriculture.

Utilization Nature of the Schemes

Here an attempt has been made to find out utilization nature of the schemes those were accepted by the beneficiaries. It is very important whether the people are utilizing the service of the scheme properly or not because it will reflect the fullest accrual of benefits of the schemes.

The total picture of utilization nature of the schemes of the beneficiary households are shown at a glance in the Table 4.2.3. It was noticed that out of 264 beneficiaries, 146 beneficiaries, i.e., 55 per cent have utilized their schemes properly and rest of the beneficiaries, i.e., 118 beneficiaries (44.70 per cent cases) the schemes are misutilized. Natures of misutilization for different types of schemes are different. Those are categorised into seven categories according to their common nature. Forty-two (44.70 per cent) beneficiaries misutilized their schemes for consumption purposes. All the schemes have included in this category which have consumed by the beneficiary households directly for food consumption at the time of crisis or any other reasons and misutilized the scope of generating income, employment, asset building or savings. Nine beneficiaries misutilized their schemes at the time of ceremonies like marriage, obsequal ceremonies etc. Three beneficiaries were identified who misutilized their schemes by savings. Though savings is quite odd to treat as misutilized but in spite of that the schemes were categorised as a type of misutilization because of the fact that the beneficiaries did not utilize the scheme as how they have to utilize it and generating income, employment, asset or savings from the generated incomes of the scheme.

There are eight beneficiaries who misutilized the scheme at the time of religious festivals. So many religious festivals are performed by all the categories of tribal people round the year. Almost all the festivals they observed at first communally at the village level and then at the household level of their own. For both the cases they have to sacrifice some animals like goat, hen, duck, pig, etc according to the nature of the *bongas* they worship. Not only that they have a social obligation also to entertain their guests by sufficient country liquor and meat curry at the time of the religious festivals. As a result, quite obviously a tribal beneficiary meet this kind of immediate necessity by the animals or poultry birds they get readily from their schemes. At that time it becomes more important than the importance of the scheme they have taken as a government loan for their future.

In case of seven beneficiaries nature of misutilization is purchase of asset. Here, the beneficiaries alter the asset of the scheme by another non-productive asset.

In case of another large number of beneficiaries nature of misutilization is midway break up of the schemes. They are 47 in number, i.e., 40 per cent cases of the total misutilized schemes. Such schemes are included in this category those were stopped after running upto a certain period. It is because of various reasons like loss of units, break down of assets, family breakage, death of beneficiary, etc. Most of the cases the unit of animal husbandry schemes were lost due to its poor quality. After the acceptance of a unit of animal husbandry scheme the beneficiary observed that the units were becoming weak and ultimately either it was died or they were compelled to sell their units with minimum price. Here lack of awareness of beneficiary, lack of proper periodical veterinary services, guidance and suggestions for the recovery of the unit is also the reasons of his loss of units.

Only two tribal individuals are there who misutilized their schemes exclusively for consuming liquor.

Utilisation and Misutilisation of Different Schemes

From the analysis of the nature of utilisation of schemes it reveals that when one scheme is properly utilised by a beneficiary the same scheme is misutilised by another beneficiary. Potential of any developmental scheme depends on its nature of utilisation. Here, an attempt has been made to depict the nature of utilisation and as well as nature of misutilisation of different schemes received by the beneficiary households.

Bullock with Cart

Thirty-four beneficiaries accepted this scheme and for 100 per cent cases it is properly utilised. It is one of the most essential equipment of cultivation in its every step. Bullocks are essential for ploughing; bullock and cart are essential for carrying cow dung or other fertilizer to the field and after harvesting it is essential to carry the production to the house from the field. Before the acceptance of the scheme, they have to depend upon the neighbour's cart and on the convenience time of him. As a result never able to maintain the proper timings which is the first and foremost criteria for better yield. The beneficiaries not only benefited by this scheme themselves, now their neighbours are also taking it when they required. Though in return a tribal neighbour do not pay in cash but become obliged to him to give his labour as and when it is necessary.

Calf Rearing

Out of twenty-four beneficiaries ten beneficiaries have found to utilize it properly. Almost all the members of a household are engaged time to time for rearing the calf. Specially the young members take the responsibility of grazing. After a certain period of two to three years when it seems that it will get a high price they sell it and from this generated income they can buy more calves, buffaloes or any other alternate assets. For some beneficiaries it was also found to buy some land for cultivation and also found to make a fixed deposit of Bank from the part of the generated income.

Fourteen beneficiaries misutilized their scheme of calf rearing and almost all the types of misutilization (as categorised by the Researcher) are observed for this scheme. Three beneficiaries were found to misutilized the scheme for ceremony. As for example, Nitai Sardar, 47 years old man of Dholtikuri village accepted the scheme of calf rearing four years ago. There are six members in his family;

Table 4.2.3
Utilization Nature of Schemes by the Beneficiary Households

l. No.	*Name of the sheme*	*No. of Benefi-ciary*	*Prop-erly utili-zed (No.)*	*Misuti-lized (No.)*	*Misutilization Nature*						
					Com-sump-tion	*Cere-moni-al*	*Savi-ngs*	*Reli-gious Festi-val*	*Pur-chase of asset*	*Mid-way break up*	*Exclu-sively for liquor pur-pose*
(1)	*(2)*	*(3)*	*(4)*	*(5)*	*(6)*	*(7)*	*(8)*	*(9)*	*(10)*	*(11)*	*(12)*
1.	Bullock with cart	34	34 (100.00)	-	-	-	-	-	-	-	-
2.	Calf rearing	24	10 (41.67)	14(58.33)	3(21.43)	3(21.43)	1(7.14)	-	2(14.29)	3(21.43)	2(14.29)
3.	STW/Pumpset	17	13 (76.47)	4(23.53)	-	-	-	-	-	4(100.00)	-
4.	Duckary	1	-	1(100.00)	-	-	-	1(100.00)	-	-	-
5.	Heifer rearing	12	5 (41.67)	7(58.33)	2(28.57)	2(28.57)	-	-	-	3(42.86)	-
6.	Rickshaw	3	3 (100.00)	-	-	-	-	-	-	-	-
7.	Piggary	1	-	1(100.00)	-	-	-	1(100.00)	-	-	-
8.	Goatary	2	1 (50.00)	1(50.00)	1(100.00)	-	-	-	-	-	-
9.	Rice processing	4	-	4(100.00)	-	-	-	-	-	4(100.00)	-
10.	Milch cow	13	5 (38.46)	8(61.54)	3(37.50)	-	-	-	-	5(62.50)	-
11.	Carpentary	6	3 (50.00)	3(50.00)	-	-	-	-	-	3(100.00)	-

Contd.

Contd.Table 4.2.3

(1)	(2)	(3)	(4)	(5)	(6)	(7)	(8)	(9)	(10)	(11)	(12)
12.	Fishary	1	1 (100.00)	-	-	-	-	-	-	-	-
13.	Bamboo work	3	3 (100.00)	-	-	-	-	-	-	-	-
14.	Business	4	1 (25.00)	3(75.00)	3(100.00)	-	-	-	-	-	-
15.	Grocery	13	5 (38.46)	8(61.54)	3(37.50)	-	-	-	-	5(62.50)	-
16.	Short term Agricultural loan	26	26 (100.00)	-	-	-	-	-	-	-	-
17.	Calf rearing + Goatary	41	7 (17.07)	34(82.93)	12(35.29)	2(5.88)	1(2.94)	2(5.88)	3(8.82)	14(41.18)	-
18.	Calf rearing + Sheep	7	-	7(100.00)	5(71.43)	1(14.29)	-	-	1(14.29)	-	-
19.	Calf rearing + rice processing	11	-	11(100.00)	7(63.64)	1(9.09)	-	-	-	3(27.27)	-
20.	Rickshaw + rice processing	1	1 (100.00)	-	-	-	-	-	-	-	-
21.	Veg. Vending +Calf rearing	4	-	4(100.00)	1(25.00)	-	1(25.00)	-	1(25.00)	1(25.00)	-
22.	Duckary + calf rearing	2	-	2(100.00)	-	-	-	2(100.00)	-	-	-
23.	Rickshaw + calf rearing	1	1 (100.00)	-	-	-	-	-	-	-	-
24.	Rickshaw van + calf rearing	2	2 (100.00)	-	-	-	-	-	-	-	-

Contd. Table 4.2.3

(1)	(2)	(3)	(4)	(5)	(6)	(7)	(8)	(9)	(10)	(11)	(12)
25.	Bullock cart + S.T. Agriculture	14	14 (100.00)	-	-	-	-	-	-	-	-
26.	Calf rearing + milch cow	1	1 (100.00)	-	-	-	-	-	-	-	-
27.	Calf rearing + S.T. Agriculture	1	1 (100.00)	-	-	-	-	-	-	-	-
28.	Bullock cart + Bomboowork	1	1 (100.00)	-	-	-	-	-	-	-	-
29.	S.T. Agriculture+ Bamboowork	1	1 (100.00)	-	-	-	-	-	-	-	-
30.	Grocery + calf rearing	5	1 (20.00)	4(80.00)	2(50.00)	-	-	-	-	2(50.00)	-
31.	STW/Pumpset + Short term	1	1 (100.00)	-	-	-	-	-	-	-	-
32.	Bamboo work +Calf rearing	3	3 (100.00)	-	-	-	-	-	-	-	-
33.	Bullock cart + Duckary	4	2 (50.00)	2(50.00)	-	-	-	2(100.00)	-	-	-
	TOTAL	264	146 (55.30)	118(44.70)	42(35.59)	9(7.63)	3(2.54)	8(6.78)	7(5.93)	47(39.83)	2(1.69)

(Figures in parenthesis indicate the percentage.)

his wife, old mother, one daughter of seventeen years and two sons of 12 years and 10 years. He has only 1.5 acres of cultivable land. Both husband wife and their young daughter was engaged in cultivation and rest of the time as agricultural labourers. Then, the young daughter's marriage was fixed up. He had to give Rs. 4000/- in cash and 7 utensils of bell metal as a dowry. Not only that he should entertain all the guests and kins of bride and neighbours of his village and kins of his own by sufficient country liquor, meat curry etc. for at least three days of marriage. As a result, Nitai Sardar was compelled to sell his asset, two young bull taken as a government scheme and rearing for last four years.

In another case Boro Baske, 42 years old Santal of village Bankajal of Kankali Gram Panchayat got two units of calf 6 years ago. He has only one acre of land of his own and in 4.5 acres leased in land cultivate as sharecropper jointly with his younger brother. There were five members in his family; old father, his wife, one 13 years old son and 23 years old young married daughter who lives in his father's house and worked as a labour in the rice mill at Bolpur. Daughter's husband worked as a labourer of Lorry outside the district and visited his father-in-law's house once or twice in a month and stayed for two to three days as a guest. Daughter or daughter's husband never gave him any kind of monetary help. Occasionally daughter gave some money to her mother or buys some cloth, food or any other things from Bolpur market. In this situation his old father was ill and hospitalised for a certain period. But ultimately he was died. After his death from cremation to the obsequal ceremony he was socially obliged to go through some social ceremonies step by step and at that time he was obliged to entertain his villagers with country liquor. Appearing before this kind of miscellaneous expenditure he sold his cow those he accepted as a loan and meet all of his social obligations.

In another case calf rearing scheme was misutilized by savings. Here also an example may be mentioned. In the village Bankajal, 28 years old young man, working as mason at Bolpur and Santiniketan area get 2 units of calf. After one and half months of his acceptance one calf became sick and they took it to the veterinary hospital at Bolpur. But ultimately it died. Immediately he contacted with the Block office with the stampt ear of the calf and the death certificate of the veterinary doctor of the Hospital. He submitted these documents to the Block office and then after four to five months he got Rs. 600/- for buying a new calf. But he did not do this. He deposited the money in his Bank Account for savings.

Two beneficiaries misutilized their schemes by purchasing another assets and in 3 cases calf rearing schemes were found to misutilize for midway break up. In case of another two beneficiaries schemes were misutilized exclusively for liquor purpose. An example may be mentioned here. Fifty five years old man popularly works as *janguru* (traditional medicine man) got four units of calf. After the acceptance of the calves he was returning to his house. But in the way he met the wholesalers and after some bargaining he sold two of the four calves. Then he returned back and handed over another two to his wife and then went for a liquor shop. His wife informed me that then he sold remaining two calves one after another and all the money was spent for liquor purpose.

Shallow Tubwell with Pump Set

The beneficiaries in 76.47 per cent cases properly use this most essential modern equipment for cultivation. These beneficiaries not only cultivating Boro paddy in the summer season but also cultivating various types of cereals, wheat, potato, sugarcane etc. by using their Shallow Tubewells with Pump Sets. Not only that they also hire it out to other farms and earn a substantial amount of money. Generally they are found to take rent of Rs. 25/- to 30/- per hour.

In case of remaining four beneficiaries the scheme was misutilized and in all the cases nature of misutilization is midway break up i.e. after running upto a certain period of acceptance the schemes were stopped. As for example, in case of a 36 years old young small farmer having 4.5 acres of land of village Patharghata of Kankali Gram Panchayat. But in the next year he saw that the water level in the field was shrinking. For its re-shrinking it was needed a lot of expenditure which was impossible for him. As a result since then his shallow tubewell remained useless.

In another case, about 60 years old Santal man is a medium farmer having 3.96 acres of land got a pump set but it was sanctioned in the name of his son. Then his son was unmarried. Upto three years they utilized it. But after his son's marriage that was a love marriage, a misunderstanding was happened and father separated his son from the house without any cultivable land. As it was sanctioned in the name of his son he took it in his own house where he lives separately in the same village. But it becomes useless to him as he has no land at all and both husband and wife working as agricultural labourers at the season time and labourers in the brick field in rest of the period.

Duckary

Only one beneficiary was there and he misutilized his scheme by using it during the religious festivals.

Heifer Rearing

One beneficiary can make a good profit from this scheme if it will used properly. Five beneficiaries were found to run their scheme successfully whereas in case of seven beneficiaries it was misutilized. Two of them misutilized their scheme by consumption. Another two beneficiaries misutilized their scheme for ceremonial purposes and for the remaining three it is due to mid way break up. Reasons behind midway break up of these three cases are poor quality of units. In one case the unit died after a certain period and in case of remaining two the beneficiaries were sold off their units in a low price.

Rickshaw

Three beneficiaries are there who have taken the scheme of Rickshaw and all of them running it successfully. It is because of the fact that these beneficiaries working place is Bolpur and Santiniketan area, which is not only a popular town area but also becoming a popular tourist spot. During the various occasion like *Paus Mela, Dol*, etc. at Santiniketan and almost round the year a large number of tourists are coming here. They get these tourists and as well as the people of the locality as their passenger. On an average, they earn Rs. 50/- per day.

Piggery

One Santal beneficiary has accepted the scheme of piggary and it was completely misutilized by using it during the religious festivals. Pig is one of the most essential animals for sacrifice at the time of their various worship of *bongas*.

Goatery

Two beneficiaries have taken the scheme of goatary of whom one beneficiary utilized it properly and another one misutilized it by consumption.

Rice Processing

Four beneficiaries have taken this scheme but in every case it was misutilized by consumption. In this case the amount of project cost is given to the beneficiary totally in cash which may be mentioned as the main cause of misutilization of the scheme. One of the beneficiaries also mentioned that his lack of intelligence for running a business successfully is the reason of failure of the scheme for him. After the acceptance of the scheme when he felt that the scheme was becoming failure he regretted for not taking the scheme of animal husbandry which he thinks easier to maintain by him. He also generalised it for themselves that means for the tribals. Because, the tribals are generally habituated to rear the calf, goat etc. from the very beginning of their childhood.

Milch Cow

Out of thirteen beneficiaries five beneficiaries utilized their schemes properly but in case of other eight beneficiaries the schemes were misutilized. In three cases (37.50 per cent) beneficiaries misutilized their schemes for consumption purposes and in five cases (52.50 per cent) scheme were misutilized by midway break up. In case of the scheme milch cow, most of the cases Jarsi cow was given to the beneficiaries. Its care, its food habit is quite different. Tribal people are not habituated to it. They need proper instruction and guidance for its maintenance but every beneficiary has complained about its lacking. Beneficiaries were informed that after few days of acceptance either their Milch cows died or becoming sick and they tried to sell it as soon as possible with a fear of a total loss. But they did not get a reasonable amount by which they can buy another one.

The beneficiaries who can utilize it properly generally used to give the milk to their children. They are also found to sell it but through a middleman who visits their village regularly to collect the milk. And by this way the beneficiaries are generating a few incomes from the scheme.

Carpentry

Though it is quite uncommon profession for a tribal of this locality but it is found that six beneficiaries are there who have taken the scheme of carpentry. Three of them used it properly and in other cases it was misutilized. In all cases the nature of misutilization is midway break up. Those are running the scheme successfully generating income not only working at the village level but also working at the town area.

Fishery

Fishing is a traditional practice of the tribal specially of the Santals. They are liking it still today and spent most of their leisure hour by hunting or fishing. But it is surprisingly found that there is only one beneficiary has taken the scheme of fishing. He utilized it properly.

Bamboo Work

It is a traditional occupation of the Mahalis known as the basket makers. Three Mahali beneficiaries have taken this scheme and used it properly. Generally they have given all kinds of instruments and some amount in cash for buying the raw materials. They make various types of basket, winnowing-platters etc. Usually they go to the market of Bolpur and sell their wares. They also sell their wares at the village level to the neighbouring Hindu Caste people. Not only that, a special kind of basket they make which is essential at the time of marriage of the Santals and the Santals should take it only from the Mahalis.

Business

There are four beneficiaries who have taken the scheme for business. Business may be of various types. Here, two of them for garment, one of them for tailoring and another one for repairing bicycles. Only the beneficiary who has taken the scheme for repairing bicycle running his scheme successfully and used it properly. He is running his business at his own village Mahisdal. He is 27 years old young man, son of a medium farmer having 6.25 acres of land. But now belongs to a separate household and earn independently from his business. The nature of misutilization for the other three beneficiaries is consumption.

Grocery

Out of thirteen beneficiaries five utilized their Grocery scheme successfully whereas this scheme is misutilized in case of the remaining eight (61.54 per cent). Three of them misutilized the scheme by consumption and for the five beneficiaries it is for the midway break up. Among these a case of a Santal young man of the village Dholtikuri, of Sarpalehana-Albandha Gram Panchayat should be mentioned. After the acceptance of the scheme he could able to run the grocery upto three years. But all on a sudden morning he saw that all the materials of his shop was stolen. Since then his grocery shop is closed. It became impossible to him to restore the grocery in his economic condition. Now he working again as agricultural labourer and cultivates his one and half bighas of land which he bought himself from the income he generated from the grocery.

Short Term Agricultural Loan

Twenty-six beneficiaries have taken only the short

term crop loan and all of them utilized it properly. Both in Rabi and Kharif season when the tribals ploughing and preparing their lands for transplanting the paddy they need the fertilizers. But then the rate of paddy in the market is low. If they did not get the agricultural loan they had to sell their production of the last season in a low price. Whereas if they get the loan from government they can use the chemical fertilizers, Mini Kit, HYV seeds without any investment and save their own production for selling it when the market price will be high. By this way the beneficiaries are utilizing this, and maintain proper timings of fertilizer application and producing better yield.

Calf rearing with Goatery

Out of forty-one beneficiaries only seven beneficiaries have utilized the scheme properly and thirty-four beneficiaries have misutilized the scheme. Here also almost all the natures of misutilization are found like the beneficiaries who have taken calf rearing and goatary scheme individually. Twelve beneficiaries misutilized the scheme by consumption, two for ceremonial purposes, one for savings, two for religious festival, three for purchase of asset, and in case of fourteen beneficiaries it is due to midway break up. Here, the reasons behind midway break up are almost same as the reasons of midway break up of the schemes of calf rearing and goatary when beneficiaries have taken separately.

Calf rearing and Rice Processing

Eleven beneficiaries are found to accept this scheme of calf rearing and rice processing but in every cases it was observe that the schemes were misutilized. Seven beneficiaries have misutilized their schemes directly for consumption purpose, one for ceremonial purpose and in remaining three cases the schemes were misutilized due to midway break up.

Rickshaw and Rice Processing

Only one beneficiary is here who have taken this scheme and he used it properly.

Vegetable Vending and Calf Rearing

Out of four beneficiaries of this scheme four have

misutilized the scheme. Among them one have misutilized the scheme by consumption purpose, one for savings, another one for purchase of asset and the last one due to midway break up. Here, the exceptional case of a beneficiary who misutilized his scheme for savings specifically is to be mentioned. He is a Sardar of the village Dholtikuri. He is working in a liquor shop. When he was applied for this scheme he was working as an agricultural labourer. After his submision of application two years past, but loan was not sanctioned. By this time he got the opportunity of working in the liquor shop. He gets Rs. 30/- per day and cloths for two times in a year and gets the lunch every day. Just after his joining in the liquor shop he was ill and took leave for one month according to the doctor's advice. During this time the loan was sanctioned and he got the instruction from Panchayat for accepting it. He accepted the loan but already determined for working in the liquor shop. So, he kept the calf for rearing but Rs. 4000/- for the purpose of vegetable vending fixed deposited in the Bank. It may also be mentioned as a result of a growing problem of dowry among the Sardars. As, he explained that from the income of both of them, husband and wife manage domestic affairs now but he should think more about the marriage of his only daughter who is eleven years old now.

Duckary and Calf Rearing

Two beneficiaries have taken this scheme and both the cases they are misutilized by religious festivals.

Van and Calf Rearing

Only two beneficiaries have taken this scheme and both of them have utilized their scheme properly.

Bullock Cart and Short Term Agricultural Loan

Like the beneficiaries who have taken the scheme of bullock with cart and short term crop loan individually here also all the beneficiaries utilised their scheme properly.

From the Table 4.2.3 it is found that there are some schemes those are taken by only one beneficiary. Those are calf rearing and milch cow, calf rearing and short-term agricultural loan, bullock cart and for bamboo work, short-term loan with bamboo work, shallow tubewell with pumps and short-term loan. Each of the case beneficiaries utilized their scheme properly.

Grocery and Calf Rearing

Five beneficiaries are there who have taken this scheme. Only one have utilized the scheme properly but in other four cases the schemes are misutilized. Two of them misutilized it by consumption and another two for midway break up. One of the two cases of misutilization is due to the death of the beneficiary. Widow of the beneficiaries can not continue the grocery and his only one son is only six years old.

Bullock Cart and Duckary

Four beneficiaries have taken this scheme. Two of them used it properly and in other two cases it may be said that partially misutilized. As both the cases bullock with cart is properly utilized but duckary was misutilized for the purpose of religious festivals.

However, from the above discussion it reveals that the short term crop loan and the schemes those are directly related to agriculture used properly by the beneficiaries. Whereas the animal husbandry schemes, poultry bird scheme, and as well as the grocery, business or rice processing schemes those are mostly accepted by the landless and the marginal farmers are misutilized. The beneficiaries, who have land, cultivation is the first and foremost source of income, which they subsidised by the income of working as agricultural labourers or any kind of daily labourers. By utilizing the agricultural equipment the landholders can increase their source of continuous income more easily. But in case of a landless beneficiary who has taken the scheme of calf rearing or goatary or heifer rearing can not get a continuous income from their scheme. Their source of income as agricultural labourers is fixed. They get an asset from which they can earn some amount after a certain period of two to three years. But during this time, there are so many immediate contingencies they have to face and also they have to meet the social obligations during the ceremonies or rituals like marriage, death etc. and various types of religious festivals those are the most integral part of their social life. For the fulfilment of these kind of unavoidable requirements they obviously use the readily available asset procured from the scheme of ITDP. On the other hand the beneficiaries have not the full responsibility for misutilization of the schemes. Lack of veterinary services, investigation, guidance, suggestions, training etc. for proper utilization and maintenance of the schemes are also responsible.

It is also revealed here that one of the most important bottlenecks of proper utilization of a scheme is its wrong and inappropriate selection for a beneficiary. It is because of the fact that in most of the cases the schemes are sanctioned in a cursory manner. Hardly any thought is given to basic infrastructure required for the proper utilization of the schemes. Not only that, required technical skills of a beneficiary to conceive a feasible project be not also properly assessed before its distribution. In fact the schemes are selected and given randomly from the package of schemes prescribed by the Government for that particular financial year.

4.3. Repayment : Attitude and Practices

Mobility of any developmental scheme depends on the repayment performance of the beneficiaries. The credit plan, which is the very basis of the developmental scheme, designed with regular repayment. Flow of credit is maintained and the success of the developmental scheme is reflected in terms of repayment performance of the beneficiaries under study is shown in the Table 4.3.1.

Out of total 264 beneficiaries 68 beneficiaries (25.75 per cent) have paid fully. Fifty-nine beneficiaries have paid partly. The partly paid beneficiaries are those who discontinued their repayment after repaying some instalments and no possibility of repayment is there in future. Eighty-two beneficiaries, i.e., 31.06 per cent of the total beneficiaries are continuing their repayment by instalment. The beneficiaries are also included in this category who crossed already the due time of repayment within five years but still continue repayment as and when and how much is possible for them. Fifty-five beneficiaries, i.e., 20.83 per cent have never paid any instalment they noticed by the bank (Table 4.3.1).

Out of thirty-nine landless beneficiaries only seven beneficiaries have paid fully. Another seven landless paid partly. Eleven of them, continuing repayment by instalment and 14 landless beneficiaries (35.89 per cent) have never paid any single instalment.

Forty-four beneficiaries out of 153 marginal farmers paid fully. Thirty-seven of them paid partly, 44 (28.76 per cent) beneficiaries are continuing repayment and remaining 28 beneficiaries (18.30 per cent) never paid any instalment.

Out of sixty-three small farmers, 15 beneficiaries had paid all the installments they were to pay. Twelve of them have partly paid. Twenty-five are continuing their repayment and eleven beneficiaries have not paid any of instalment.

Among the medium farmers who are only six in number, one beneficiary have paid fully, 2 have paid partly and two are continuing and remain one have never repaid.

Out of only three large farmers one had paid fully and another two had paid partly (Table: 4.3.1).

Though in case of landless and marginal farmers it has been largely found that the repayment performance of the beneficiaries are related with their land size but the overall performance does not reveal that the land size of the beneficiaries is the only major factor for their good repayment performance. It is quite obvious, because among the landless beneficiaries whose only source of income is agricultural labourers, deficiency exists round the year and the income they generated from the scheme all are spent for consumption. They don't have any surplus income. On

Table 4.3.1

Repayment Performance of the Beneficiary (by Land Size)

Land Size (in Acre)	*Fully Paid*		*Partly Paid*		*Continuing*		*Unpaid*		*Total*	
	No.	*(%)*	*No.*	*(%)*	*No.*	*(%)*	*No.*	*(%)*	*No.*	*(%)*
LAND LESS	7	17.95	7	17.95	11	28.21	14	35.89	39	100.00
0.1 - 2.50	44	28.76	37	24.18	44	28.76	28	18.30	153	100.00
2.51 - 5.00	15	23.81	12	19.05	25	39.68	11	17.46	63	100.00
5.01 - 7.50	1	16.67	2	33.33	2	33.33	1	16.67	6	100.00
ABOVE 7.50	1	33.33	2	66.67	-	-	-	-	3	100.00
TOTAL	68	25.76	60	22.35	82	31.06	55	20.83	264	100.00

the other hand, it is to be said that the scheme they were mostly accepted did not give them a continuous income, which help them for a regular repayment. The situation is almost same to a marginal farmer. They have not a sufficient land account, which give them a surplus production after fulfilling their familial requirements.

A good number of beneficiaries are found who paid partly that is after paying two or three installments the beneficiaries discontinued their repayment. Among the landless and the marginal farmers who have a little amount of land, deficiency exists round the year. It is a very common experience of them that after paying two or three instalments if any one miss the next instalment due to any immediate contingency or due to deficiency in domestic affairs in the next time bank noticed him to pay back a heavy amount of instalment. As, bank counted the amount of the instalment with the last unpaid instalment with interest. As a result, in this time again he may not able to repay the full amount of the noticed instalment after meeting all the familial requirements. But the amount of instalment is increasing continuously. By this way if the due time of five years is crossed, rate of interest of marginal money of his project cost is increased from 4 per cent to 10 per cent and the amount of instalment is increased more and more and the beneficiaries become frustrated and stopped to repay the loan. As, by this time after a long period of repayment he knew that perhaps it will running for ever and ever and he will never be able to release from the indebtedness to the Government. Beneficiary became frustrated about this complicated and long-term system of cash repayment of the institutional credit.

Best repayment performance of the beneficiaries is noticed in case of the crop loan which is the only scheme given for short term (Table 4.3.2). Twenty-two beneficiaries (84.62 per cent) of this scheme have paid fully, one beneficiary paid partly, two beneficiaries are continuing and only one is there who paid nothing. Whereas, in case of other schemes those are the entire medium term loan given for five years, performances are not so good. As for example in case of the scheme bullock with cart, out of thirty-four beneficiaries twelve have paid partly, ten of them continuing their repayment and in three cases loan is totally unpaid. In case of calf rearing scheme, out of twenty-four beneficiaries, ten have paid fully, four have paid partly, three are continuing and seven are totally unpaid.

Out of seventeen beneficiaries who have taken the scheme of shallow tube well with pump set two beneficiaries paid fully, five beneficiaries paid partly, seven are continuing and in three cases it is totally unpaid.

Like these no schemes are there for which percentage of fully paid beneficiary have crossed at least fifty per cent without three exceptional cases where each beneficiary take a particular scheme and paid fully. These are the schemes of fishery, bullock with cart and bamboo work, calf rearing and short-term agricultural loan. To a landholder crop loan becomes essential as it helps them to purchase HYV seeds, chemical fertilizers, minikit etc. and they can save their last time production. On the other hand repayment of this loan is comparatively easy, as its amount is not so high and can repay their loan after harvesting. Not only that the beneficiary who can realize the facility of the scheme from the previous experience feels interest to take it again. As a result, he has an urge to repay the loan. It is because of the fact that, he has to submit a no dues certificate when he will apply for the next term. Whereas, in case of any medium term loan as the amount is high, can not get any immediate action from the scheme and have to continue the repayment for minimum up to five years, in so many cases the beneficiary cannot continue their repayment and it may be for various reasons.

On an average, the beneficiaries of the study area have repaid only 40 per cent of the total received amount. In case of short term crop loan average received amount is Rs.1019.61/-, which is the lowest amount among the thirty-three types of schemes received by the beneficiaries. Average 98.86 per cent of the total received amount for this

Table 4.3.2

Schemewise Repayment Performance of the Beneficiaries

Sl. No.	Name of the schemes	Fully paid No.	Fully paid %	Partly paid No.	Partly paid %	Continuing No.	Continuing %	Unpaid No.	Unpaid %	Total
1.	Bullock with cart	12	35.29	9	26.47	10	29.41	3	8.82	34
2.	Calf rearing	10	41.66	4	16.66	3	12.5	7	29.16	24
3.	STW with pump set	2	11.76	5	29.41	7	41.17	3	17.46	17
4.	Duckary	-	-	-	-	1	100.0	-	-	1
5.	Rickshaw	-	-	1	33.33	2	66.66	-	-	3
6.	Piggary	-	-	-	-	-	-	1	100.0	1
7.	Goatary	-	-	-	-	1	50.00	1	50.00	2
8.	Rice processing	-	-	1	25.00	1	25.00	2	50.00	4
9.	Milch cow	5	38.46	5	38.46	2	15.38	1	7.69	13
10.	Carpentry	-	-	2	33.33	1	16.66	3	50.00	6
11.	Heifer rearing	-	-	3	25.00	8	66.66	1	0.33	12
12.	Fishery	1	100.0	-	-	-	-	-	-	1
13.	Short term Agriculture	22	84.62	1	3.85	2	7.69	1	3.85	26

Contd.

Contd. Table 4.3.2

Sl. No.	Name of the schemes	Fully paid No.	Fully paid %	Partly paid No.	Partly paid %	Continuing No.	Continuing %	Unpaid No.	Unpaid %	Total
14.	Bamboo work	1	33.33	1	33.33	1	33.33	-	-	3
15.	Business	1	25.00	1	25.00	1	25.00	1	25.00	4
16.	Grocery	1	7.69	5	38.46	5	38.46	2	15.38	13
17.	Calf rearing + Goatary	7	17.00	13	31.70	3	7.31	18	43.90	41
18.	Calf rearing + Sheep	-	-	-	-	2	28.57	5	71.42	7
19.	Calf rearing + Rice Pr.	1	9.09	2	18.18	7	63.63	1	9.09	11
20.	Calf rearing + Veg Vending	-	-	-	-	4	100.0	-	-	4
21.	Calf rearing + Duckary	-	-	-	-	1	50.00	1	50.00	2
22.	Rickshaw + Calf rearing	-	-	-	-	1	100.0	-	-	1
23.	Van + Calf rearing	-	-	-	-	2	100.0	-	-	2
24.	Bullock cart+ Short term Ag.	2	14.28	2	14.28	10	71.42	-	-	14
25.	Bullock cart+ Bamboo work	1	100.0	-	-	-	-	-	-	1
26.	Short-term Ag.+Bamboo work	-	-	1	100.0	-	-	-	-	1
27.	Grocery + Calf rearing	-	-	-	-	1	20.00	4	80.00	5
28.	STW Pump Set+Short-term	-	-	1	100.0	-	-	-	-	1
29.	Bamboo work+ Calf rearing	1	33.33	1	33.33	1	33.33	-	-	3
30.	Bullock cart + Duckary	-	-	-	-	4	100.0	-	-	4

Contd.

Contd. Table 4.3.2

Sl. No.	Name of the schemes	Fully paid No.	Fully paid %	Partly paid No.	Partly paid %	Continuing No.	Continuing %	Unpaid No.	Unpaid %	Total
31.	Calf rearing + Short term Ag.	1	100.0	-	-	-	-	-	-	1
32	Calf rearing + Short term Ag.	-	-	-	-	1	100.0	-	-	1
33	Rickshaw + Rice Processing	-	-	1	100.0	-	-	-	-	1
	Total	68	25.76	59	22.35	82	31.06	55	20.83	264

scheme is repaid which may be mentioned as the one of the best performance of all the schemes (Table 4.3.3). Besides the short-term crop loan very few schemes are noticed where almost hundred per cent or sometimes above hundred per cent of the received amount was repaid by the beneficiaries. These schemes are fishery, calf rearing and milch cow, bullock cart and bamboo work, shallow tube well with pump set and short-term crop loan. It is to be mentioned here that for each of the cases only one beneficiary received the scheme (Table 4.3.3). Most worth performance is noticed for the scheme piggery where the beneficiary has paid nothing.

Reasons for Non-Payment

Repayment of loan depends on various factors. Factors may be related to social or economic aspects of the beneficiary households or it may be due to accident or lacuna in the scheme itself. The analysis of the reasons behind non-payment of loan is important because it may help in removing the constraints of successful operation of the scheme. Twelve different reasons have identified for non-payment of loan and these are on the basis of peoples' perception (Table 4.3.4). Nine beneficiaries of the total number of non-paying beneficiaries have identified who have not repaid, as they could not generate desirable income from their scheme. As for example, one beneficiary, had taken short-term crop loan, utilized his scheme properly but due to heavy rain just before and during harvesting, crops were ruined and he was felt in a total loss for that season and could not repay his loan.

In case of 24 beneficiaries (21.05 per cent) as all the income generated from the scheme was spent on family consumption, the loans were remained unpaid. For the landless and the marginal farmers deficiency for household affairs is a crucial problem and exists for round the year. To solve this problem they spent all the income generated from the scheme for domestic affairs or for other immediate contingencies and loans remained unpaid.

Table 4.3.3

Average Amount of Loan Received and Repaid by the Beneficiaries (Schemewise)

Sl. No.	*Name of the Scheme*	*Average Amount (in Rs.)* Received	Repaid
1.	Bullock with cart	7149.69	3917.97 (54.80)
2.	Calf rearing	3856.66	1502.17 (38.95)
3.	STW with pump set	18762.50	6510.05 (34.60)
4.	Duckary	1200.00	3750.00 (31.25)
5.	Heifer rearing	8708.33	1989.00 (22.50)
6.	Rickshaw	10053.33	5100.00 (50.73)
7.	Piggary	1200.00	-
8.	Goatary	2780.00	787.50 (28.30)
9.	Rice Processing	8077.50	1530.00 (18.94)
10.	Milch cow	3781.53	1503.54 (36.76)
11.	Carpentry	3416.66	860.33 (25.17)
12.	Fishery	5000.00	5000.00 (100.00)
13.	Bamboo work	1500.00	1002.33 (66.80)
14.	Business	5000.00	3504.99 (70.08)
15.	Grocery	7820.00	2692.96 (36.25)
16.	Short term agriculture	1019.61	1008.19 (98.86)
17.	Calf rearing + Goatary	5652.19	1147.96 (20.29)
18.	Calf rearing + Sheep	7428.00	1395.72 (18.79)
19.	Calf rearing + Rice Processing	6871.45	1538.52 (22.39)
20.	Rickshaw + Rice Processing	15750.00	6500.00 (41.26)
21.	Veg. Vending + Calf rearing	11495.00	870.00 (7.56)
22.	Duckary + Calf rearing	6880.00	472.50 (6.86)
23.	Rickshaw + Calf rearing	15150.00	1500.00 (9.90)
24.	Van + Calf rearing	11500.00	1830.00 (15.91)
25.	Bullock cart + Short term	8785.71	4762.73 (54.21)
26.	Calf rearing + milch cow	6060.00	6775.00 (111.79)
27.	Calf rearing + Short term	4500.00	2050.00 (45.55)
28.	Bullock cart + Bamboo work	9500.00	8560.00 (90.10)
29.	Short-term + Bamboo work	2500.00	2500.00 (100.00)
30.	Grocery + calf rearing	5200.00	394.16 (7.58)
31.	STW/Pump Set + Short term	12600.00	12600.00 (100.00)
32.	Bamboo work + Calf rearing	4500.00	2234.70 (49.66)
33.	Bullock cart + Duckary	11000.00	265.00 (2.40)
	Total	234694.00	96055.32 (40.00)

(Figures in the parenthesis indicate the percentage).

Table 4.3.4
Reasons for Non-payment (Partly/Unpaid) of Loans (Peoples' Opinion)

Sl. No.	*Reasons*	*No.*	*% of Total Beneficiary*
1.	Additional income could not be generated	9	7.89
2.	Income generated was spent on family consumption	24	21.05
3.	Break down of assets/loss of units	14	12.28
4.	Used in purchase of alternate assets	5	4.39
5.	Incomplete unit was given	4	3.51
6.	Death of beneficiary	4	3.51
7.	Family breakage	5	4.39
8.	For bad quality of units	21	18.42
9.	Form an idea that loan is remitted	10	8.77
10.	Breach of promise of political leaders	4	3.51
11.	Never noticed	4	3.51
12.	Willing defaulter	10	8.77
	Total	114	100.00

There are 14 beneficiaries which is 12.28 per cent of the total defaulters can not repay their loans for break down of the assets that was given him as a loan. As for example in case of a scheme shallow tube well with pump set after 3 years of acceptance the pump set was broken down. After some days when he contacts with a mechanic, he suggested him to replace one parts of the machine. But it was not possible to him to provide the cost of that parts at that time. As a result to save the crops he take water from his neighbour's pump set and returned the cost of water by paddy just after the harvesting but the installment of Government loan remained unpaid.

In another case for the same scheme after two years of acceptance the water level was shrinking and since then the pump set became useless and loan is remained unpaid.

Five beneficiaries were identified who used all the generated income from the scheme to purchase alternate assets or another asset. As for example one Santal landless beneficiary inhabitant of village Dholtikuri got an information that one of his neighbour will sell his 17 Kathas of land in a low price. He was becoming interested to buy the land and contact with him. Then he sold his two cows get from the government scheme and obviously his loans remained unpaid.

In another case, one Santal beneficiary of village Bankajal, save all the money generated from his scheme of shallow tube well with pump set. By this saved money he used to buy land but did not repay loan after paying the first two instalments.

Another case may also be mentioned here. One beneficiary reared his two calves up to two and a half years, then he bought two buffaloes by selling his calves. He had to pay some extra money, as the amount he got by selling the calves was not sufficient enough. To make up this deficiency he had to sell some paddy also. As a result he did not repay all of his instalments he had to pay.

In case of four beneficiaries (3.51 per cent) reason of non-payment is that they have a complaint against the units. As for example one beneficiary of village Patharghata has complained that one part of his bullock cart was not given when he was given it from the LAMP society. He reported it to the Panchayat member. According to his advice he went to the LAMP society for 3-4 days. Moreover, Society had taken Rs. 20/- from him. He also submitted an application. But the result was zero. He says that due to this reason he did not repay his loan.

In four cases due to death of the beneficiary, loans remained unpaid or partly paid. In these cases his family members didn't take the responsibility of repayment. As for example the widow of a dead beneficiary has stated that, "as the loan was not sanctioned in my name, I will not take the responsibility of his debt. If I do not repay it I should not be punished".

For five beneficiaries family breakage is the reason for non-payment of loan. In case of a household of Damdama, the beneficiary who is now sixty years old took the scheme of shallow tube well with pump set. He said that his elder son was separated from the household two years ago after marriage and his younger son who studied upto class IX does not help him and is always reluctant to work in the agricultural field. The old man was thus not in condition to manage the domestic affairs nor to repay the instalments.

To a good number of beneficiaries the reason for non-payment of loan is for bad quality of units. Twenty beneficiaries of the total defaulters did not repay their loans due to this reason. One beneficiary of village Baradanga of Sarpalehana Gram Panchayat got 4 units of goat. Two of them were weak when given. They became sick more after his acceptance and ultimately within two weeks they all died. The beneficiary says that he is not unwilling to repay the loan but why should he pay for those whom he could not use at all. Bank noticed him to pay off the installment on the basis of the total project cost, which includes the cost of the dead units also. But the man did not pay any of the instalments.

There were ten beneficiaries among the defaulters who formed an idea that loan is remitted. In these cases generally the beneficiaries are misguided by the local political leaders, panchayat members or by some local progressive fellows. These people are trying to make a good image in front of the village people for their self-interest. Beneficiaries are also stopped to repay the loans on the basis of the oral information of these fellows. They never got any official information.

Four beneficiaries (3.51 per cent) of village Sarbanandapur of Kankali Gram Panchayat determined that they do not repay their loan due to breach of promise of political leaders. A 28 years old young man said that he himself was a supporter of CPI but he thinks that the Front Government did nothing for them. Before the last Panchayat election the political leaders promised to arrange a submersible pump set and also a tubewell for their village. Then two years passed, the leaders enjoy the power of Panchayat but the work was not done. Villagers have been suffering from water scarcity. The young man decided that he would not pay off any installment as long the panchayat members keep their promise and arrange a submersible pump set and a tubewell for them.

Four beneficiaries have never noticed for repayment. All of them are taken the loan through the LAMP society, which is at present in a dilapidated condition.

Ten beneficiaries have identified as willing defaulter. These beneficiaries do not response against the notice of Bank intentionally. Laxmiram Murmu is an ex-member of Panchayat and Malati Murmu, his wife, the present member of Panchayat thinks that this kind of scheme are for the source of income of Bank and it is nothing but a business. Due to this reason Bank always interested about the repayment of loan. Because after the full repayment they can give him another loan and their income will be increased. Side by side he also says that by this way they are also benefited by getting valuable assets without any investment. The loan was sanctioned in the name of his father. Then he was the member of Panchayat. Eight years have passed after the acceptance of a scheme of shallow tube well with pump set. By this time he purchased about 12 bighas of land from the income generated with the help of the scheme, but never paid any single instalment. He never deposited his money in the Bank account of his own but saved money by fixed deposit. Because, he formed an idea that if he deposited money in his account the Bank Manager may draw money from his account and repay the loan.

Regarding these default cases, it seems that the beneficiaries are often reluctant to pay back the loans owing their power linkage to the local statutory bodies entrusted to look after the implementation and monitoring of the programmes. The people did not pay back their loans and took undue advantage of their positions in the local bodies.

Attitude of the Beneficiaries about Repayment

Regarding the repayment of government loans the views,

expressed by the beneficiaries are different. These are also reflected on their performances of repayment. Some beneficiaries feel gratefulness to the government for giving them a scope to get an asset without investment, which may have helped them to achieve a better economic condition. They believe that all these facilities, government arranged for their betterment and they should liable to the Government. Not only that, they should liable to their society also. Because of the fact that if they will mark as defaulters they should lost the faith of Government upon them and then their tribal society will be suffered. Perception of these beneficiaries is, non-payment of loans not only be going against the customary rules of their own community but also be lowering down the prestige of the other community members including those of their own family to the eyes of the administrators and welfare workers. No one will believe them. From this point of view, Laxmiram Tudu, one 62 years old Mahali of village Dighidanga of Sarpalehana Panchayat suggested that it will be better to discuss with the villagers before the selection of beneficiary and also about the scheme selected for him. He believes that it will helpful for better recovery, as they know their own villager than others.

Another group of beneficiaries is interested to repay the loan from the willingness to get a government loan again. They know that any defaulter will not be allowed to get a loan. These beneficiaries are annoyed about the defaulters of their own community.

Above two categories of people are obviously those who can implement their schemes properly and able to generate income from the scheme. But the beneficiaries who have not successful in implementation of the scheme and hence, benefit accrued by them had been partial or nothing, attitude about repayment should not be spontaneous. Among these beneficiaries some are unable to arrange it and the others are not willing to repay fully or partially.

Another category of beneficiaries thinks that they should repay their loan and they told it from their fear. As for example some beneficiaries have opined that they should repay their loan fully during their lifetime otherwise it will devolve on the next generation and they will blame them. Some other beneficiaries have a fear of increasing interest of the loan. They think that the loan of government should be repaid in someday or other in future. Thus, for nothing non-payment will increase the amount with interest.

In case of another beneficiary it is found that he has a fear of punishment for non-payment. He formed an idea that if his loan will be unpaid their domestic animals will be seized. But by whom, it is not clear to him and there is no instance in front of him.

Lastly there are some beneficiaries who are found to ignore the system of repayment desperately. These people are specifically those who are directly or indirectly engaged in politics or conscious about the modern political system or influenced by these people. As for example, one ex-member of panchayat, now whose wife is the member due to reservation still active as a member. He is the son of a defaulter. He says that he is in power. So, no one will be audacious to send him a reminder. Not only that he also says that now he makes his family fully secured and he has no need of any financial assistance from Government. In future, he will never apply for it.

However, it is to be said that, though overall performance of repayment of the beneficiaries are not desirable but to a majority of them non-payment is not always intentionally or not for ignoring the system. To them the scheduled and routine system of repayment itself became the implicit reason of their non-payment. Side by side, their deficiency, emergency familial requirements, inability to supplement the schemes are also behind their non-payment. But all these are true for the landless or marginal farmers and sometimes for the small farmers also. They were compelled to become a defaulter but sometimes they are suffering by their sting of conscience. But it is more significant to notice that the beneficiaries having comparatively better land

account, better economic condition and moreover, politically concerned, are ignoring the system unscrupulously. They are not indifferent about making more profit, which is generally totally absent in a tribal economy.

4.4. Development Schemes : Percepts and Attitude

Since 1983, various family benefit schemes of Integrated Tribal Development Project are actively running in the District of Birbhum as well as in the study area. From the entire study it reveals that the schemes could not make similar impact on the beneficiary households. The families with the same type of scheme could not have the same economic benefit. It involves activities and responsibilities both of the project functionaries and the beneficiaries themselves. Now, an attempt has been made to understand the perception and attitude of the beneficiaries about the ITDP schemes.

Attitude of the Beneficiaries for Accepting Further Loans

To analyse the attitude and perception about the scheme an attempt was made to know either the beneficiaries are willing or unwilling to accept it further. It was found that 58.33 per cent of the total tribal beneficiaries are willing and 41.67 per cent of total beneficiaries are unwilling to accept the government loan again (Table 4.4.1). It was

Table 4.4.1

Attitude of the Beneficiaries for Accepting Further Loans

Name of the Tribe	*Willing*		*Un-willing*		*Total*
	No.	*(%)*	*No.*	*(%)*	
Santal	129	57.85	94	42.15	223
Mahali	13	72.22	5	27.78	18
Kora	2	40.00	3	60.00	5
Sardar	10	55.56	8	44.44	18
Total	154	58.33	110	41.67	264

noticed that 58 per cent of total tribal Santal beneficiaries are willing and 42 per cent are unwilling to take any loan from Government. In case of Mahali beneficiaries, 72.22 per cent are willing and 27.78 per cent are unwilling. Out

of five beneficiaries of Kora community two are willing beneficiaries and three are unwilling. Among the eighteen Sardar beneficiaries, ten are willing and remaining eight are unwilling. Thus, in every community most of the beneficiaries have a desire to take further financial assistance from Government for their economic upliftment.

It is found that most of the unwilling beneficiaries are marginal farmers (Table 4.4.2). Sixty-three per cent

Table 4.4.2
Unwilling Beneficiaries for Accepting Further Loan
(By Land Size)

Land Size (in Acre)	*Santal*		*Mahali*		*Kora*		*Sardar*		*Total*	
	No.	*(%)*	*No.*	*(%)*	*No.*	*(%)*	*No.*	*(%)*	*No.*	*(%)*
Landless	23	24.47	1	20.00	1	33.33	2	25.00	27	24.55
0.1 - 2.50	57	60.64	4	80.00	2	66.67	6	75.00	69	62.73
2.51 - 5.00	12	12.77	-	-	-	-	-	-	12	10.91
5.01 - 7.50	-	-	-	-	-	-	-	-	-	-
Above 7.50	2	2.13	-	-	-	-	-	-	2	1.82
Total	94	100.00	5	100.00	3	100.00	8	100.00	110	100.00

marginal farmers and twenty five per cent landless beneficiaries were identified as unwilling and reluctant to take the Government assistance further. This is true for every community. Beside this, twelve Santal small farmers and two Santal large farmers were also found to reluct to receive loans for the second time. To get a government scheme every tribal individual has to communicate regularly with the Panchayat, Block Office, Cooperative Society, and Bank to satisfy all the official procedures. It seems that majority of the marginal farmers and landless beneficiaries are disinterested to loss one manday instead of a day spending for a loan which have no surety to get and also have no assurance of economic upliftment.

Reasons of Unwillingness

The marginal farmers and the landless beneficiaries are afraid about the repayment in cash by instalment. From their previous experience they lost their faith upon

themselves. Some of them are still defaulter. But the beneficiaries, who have repaid fully, bring in their difficulties of paying the loans in cash. Cash among these people is considered scarce, and is preferred. Thus, instead of cash they feel it more convenient to pay back any debt in terms of kind or labour. But there is no scope for paying the bank loans in kind or labour. Sometimes beneficiaries have the experience that when they receive the bank notice for payment of instalment at a time then it becomes quite impossible for them to pay after fulfilling all the immediate requirements for their families.

Sometimes it was noticed that the beneficiaries have a bad experience of inadequacy in financial assistance. They were given the unit according to sanctioned project always in kind not in cash. But then they did not get any financial assistance to obtain and maintain the assets economically. All the responsibilities were devolved on the beneficiaries after the acceptance of the scheme. They have to procure all the required feed and fodder and also the required infrastructure for the animal husbandry scheme privately. In case of other scheme also they have to provide some money for its successful implementation and maintenance. Sometimes the landless and the marginal farmers were too poor to subsidize their schemes privately.

They also have a bad experience of substandard quality of assets, from which they did not generate income but remain indebted to Government forever.

From the previous experience some beneficiaries are frustrated about the long-term official processes and formalities. It reported by the beneficiaries that they have to spend a number of days in the official process of getting papers ready for having a loan. The entire exercise in this connection may even fail to materialize. They thus think that if they work on those days, they can earn some money instead of wasting time this way.

Some beneficiaries are reluctant to take it again due to a long term repayment procedure. In such cases, the loans have to be paid in instalments within a time schedule of three years. The instalments have to be paid with interest and the repayment would start after two years from the date of receipt. The loans are subsidised, and the repayment instalments are ascertained excluding the subsidised amount; the beneficiaries, however, do not understand the advantageous means of this long-term procedure of repayment nor do they feel free with a burden of indebtedness to the government for such a long time. Some of the beneficiaries were also found to calculate that they do not, in reality, get any subsidy and the entire amount of loan with interest is becoming equivalent with the actual project cast through this system.

A few beneficiaries also think that they don't need any further assistance. They are able to make their family secured by the first time assistance. Their perception is that, generated income from the first time assistance is sufficient to make their family income secure. No doubt these beneficiaries could effectively run the schemes and able to raise their income level. But due to their limited want they think it sufficient instead of taking the opportunity to make the income level more high. Side by side it is also to be mentioned here that sometimes these beneficiaries are defaulters and only chiefly interested in grabbing the assistance.

Preference of Schemes of the Willing Beneficiaries

An attempt had been made to know what kinds of schemes the willing beneficiaries prefer for their further acceptance (Table 4.4.3). It reflects the perception and attitude of the beneficiaries about the schemes of these existing developmental projects for them. If the preferable schemes of the beneficiaries are analyzed it is found that two landless preferred calf rearing scheme, one preferred business, five for milch cow and another two have preferred calf and goatary scheme. Most of these schemes belong to the animal husbandry sector. Though there are instances of failure in these schemes, and the beneficiaries had faced problems in the past in running the projects effectively,

Table 4.4.3

Willingness of Beneficiaries for Accepting Further Loans (by Land Size)

Land Size (in Acre)

Sl. No.	Name of the Scheme	Landless	0.1-2.50	2.51-5.00	5.01-7.50	Above-7.50	Total
1.	Short-term loan	-	29(34.94)	26(50.98)	2(33.33)	-	57(37.01)
2.	Milch cow+Short-term	-	-	1(1.96)	-	-	1(0.65)
3.	Goatary + Sheep	-	1(1.20)	-	-	-	1(0.65)
4.	STW with pump set	-	2(2.42)	5(9.80)	2(33.33)	1(100.00)	10(6.49)
5.	Calf rearing	2(15.38)	8(9.65)	5(9.80)	-	-	15(9.74)
6.	Bullock with cart	-	2(2.42)	1(1.96)	-	-	3(1.95)
7.	Bullock cart+Short-term	-	1(1.20)	3(5.88)	-	-	4(2.60)
8.	Craft	-	7(8.43)	-	-	-	7(4.55)
9.	Business	1(7.69)	-	1(1.96)	-	-	2(1.30)
10.	Craft+Short-term	-	1(1.20)	2(3.92)	-	-	3(1.95)
11.	Duckary	-	-	1(1.96)	-	-	1(0.65)
12.	Milch cow	5(38.46)	9(10.85)	3(5.88)	1(16.67)	-	18.(11.69)
13.	Goatary + Short-term	-	1(1.20)	-	-	-	1(0.65)
14.	Rice Pro. + Short-term	-	1(1.20)	-	-	-	1(0.65)

Contd

Contd. Table 4.4.3

Sl. No.	*Name of the Scheme*	*Landless*	*0.1-2.50*	*2.51-5.00*	*5.01-7.50*	*Above-7.50*	*Total*
15.	Grocery	-	1(1.20)	-	-	-	1(0.65)
16.	Grocery + Calf rearing	-	1(1.20)	-	-	-	1(0.65)
17.	Calf + Sheep	-	2(2.42)	-	-	-	2(1.30)
18.	Calf + Goatary	2(15.38)	3(3.61)	1(1.96)	-	-	6(3.90)
19.	Fishery	-	1(1.20)	-	-	-	1(0.65)
20.	Rice Processing	-	-	1(1.96)	-	-	1(0.65)
21.	Pump set + Short-term	-	-	1(1.96)	1(16.67)	-	2(1.30)
22.	Goatary	-	1(1.20)	-	-	-	1(0.65)
23.	Rickshaw	-	1(1.20)	-	-	-	1(0.65)
24.	Poultry	-	1(1.20)	-	-	-	1(0.65)
25.	Thatching	-	1(1.20)	-	-	-	1(0.65)
26.	For improvement of grocery	-	2(2.42)	-	-	-	2(1.30)
27.	Any kind of loan	1(7.69)	2(2.42)	-	-	-	3(1.95)
28.	Don't know	2(15.38)	5(6.02)	-	-	-	7(4.55)
	Total	13(100.00)	83(100.00)	51(100.00)	6(100.00)	1(100.00)	154(100.00)

(Figures in the parenthesis indicate the percentage).

they preferred these schemes to others. They say that they have knowledge in animal husbandry compared to the schemes of other sectors. To speak otherwise, it seems that the beneficiaries feel somewhat at ease with schemes of animal rearing, which is quite in conformity with their traditional habit and schemes. The problems they have to face now is primarily the increasing lack of communal resource base in terms of grazing land, natural water pools and the infrastructural facility for farm of birds. The lack of adequate veterinary facilities to the new variety of birds and animals about which the people seem to have little or no knowledge is also a problem they have to face.

Besides these, one landless expressed that he is willing to accept any kind of loan. Another two landless beneficiaries said that they don't know what kind of schemes will be suited for them and for what scheme they have sufficient skill and capabilities for its effective implementation. Thus, it is to be said that these kinds of beneficiaries are chiefly interested in grabbing the assistance rather than running the scheme.

The marginal farmers prefer almost all types of schemes. But the most preferable scheme is short-term agricultural scheme. Twenty-nine willing marginal farmers are found to prefer this scheme. On the other hand, one marginal farmer prefers this scheme with another agriculturally associated scheme, bullock with cart. Another two have preferred this scheme, one with a goatary scheme and another with rice processing. Marginal farmers are not interested to take medium term loan, though they are eligible for it. From their previous experience they learnt that it was a problem for them to repay the medium term loan in the prescribed manner, though there is a scope to get 50 per cent subsidy on his project cost. Short-term scheme has no subsidy at all, and the entire loan is to be paid immediately after six months. From their previous experience or by sharing the experience of the neighbours they have learnt that it is comparatively easy to get loans under this and achieve an immediate gain. They can use chemical fertilizers, HYV seeds, necessary for good harvest without any own investment and stored up their crops for the lean period. Another advantage of this scheme is that they have to repay a smaller amount of loan, which is comparatively easy to them. Next preference of the marginal farmers is the animal husbandry and poultry bird scheme. Only one beneficiary is there who want to take the grocery scheme again and other one, the short-term scheme with calf rearing. There is one marginal farmer who does not want to take any scheme further. Instead he would like to have some financial assistance for thatching his huts. While talking of his own preference he told that every year they have to bear a heavy expenditure for repairing their huts specially before the rainy season. To fulfill this requirement most of the time they have to take loans from private sources like their landowner, professional moneylenders, and *aratdars*. He, therefore, feels some provision of loan for this kind of work would be of more useful to them.

Two marginal farmers who have taken the scheme of grocery and effectively implementing it have felt an inadequacy for its maintenance. They want to get financial assistance of the project for improvement of their grocery rather than any new scheme.

Like the landless beneficiaries two marginal farmers are also identified who don't know what types of schemes they can take again for their economic betterment but he is willing to take it definitely.

To the small farmers the most preferable scheme is also the short-term agricultural loan. Fifty-one per cent of them are found willing to take this scheme again and again. Their next preference is shallow tubewell with pump set by which, they think; they would be able to minimize their cost of expenditure for cultivating the Boro Paddy. It is a common experience to them that they could not cultivate their land in the Boro season due to inadequacy of money for irrigation. They also have an experience that after acquiring money they could not able to irrigate his land in a proper time, as they have to depend upon others for irrigation purpose. Five willing small farmer beneficiaries however, expressed their eagerness to obtain this essential equipment of modern agricultural practices. Another five small farmers prefer calf rearing scheme to others. One of them is willing to acquire a bullock with cart, as he does not have it. He wants to acquire this by a loan with 50 per cent subsidy. Three beneficiaries are willing to take the same scheme as well as the short-term agricultural scheme. Besides these, only one small farmer is willing to take the scheme of business, two opt for craft and short-term scheme, one, for duckary, three, for milch cow, one, for calf and goatary and another one, for rice processing scheme.

Out of six willing medium farmer beneficiaries two are willing to take the short-term agricultural loan and two, for Shallow Tube well with pumpset scheme. One has a desire to obtain a milch cow and the other, wants to take a pumpset as well as short term scheme.

There is only one large farmer, who is willing to take government scheme again. His willingness is for obtaining a shallow tubewell with pumpset without own investment and with the facility for fifty per cent subsidy.

Thus, from the above discussion it is revealed that the majority of landless beneficiaries and a part of marginal farmers prefer the animal husbandry schemes for the next time. A good number of marginal farmers and most of the small farmers prefer the scheme in terms of a short-term loan. A few of these two categories preferred to take a medium term scheme of shallow tubewell with pump set for the next time. Medium farmers have the desire equally for short-term and medium term scheme, obviously for irrigation purpose. Lastly the large farmers are desirous only for the medium term scheme of irrigation.

The landless and marginal farmers are more in number, they are also poorer than other beneficiaries. They are willing to have benefits of the schemes, all of which are not accessible to them. Moreover, they are afraid of the long-term complicated system of cash repayment. Whereas, the large farmers are willing to utilize the opportunity of 50 per cent subsidy of a government scheme and acquiring a valuable asset like shallow tube well with pump set without any own investment. They don't bother about the procedure of repayment and amount of the project cost of the scheme.

To the landless and marginal farmers the canvas of needs is so broad. Sometimes it is found that they themselves are not clear about their actual need. In many cases they are ready to receive any scheme they offered. But to the landholders need, expectation and want is clear and restricted.

4.5. Private Credit as a Complementary System

From the discussion of previous chapters it is clear that, the scope of family benefit schemes is quite large, but this kind of institutional credit covers only a part of the poor tribal people's huge canvas of needs. More precisely, it may be said that the institutional credit deals with the situations, which have some limitations;

(i) institutional loans are not easily available;

(ii) benefit from the underlying project depends on its marketable surplus;

(iii) it goes through a contractual obligations which may be called enforceable but through a codified legal system;

(iv) it never gives support when the poor tribals required a financial assistance purely for consumption and contingent activities.

In the foregoing analysis of this chapter an attempt has been made to find out how and in which way the tribals solve the problems and how an alternative collateral system of informal credit exists with the institutional credit system of Integrated Tribal Development Programme.

Source of Private Loans

During the field investigation it was found that in spite

of taking loans from institutional sources of Integrated Tribal Development Programme, 70.45 per cent of the total beneficiaries have also taken loans from different informal sources (Table 4.5.1). It was found that 3.79 per cent of them

Table 4.5.1

Source of Private Loans Taken by the Beneficiary Households

Sources	*No.*	*(%)*
Private Money Lender	10	3.79
Aratdar (Local assembler)	60	22.73
Land owner	97	36.74
Friend / Relative	7	2.65
Others	12	4.55
Not indebted	78	29.55
Total	264	100.00

have borrowed money from the private moneylenders. From the local assemblers (*aratdar*) six beneficiaries (22.73 per cent) have borrowed loans. Another significant number of beneficiaries (36.74 per cent) have borrowed loans from the landowners. Among them the tenant cultivators are most numerous, followed by the agricultural labourers. Here, in most of the cases the land owners are the neighbouring Hindu Caste people, in whose land the landless tribals are working as agricultural labourers round the year, sometimes generation after generation and the share croppers sharing lands with them and at the rest of the time working as agricultural labourers in their land. On the other hand seven beneficiaries have found to take loans from their friends or relatives. Other twelve borrowed money from other sources like the owner of shaw mill, rice mill, brick kiln etc. where they work as labourers. Lastly, it was found that 29.55 per cent of the beneficiaries are not indebted, by any informal sources. But, in reality, the fact is that though they are not indebted now but sometimes they also borrow money from these sources as and when they require.

Purposes of taking Loans from Private Sources

The tribal beneficiaries are used to borrow money from

the private agencies for various purposes. From Table 4.5.2 it is found that twenty seven (10.23 per cent) beneficiaries have taken loans for their immediate contingency purposes like, sudden illness, sudden death or due to essential requirement for repairing hut etc. Thirty-nine beneficiaries (14.77per cent) have borrowed money for production/income purpose. Though, the tribal people are financially assisted for agriculture purposes by the schemes of Integrated Tribal Development Project but due to some limitations of the project every one cannot avail the facilities according to their requirements. Sometimes it is also noticed that the amount is inadequate to their requirements and they have to borrow money from any private agencies to supplement it. When one beneficiary gets a short term agricultural loan he can save money for the investment due to chemical fertilizer, HYV seeds etc. But the saved money was not sufficient for irrigating his land. Thus, if he cannot avail it himself, he has to depend upon the informal credit system obviously. In case of other schemes also due to financial

Table 4.5.2

Purposes of Taking Loans from Private Agencies by the Beneficiary Households

	Purposes of Taking Loans	*No.*	*%*
1.	Immediate Contingency	27	10.23
2.	Production / Income	39	14.77
3.	Deficiency	83	31.44
4.	Immediate contingency + deficiency	17	6.44
5.	Immediate contingency + production	4	1.51
6.	Deficiency + production	8	3.03
7.	Others	8	3.79
8.	Not indebted	78	29.55
	Total	264	100.00

inadequacy the beneficiaries borrowed money from private sources for its maintenance and successful continuation, because they were given the unit of the scheme in kind not in cash. After acceptance they did not get any financial assistance to obtain and maintain the assets economically.

A significant number of beneficiaries were found to depend on the informal credit for supplementing their familial requirements at the time of deficiency specifically during the lean period. Eighty-three beneficiaries, who is 31.44 per cent of the total beneficiaries borrowed money due to deficiency. Another seventeen beneficiaries borrowed money for both immediate contingency purpose and deficiency and four for immediate contingency and production purposes. Again eight beneficiaries were found to depend on this system for the requirements at the time of deficiency and as well as for production purposes. Eight beneficiaries were found to borrow money for other purposes, like, requirements for meeting some social obligations at the time of religious festivals or during the ceremonies, fulfillment of dowry etc.

Here, the most significant feature is that most of the landless beneficiaries and a good number of marginal farmers depend on the private sources to overcome their round the year deficiency. Out of thirty-nine landless beneficiaries twenty-five (64.10 per cent) and fifty-four marginal farmers out of hundred fifty-three (33.99 per cent) have borrowed money for deficiency purpose specially during the lean period. Their next requirement is for immediate contingency purposes. Six landless and sixteen marginal farmers were found to take loan for the fulfilment of immediate contingency. Another four (10.26 per cent) landless have taken loan for both immediate contingency and due to deficiency. Only one landless beneficiary has taken loan for both deficiency and production purposes and another one, for his immediate contingency purpose as well as production purpose. Only two landless were not indebted (Table 4.5.3). On the other hand twenty-four marginal farmers have taken money for production/income purposes, nine for both immediate contingency and deficiency purpose, six for deficiency and production purposes and only two for both immediate contingency and production purposes.

Table 4.5.3

Purposes of Taking Private Loans According to the Land Size of the Beneficiaries

Purpose / *Land Size* (in acres)	*Immediate contingency*		*Production/Income*		*Deficiency*		*Immediate contin-gency + deficiency*		*Deficiency+ Produ-ction*		*Immediate contingency + Produ-ction*		*Others*		*Not indebted*		*Total*	
	No.	%	No.	%	No.	%	No.	%	No.	%	No.	%	No.	%	No.	%	No.	%
Landless	6	15.38	-	-	25	64.10	4	10.26	1	2.56	1	2.56	-	-	2	5.13	39	100.00
0.1 - 2.50	16	10.46	24	15.69	52	33.99	9	5.88	6	3.92	2	1.31	7	4.58	37	24.18	153	100.00
2.51 - 5.00	5	7.94	13	20.63	6	9.52	4	6.35	1	1.59	1	1.59	1	1.59	32	50.79	63	100.00
5.01 - 7.50	-	-	1	16.67	-	-	-	-	-	-	-	-	-	-	5	83.33	6	100.00
Above 7.50	-	-	1	33.33	-	-	-	-	-	-	-	-	-	-	2	66.67	3	100.00
Total	27	10.23	39	14.02	83	31.44	17	6.44	8	3.03	4	1.52	10	3.79	78	29.55	264	100.00

Remaining seven marginal farmers were found not indebted. Among the small farmers only 9.52 per cent have taken loan from non-institutional sources for deficiency purposes, 20.63 per cent for production/income purposes and 7.94 per cent for immediate contingency purposes. For the purpose of immediate contingency and deficiency, it was found that only four (6.35 per cent) small farmers have borrowed money from the informal sources. On the other hand, only one have borrowed for deficiency and production purposes, another one for immediate contingency and production purposes and remaining one for other purpose. It was also noticed that the percentage of not indebted beneficiaries among the small farmers is 50.79 per cent. Among six medium farmers, five was found to remain not indebted and only one was dependent on the informal credit system for betterment of his production/income. Among three large farmers, two were identified as not indebted and the other one has taken it for production purposes (Table 4.5.3). Thus, from the above facts and figures, it reveals that intention of the landless and the marginal farmers are always to recover their round the year deficiency and immediate contingency from the non-institutional sources. Whereas, majority of the higher land holders whether they are small farmers or medium farmers or large farmers always borrowed money with an intention of improving their production capacity, as well as their income. However, the landless and marginal farmers to whom the financial assistance is more essential, have remained at the same situation. After the financial assistance from government still they have to think about their own salvation from round the year deficiency and immediate contingency.

Interest Pattern of Non-institutional Sources

Seventy-six beneficiaries (40.86 per cent) have borrowed money from the private agencies with interest (Table 4.5.4). These beneficiaries have taken money with a contract of repayment in cash with interest, which vary according to the source of debt. Generally, these lenders

Table 4.5.4

Pattern of Interests Taken By the Private Agencies from the Beneficiary Households

Interest Pattern	*No.*	*(%)*
With Interest	76	40.86
Without Interest	108	58.06
Contractual	2	1.08
Total	186	100.00

are the professional moneylenders and the *aratdars*. Professional moneylenders lend their money in cash. At the time of lending, moneylender makes a contract with the borrower regarding duration of time of lending and about the rate of interest. *Aratdars* lend paddy to the tribal people. Most of the cases the landowner tribals borrow paddy from the *aratdars* at the time of deficiency or immediate contingency purposes or as seed for cultivation. Borrowers pay back the paddy just after harvesting. They have pay back more or less 5 kgs. of paddy for every 20 kgs. of paddy.

A significant number of beneficiaries (58.06 per cent) have borrowed money without interest. Only two beneficiaries have taken loan from the private sources with a contract of a certain period. Within the due time if the borrower can repay the money the lender will not take any interest but if the borrower fail to repay within the stipulated time he will have to repay with a high rate of interest still his total repayment. In the Table 4.5.4 these two beneficiaries categorised as contractual.

Here, almost all of those significant numbers of beneficiaries have borrowed money without interest from their landowners. It is already mentioned that these landowners are mostly the neighbouring Hindu Caste people, in whose land the landless tribals are working as agricultural labourers round the year or the share croppers, sharing land with them and at the rest of the time working as agricultural labourers on their lands. At the lean period when they have to confront an unavoidable deficiency or at the time of any other unavoidable immediate contingencies they borrow some amount of money either in cash or in kind from their landowners. They pay-off their borrowed money never in cash. At the season time the landless labourers give their labour without any remuneration since their borrowed money is fully repaid. Here, the most significant feature is that their wage rate is counted not according to the wage rate of this season time but according to the wage rate of that lean period when it was very low. When, any tribal sharecropper borrowed money from their landowner, pay-off the money either in cash or by crops. But they are obliged to pay-off it just after harvest. As a result, they are compelled to sell their production in low price, if they pay-off in cash. When they repay it by crops, then their repaid amount of crop is counted according to the rate of market price of that time of borrowings.

Thus, the system of borrowing money without interest from the landowners is not simple as it looks. An implicit interest is exist. Here, the most significant feature is that regarding this kind of implicit interest the tribal beneficiaries are also conscious. They take it consciously but helplessly, as they have no scope to get any financial help from government during their crucial time. Naturally to get rid off from that crucial situation they are compelled to borrow from their reclaimers, the landowners.

Here, the long term tenant-cultivator relationship and the superb minute adjustment in the entire range of terms and conditions of this informal credit system standing as complementary to tribal beneficiaries rather than substitute of the formal credit system. While the informal system concentrate to consumption and contingency loan the formal sector centralise its attention in production and investment loans. As a result, neither source can fully meet the needs of the poor tribal borrowers as it was found that dependence on the informal sources being high for the borrowers who are belonging to inferior economic conditions. Another important point for dependence on informal sources is the rationing system of loan disbursement by the institutional sources. Whereas, the informal credit has its capabilities to supply loans as well as to receive repayments in a variety of forms and without any specific schedule of payment and repayment.

4.6. ITDP : Its Impact and Constraints

After a brief discussion about the acceptance pattern of the schemes by the beneficiaries, their utilization pattern and repayment performance an attempt has been made here to find out whether the tribal people can implement the scheme or not. To measure the performance of the schemes it is essential to find out the viability of the schemes to the beneficiaries, which is the prime condition to get a positive impact from any developmental scheme.

Table 4.6.1 depicts the performance of the schemes. Here, the scheme for a beneficiary have been considered as economically viable which fulfil at least one of the following criteria:

(1) When a profitable income is generated from the scheme.

Table 4.6.1
Performance of the Schemes

	Name of the Scheme	*No. of Beneficiary*	*Viable (No.)*	*Non-Viable (No.)*
1.	Bullock with cart	34	34(100.00)	-
2.	Calf rearing	24	4(16.67)	20(83.33)
3.	STW/Pump set	17	11(64.71)	6(35.29)
4.	Duckary	1	-	1(100.00)
5.	Heifer rearing	12	4(33.33)	8(66.67)
6.	Rickshaw	3	3(100.00)	-
7.	Piggary	1	-	1(100.00)
8.	Goatary	2	1(50.00)	1(50.00)
9.	Rice processing	4	-	4(100.00)
10.	Milch cow	13	6(46.15)	7(53.85)
11.	Carpentry	6	4(66.67)	2(33.33)
12.	Fishery	1	-	1(100.00)
13.	Bamboo work	3	-	3(100.00)
14.	Business	4	1(25.00)	3(75.00)
15.	Grocery	13	7(53.85)	6(46.15)
16.	Short term agriculture	26	25(96.15)	1(3.85)
17.	Calf rearing + Goatary	41	12(29.27)	29(70.73)

Contd.

Contd. Table 4.6.1

	Name of the Scheme	No. of Beneficiary	Viable (No.)	Non-Viable (No.)
18.	Calf rearing + Sheep	7	2(28.57)	5(71.43)
19.	Calf rearing + Rice Processing	11	4(36.36)	7(63.64)
20.	Rickshaw + Rice Processing	1	1(100.00)	-
21.	Veg. Vending + Calf rearing	4	1(25.00)	3(75.00)
22.	Duckary + Calf rearing	2	-	2(100.00)
23.	Rickshaw + Calf rearing	1	1(100.00)	-
24.	Rickshaw van + Calf rearing	2	2(100.00)	-
25.	Bullock cart + Short term	14	14(100.00)	-
26.	Calf rearing + milch cow	1	1(100.00)	-
27.	Calf rearing + Short-term	1	1(100.00)	-
28.	Bullock cart + Bamboo work	1	1(100.00)	-
29.	Short term + Bamboo work	1	1(100.00)	-
30.	Grocery + calf rearing	5	2(40.00)	3(60.00)
31.	STW/Pump Set + Short term	1	1(100.00)	-
32.	Bamboo work + Calf rearing	3	1(33.33)	2(66.67)
33.	Bullock cart + Duckary	4	2(50.00)	2(50.00)
	Total	264	138(52.27)	126(47.73)

* Figures in parenthesis indicate percentage of viable/non-viable schemes in number of Beneficiary.

(2) When the scheme is directly or indirectly related to the employment generation for the beneficiary household.

(3) When beneficiary can procure an asset from the scheme.

(4) When beneficiary obtain some savings by the proper implementation of the schemes.

From the Table 4.6.1 it is found that 138 beneficiaries, i.e., 52.27 per cent of the total beneficiaries are running the schemes viably whereas for 126 beneficiaries, which is 47.73 per cent of the total beneficiaries the schemes are become non-viable.

Performance of Agricultural Schemes

Eighty-eight per cent of the total beneficiaries in the study area are landholders and 83.52 per cent of the total population of beneficiary household earn their livelihood from agriculture, as cultivators or as agricultural labourers. Therefore, it is expectcd that the performance of the schemes related with agriculture will be more distinctive rather than any schemes of other sectors. It was noticed that 100 per cent cases the scheme of bullock with cart, was viable for the beneficiaries. For the scheme of shallow tube well with pump set, out of seventeen, eleven beneficiaries have run the scheme viably and in six cases the same scheme become non-viable. Out of twenty-six beneficiaries of short-term agricultural scheme twenty-five cases the scheme was viable. Only in case of one beneficiary it became non-viable. In this case due to heavy rainfall just before harvesting all the crops were ruined. Fourteen beneficiaries have taken the scheme of bullock with cart and short-term loan. For each of the cases the schemes were viable for the beneficiaries. For the other four beneficiaries who have taken four different types of schemes like, calf rearing and short-term crop loan, bullock cart and bamboo work, short-term crop loan and bamboo work, shallow tube well with pump set and short-term agricultural loan, each of the cases schemes were viable. In case of four beneficiaries of the scheme of bullock cart and duckary two have run the scheme viably and in other two cases it was non-viable. That is, on an average ninety-one per cent cases the agriculturally associated schemes are running viably (Table 4.6.1). This kind of successful implementation is obviously reflected on the cropping pattern, cropping intensity and production and productivity of the major crops cultivated by the beneficiary households who were facilitated by the agriculturally associated schemes.

Impact on the Cropping Pattern and Cropping Intensity

It was found that the beneficiary households of every tribal community of the study area are cultivating local variety paddy, HYV paddy, Boro paddy, wheat, mustard, potato, vegetable, sugarcane and pulses. The gross cropped area among the Santals is 2.242 acres, among the Mahalis it is 2.216 acres, among the Koras it is 1.445 acres and 2.517 acres among the Sardar Community. Whether their net cropped area are, 1.72 acres, 1.85 acres, 1.12 acres and 2.06 acres respectively (Table 4.6.2). It is no doubt the positive impact of the introduction of modern irrigational facilities and other agricultural equipment by which they are facilitated by the government schemes. Now, they are not dependent upon the monsoon rainfall only. They are cultivating their land round the year and as a result cropping intensity is increasing. District Birbhum is a mono-cropped area and average cropping intensity of the district is 100-110 per cent. Whereas, it is found that the cropping intensity among the Santal community is 130.35 per cent, 119.78 per cent for the Mahalis, and 129.91 per cent for the Koras and in case of Sardar community it is 122.18 per cent. That is, for each of the category cropping intensity of the beneficiary households are higher than the average cropping intensity of the district. However, the beneficiary households are engaged in cultivation round the year. Thus, the employment generation is also increased.

Impact on the Production and Productivity of Major Crops

In the Table 4.6.3 an endeavour has been made to measure the impact of the schemes associated with agriculture on the production and productivity of major crops of the beneficiary households. It has been measured in terms of a comparison between the production and productivity of the beneficiary households assisted by the agriculturally associated schemes with the production and productivity of the beneficiary households have not assisted by such schemes. These two categories of beneficiaries have been mentioned in the table as agricultural loan beneficiary and non-agricultural loan beneficiary respectively. It is found that for every major crops area as

Table 4.6.2
Average Cropping Pattern and Cropping Intensity

Area under different Crops (Acre)

Name of the Tribe	*Aman TV*	*Aman HYV*	*Boro*	*Wheat*	*Mustard*	*Potato*	*Vegetable*	*Sugar-cane*	*Pulses*	*Gross cropped area*	*Net cropped area*	*Cropping Intensity (%)*
Santal	0.46	1.25	0.28	0.19	0.01	0.03	0.008	0.01	0.004	2.242	1.72	130.35
Mahali	0.49	1.35	0.20	0.12	0.01	0.028	0.007	0.008	0.003	2.216	1.85	119.78
Kora	0.44	0.67	0.19	0.11	0.01	0.015	0.008	0.003	0.002	1.455	1.12	129.91
Sardar	0.42	1.63	0.22	0.18	0.02	0.03	0.006	0.007	0.004	2.517	2.06	122.18

Table 4.6.3

Average Area, Production and Productivity of Major Crops

Major Crops	*Agricultural Loan Beneficiary*			*Non Agricultural Loan Beneficiary*		
	Area (Acre)	*Production (Q)*	*Productivity*	*Area (Acre)*	*Production (Q)*	*Productivity*
Amon TV	0.41	5.00	12.20	0.49	5.75	11.73
Amon HYV	1.42	27.96	19.69	1.04	17.94	17.25
Boro	0.27	5.76	21.33	0.18	3.375	18.75
Wheat	0.14	1.05	7.5	0.16	1.184	7.40
Mustard	0.013	0.0585	4.5	0.012	0.0528	4.40
Potato	0.03	1.944	64.80	0.02	1.0032	50.16

well as production of the agricultural loan beneficiaries are higher than the non-agricultural loan beneficiaries. Hence, the productivity of every crop of agricultural loan beneficiaries is higher than the non-agricultural loan beneficiaries. It was found that average productivity of local variety paddy is 12.20 quintal per acre in case of agricultural loan beneficiaries whereas it is 11.73 quintal per acre among the non-agricultural loan beneficiaries. In case of HYV paddy productivity of agricultural loan beneficiary is 19.69 quintal per acre whereas 17.25 quintal per acre in case of non-agricultural loan beneficiaries. In case of Boro Paddy productivity of agricultural loan beneficiary and non-agricultural loan beneficiary is 21.33 quintal per acre and 18.75 quintal per acre respectively. For the other three crops wheat, mustard and potato it is also same. In case of agricultural loan beneficiary's productivity of these crops are 7.5, 4.5 and 64.80 quintal per acre respectively. On the other hand productivity of those crops for the non-agricultural loan beneficiaries is 7.40, 4.40 and 50.16 quintal per acre respectively. Hence, it is no doubt a positive impact of the schemes those are associated with agriculture.

Performance of Non-agricultural Schemes

Besides agricultural schemes, a large number of beneficiaries are found to take the schemes of animal husbandry sector. These schemes have specially taken by the landless and marginal farmers. For the scheme of calf rearing out of twenty-four, only four beneficiaries have found to run the scheme viably. In case of one beneficiary of the duckary scheme, the scheme became non-viable. Among twelve beneficiaries of heifer rearing scheme only four can run the scheme viably and for the remainders it was non-viable. In case of only one beneficiary of piggery scheme the beneficiary could not implement the scheme and it was same for the beneficiary of goatary scheme. Among thirteen beneficiaries of the scheme of milch cow only in six cases the schemes are running viably and in remaining seven cases it becomes non-viable. Only one beneficiary of the fishery scheme could not run the scheme viably though it was mentioned in the previous chapter as a scheme, which was utilized properly. He was also generating income from the scheme upto four consecutive years after acceptance of the scheme but could not form a sufficient capital for the maintenance of the scheme for its successful continuation. During the field survey it was not existed and the beneficiary was found to return back to his old profession of agricultural labourers. A good number of landless and marginal farmers have taken the scheme of calf rearing and goatary. But only twelve of them (29.27 per cent) could run the scheme viably and twenty-nine (70.73 per cent) beneficiaries could not implement the scheme successfully. In case of the scheme of calf rearing and sheep only two of seven beneficiaries could run the scheme viably and for remaining five cases the scheme became non-viable. The same picture of higher percentage of non-viability of the animal husbandry schemes also observed in every cases when the beneficiaries have taken it associated with other categories of schemes (Table 4.6.1).

The trade and business sector and the sector of small-scale industry are included the schemes of business, grocery, vegetable vending, rice processing and carpentry. For each of the two beneficiaries of rice processing scheme it was found to become non-viable. In case of carpentry scheme out of six beneficiaries, four beneficiaries were found to run the scheme viably. For the scheme of business, only one beneficiary could run the scheme viably and in other three cases the scheme became non-viable. The grocery scheme is viable for seven beneficiaries whereas for the remaining six it was non-viable. Four beneficiaries have taken the scheme for vegetable vending associated with calf rearing scheme. But for only one of them it was found viable. Another five beneficiaries have taken the grocery scheme with calf rearing and only two of them could implement the scheme viably whereas for other three beneficiaries it became non-viable.

Here, more or less the same picture of higher rate of non-viability is noticed as the animal husbandry sector.

And another point was significantly noticed here that the schemes of this sector are also accepted specially by the landless and marginal farmers.

The schemes of Rickshaw and Rickshaw Van are another two important schemes for employment and income generation especially for the landless and as well as for the marginal farmers. It was found as a hundred per cent viable scheme to the beneficiaries. Three beneficiaries have taken the scheme of rickshaw individually and in every case they are running it successfully. In case of other two beneficiaries, one has taken it with rice processing scheme and the other one with calf rearing scheme. Both the cases the schemes were viable to the beneficiaries. Besides these, two beneficiaries have accepted the scheme of rickshaw van with calf rearing. For both the cases the schemes were also viable. The landless or marginal farmer beneficiaries who have taken the scheme of rickshaw/rickshaw van are found to shift their occupation from agricultural or other kind of daily labourers to a rickshaw pooler. The other members of the households maintain the associated schemes rice processing or calf rearing. It was found that these beneficiary households feel economically more secured than the days when their only source of income was agricultural labourers or other labourers and employed for only 120-130 days in a year which also varied from year to year.

The scheme of craft, which is, officially mentioned as bamboo work, is specifically for the Mahalis. Traditional occupation of the Mahalis is basket making and they are popularly known as basket makers. Three Mahali beneficiaries have taken individually the scheme of bamboo work but surprisingly it was noticed that in every case it became non-viable to the basket makers. It was significantly noticed here that these three beneficiaries are marginal farmers having a little amount of land and may called as more or less landless. After all the raw materials used up, these beneficiaries faced an inadequacy of it. This is because of the fact that the income they obtained from the scheme was not sufficient for the purpose of acquiring good quality raw materials due to its high price and not availability. Whereas, in other two cases where two beneficiaries have taken the scheme with other schemes, like bullock cart in one case and short-term crop loan in another case, interestingly found that the same scheme became viable to the beneficiaries. Here, both the beneficiaries are also marginal farmers but have a better amount of land and they can support their favourite scheme by their primary occupation of cultivation.

All the basket maker Mahali beneficiaries are facing a problem of lack of adequate market facilities. Bolpur is the only market place where they go themselves to sell their wares but in most of the cases they can not sell it in a profitable amount. Introduction of plastic and various types of attractive fiber materials is also a remarkable cause for the decreasing market of the traditional bamboo wares.

Impact on Income and Employment Generation

After measuring the performance of the schemes, an attempt has been made to measure the impact of such schemes on the income and employment of the sampled beneficiaries.

Impact on Income and Employment of the Landless Beneficiaries

From the acceptance pattern of the schemes of the landless it was noticed that majority of them accepted the animal husbandry schemes. It is very difficult to measure the accurate income generated from an animal husbandry scheme. To a landless utility of any scheme of this sector is to procure an asset. Their perception is that this kind of asset will give them salvation during any kind of emergency requirement. Generally, almost all the responsibilities for rearing the animals devolved on the children and old members of household. The beneficiary engaged himself as agricultural labourer or other kind of daily labourer. After rearing an animal for two to three years when they assume that it will give him a considerable amount, try to sell it. Then they got a consolidated amount by which they could get a scope for procuring more animals by his own investment. But from the Table 4.6.4, it reveals that beneficiaries whose average income is Rs. 10, 260/- could not rear the animals properly. As a result, generated income from the scheme of this sector is not remarkable. From the scheme of calf rearing they could not generated any income. Two landless have taken the Heifer rearing scheme and average annual income generated from this scheme is only Rs. 516/-. It was not sufficient for economic upliftment of a landless. Again, two landless of the scheme of milch cow could not generated any income like the scheme of calf rearing. Thirteen landless have taken the scheme of calf rearing and goatary and majority of them has failed to generate income from the scheme. On an average, only Rs. 410/- has generated from the scheme, which was not enough for economic upliftment of a landless. In case of calf rearing and sheep scheme there are four landless beneficiaries and none of them could generate income from the scheme.

Besides animal husbandry schemes, they were also found to accept the schemes from the trade and commerce sector. Two of them were found to take the scheme of business, one for grocery and another one for the scheme of rice processing. But in every case their schemes are not existed. They could not generate income from these schemes.

Impact on the income of a landless is remarkably noticed in case of rickshaw or rickshaw van scheme which was also found to accept associated with the scheme of rice processing and calf rearing. One landless beneficiary, who accepted the scheme of rickshaw, now shifted his occupation from an agricultural labourer to a rickshaw-pooler. He is generating average income of Rs. 9800/- per annum. Though it is quite impossible here to measure the accurate increasing income due to the conversion of his occupation but seems that it has made a remarkable positive impact on the income of his family. Other members of his family still continue their occupation as agricultural

Table 4.6.4

Income Generation from Different Schemes Among the Landless Beneficiary Households

(In Rs.)

Nature of the Scheme	*No. of Beneficiary*	*Average Income Generated per annum*
1. Bullock with cart	—	—
2. Calf rearing	4	—
3. STW with pump set	—	—
4. Duckary	—	—
5. Heifer rearing	2	516
6. Rickshaw	1	9800
7. Piggary	—	—
8. Goatary	—	—
9. Rice processing	1	—
10. Milch cow	2	—
11. Carpentry	—	—
12. Fishery	—	—
13. Bamboo work	—	—
14. Business	2	—
15. Grocery	1	—
16. Short term agriculture	—	—
17. Calf rearing + Goatary	13	410
18. Calf rearing + Sheep	4	—
19. Calf rearing + Rice Processing	3	—
20. Rickshaw + Rice Processing	1	9964
21. Veg. Vending + Calf rearing	2	—
22. Duckary + Calf rearing	1	—
23. Rickshaw + Calf rearing	—	—
24. Van + Calf rearing	1	10300
25. Bullock cart + Short term	—	—
26. Calf rearing + milch cow	—	—
27. Calf rearing + Short term	—	—
28. Bullock cart + Bamboo work	—	—
29. Short term + Bamboo work	—	—
30. Grocery + calf rearing	1	1656
31. STW/Pump Set + Short term	—	—
32. Bamboo work + Calf rearing	—	—
33. Bullock cart + Duckary	—	—

labourers. Assemblage of the income of all the members improves the economic status of the household. As per opinion of the beneficiary, he feels now more secured and independent. It is same for the other two beneficiaries where one have taken it with rice processing and another one with calf rearing scheme. The average income generated from these schemes are Rs. 9,964/- and Rs. 10,300/- respectively. Here, additional income from the scheme of rice processing and calf rearing are added and they have generated more income. It makes a positive impact on the economic status of the beneficiary household (Table 4.6.4).

Impact on Income and Employment of the Marginal Farmers

Marginal farmers are found to take almost all categories of schemes. Majority of them preferred the animal husbandry schemes. Though, just a little but it was noticed that impact on the income among this category of beneficiaries is better than the landless. From the calf rearing scheme sixteen marginal farmers have generated on an average Rs. 716/-. In case of heifer rearing scheme it was found that ten numbers of marginal farmers have generated average annual income of Rs. 685/-. Eleven marginal farmers of milch cow scheme have generated on an average Rs. 1720/-. In most of the cases they sell the milk to a milkman who visits their village regularly and generally of the caste people. All the beneficiaries were found to sell their cow milk in a very low price than the retail market price. The same picture of the low income generation from the other animal husbandry schemes, like calf rearing and goatary or calf rearing and sheep was noticed

Better impact on the income of marginal farmers was also noticed in case of the schemes of trade and commerce sector. Two marginal farmers were found to accept the scheme of business. Average income generated from the scheme is Rs. 3,600/- per annum. In case of the scheme of grocery, ten beneficiaries were found to generate on an average income of Rs. 8,100/- per annum. In these cases the beneficiary himself shifted his occupation but the generated income of the grocery scheme makes an indirect impact on his farm activities. It helps to purchase fertilizers and other inputs as and when required. Other members of the household have taken all the responsibilities of cultivation in their few landholding.

From the scheme of rickshaw or rickshaw van the marginal farmers were also found to achieve a positive impact on their income. Two marginal farmers were accepted the scheme of rickshaw, one have accepted it with a scheme of calf rearing and another one have found to take the scheme of rickshaw van with calf rearing scheme. From the scheme of rickshaw on an average Rs. 9,870/- was found to generate and for the other two it was Rs. 10,278/- and Rs. 10,570/- respectively.

A good number of marginal farmers accepted the schemes of agriculture and irrigation sector. Twenty of them have taken the scheme of bullock with cart, four have taken shallow tube well with pump set and twelve of them have taken the short-term agricultural schemes. All these schemes in almost all the cases have achieved a positive impact on their family income. As in every case the scheme whatever it may be helped the farmer in procuring a better yield and higher productivity. When one beneficiary have taken a scheme of bullock with cart it is used in every step of his cultivation. After its acceptance one did not have to depend on his neighbour's bullock for ploughing or for a cart to carry manure or for carrying the production from the field. Now, the beneficiaries are self- sufficient and maintain the proper timings of ploughing, application of fertilizers or for bringing the production to the house. Now, they don't have to loss any manday for meeting the obligation to his neighbour for lending him the bullock or the cart. Moreover, the beneficiary now lending his own bullock or the cart to his neighbours who have not it. Thus, it is very difficult to measure the accurate increasing income generated from the scheme. It was calculated that on an average Rs. 2,622/- was generated from a scheme of bullock with cart.

Most significant impact on the income of a beneficiary household was noticed in case of the scheme of shallow tube well with pump set. After the introduction of this modern irrigation facility they are not depending upon the monsoon rainfall. They converted their mono-cropped land to a double cropped land. It makes a positive impact on the income of a household as it has increased the cropping intensity, production and productivity of major crops. Hence, it has increased their income than the income of those days when they were not facilitated by the scheme. Moreover, these beneficiaries earn more by lending it to their neighbours. They take the rent of Rs. 25-30 per hour. By assembling all the income from increased production and the income by lending it to the neighbours, it was calculated that on an average Rs. 5,854/- they can earn with the help of the scheme of shallow tube well with pump set. Another most important scheme, which makes a positive impact on the income of a beneficiary, is the short-term crop loan. It gives them HYV seeds, chemical fertilizers, minikit, pesticides etc. those are most essential for a better production. Before facilitated by this scheme they were never able to invest for these essential requirements. If they wanted to utilize it either they have borrowed money from the landowners or procured by working as labourers in the lands of others. As a result, in most of the times they did not maintain the proper timing of transplantation, application of fertilizer etc. But when they received this scheme they have not lost a manday; not became in debt and utilized these in a proper time.

Among the marginal farmers, income generation from the scheme of bamboo work is not so remarkable. This scheme is specially accepted by the Mahalis, whose traditional occupation is basket making. It was observed that most of the members of a Mahali household are fond of engaged in this occupation in the resting period after fulfilling their agricultural works in the field. They are used to sell their wares in the market at Bolpur town and also in the locality. But, it was revealed that three Mahali marginal farmer beneficiary's average annual income generated from the scheme of bamboo work is only Rs. 514/-. It makes a very low impact on their income. In fact, the income from cultivation of a marginal farmer is inadequate to supplement the scheme. Required good quality raw materials to continue the scheme successfully is not only rarely available but also high priced. Another two marginal farmers also accepted the scheme. One has taken the scheme with bullock cart and another with Short-term agricultural loan. Here also income generation from bamboo work is not so desirable.

Four marginal farmers were found to take the scheme of carpentry. Here, every one is Santal. Among them only one was observed whose intention was just to grab the assistancè not to implement the scheme successfully. But the other three beneficiaries were found to work independently not only in the local village area but also in the town area. Here also, the beneficiary himself shifted his main occupation as cultivator to a carpenter. But the other members of the household are continuing cultivation and they also working as agricultural labourer or as other types of daily labour. Thus, the additional income from the scheme of carpentry is increased their family income and it must be the positive impact of the scheme on the income and as well as employment generation. On an average the generated income from this scheme is Rs. 1,784/- (Table 4.6.5).

Impact on Income and Employment of the Small Farmer Beneficiary Households

Fourteen small farmers are the beneficiaries of the scheme of bullock with cart. Eleven small farmers were found to accept the scheme of bullock cart with short-term agricultural scheme and two have taken the scheme of bullock cart with duckary. Their benefits from the scheme

Table 4.6.5
Income Generation from Different Schemes Among the Marginal Farmer Beneficiary Households

(In Rs.)

Nature of the Scheme	*No. of Beneficiary*	*Average Income generated per annum*
1. Bullock with cart	20	2622
2. Calf rearing	16	716
3. STW with pump set	4	5854
4. Duckary	1	—
5. Heifer rearing	10	685
6. Rickshaw	2	9870
7. Piggary	1	—
8. Goatary	2	236
9. Rice processing	2	—
10. Milch cow	11	1720
11. Carpentry	4	1784
12. Fishery	1	—
13. Bamboo work	3	514
14. Business	2	3600
15. Grocery	10	8100
16. Short term agriculture	12	2357
17. Calf rearing + Goatary	26	512
18. Calf rearing + Sheep	1	—
19. Calf rearing + Rice Processing	6	1222
20. Rickshaw + Rice Processing	—	—
21. Veg. Vending + Calf rearing	2	1333
22. Duckary + Calf rearing	1	—
23. Rickshaw + Calf rearing	1	10278
24. Van + Calf rearing	1	10570
25. Bullock cart + Short term	3	3896
26. Calf rearing + milch cow	1	2015
27. Calf rearing + Short term	—	—
28. Bullock cart + Bamboo work	1	1814
29. Shot term + Bamboo work	1	2423
30. Grocery + calf rearing	4	5066
31. STW/Pump Set + Short term	—	5997
32. Bamboo work + Calf rearing	3	485
33. Bullock cart + Duckary	1	1608

are as the marginal farmers. But, here, it was significantly noticed that the average generated income from the scheme is better than the marginal farmers. From the scheme of bullock with cart they were found to generate income of Rs. 3,260-. For the other two schemes the average generated income were Rs. 4,900- and Rs. 2,060/- respectively (Table 4.6.6).

This was same for the other two schemes those are directly related with agriculture, i.e., the scheme of shallow tube well with pump set and short-term agricultural schemes. The small farmer beneficiaries are found to accept these two schemes either individually or as an integrated scheme. Average income generated from the scheme of shallow tube well with pump set is Rs. 5,990/- and from the short-term agricultural scheme Rs. 3,160/-. In case of another beneficiary who has taken these two

Table 4.6.6
Income Generation from Different Schemes Among the Small Farmer Beneficiary Households

(In Rs.)

Nature of the Scheme	*No. of Beneficiary*	*Average Income Generated per annum*
1. Bullock with cart	14	3260
2. Calf rearing	3	1333
3. STW with pump set	10	5990
4. Rice processing	1	—
5. Carpentry	1	3206
6. Grocery	2	10220
7. Short term Agriculture	12	3160
8. Calf rearing + Goatary	1	1655
9. Calf rearing + Sheep	2	1050
10. Calf rearing + Rice processing	2	1560
11. Bullock cart + Short term	11	4900
12. Calf rearing + Short term	1	4493
13. STW with pump set+Short term	1	6720
14. Bullock cart + Duckary	2	2060

schemes as an integrated scheme have generated about Rs. 6,720/- per annum. However, it is no doubt that the incomes generated from agriculturally related schemes are able to improve the economic condition of a small farmer beneficiary household. The beneficiaries are now felt independent than those days when they were not facilitated by the schemes.

The small farmer beneficiaries are also found to take the animal husbandry schemes. Here again, it was significantly noticed that the generated income from the schemes is better than a landless or marginal farmer. As for example in case of calf rearing scheme average generated income of three small farmers is Rs. 1,333/-. One beneficiary of calf rearing and goatary scheme and two beneficiaries of calf-rearing and sheep scheme have generated average income of Rs. 1,655/- and Rs. 1,050/- respectively. In fact, due to higher land account, a small farmer can give better feed and fodder to the animals. Not only that one small farmer can wait for those days for acquiring a better market price.

Two small farmers were found to receive the scheme of grocery. They can procure average Rs. 10,220/- from this scheme. Here also, the beneficiary himself shifted his occupation as cultivator to a shopkeeper. But the other members of the household continue the cultivation. Not only that, additional income from the grocery scheme have indirectly improved their cultivation. As, the beneficiary can provide fertilizer, or other required inputs as and when needed. It is, therefore, the positive impact of the scheme.

One small farmer beneficiary of carpentry was found to achieve a positive impact on his family income. He can procure about Rs. 3,206/- from his scheme. Almost round the year he is actively working as a carpenter in the Bolpur and Santiniketan town area and side by side participates in cultivation, as and when required. Other members of the household take the responsibility of farm activities. However, the assembled income of cultivation, agricultural labourers and additional income from carpentry have improved their economic condition.

Impact on Income and Employment of the Medium Farmer Beneficiary Households

Six medium farmers have taken six different schemes. One has taken shallow tube well with pump set, one for short-term agricultural scheme and another one for bullock cart and duckary. In every case the beneficiaries were found to obtain a considerable amount of money from the schemes and sometimes it is better than the marginal farmers and small farmers also. Average generated amount was calculated about Rs. 8,060/-, Rs. 3,200/- and Rs. 2,060/- respectively. Other two medium farmers were found to take the scheme of carpentry and calf rearing with goatary. In these cases also they can generate some amount, which make a positive impact on their family income (Table 4.6.7).

Table 4.6.7
Income Generation from Different Schemes Among the Medium Farmer Beneficiary Households

(In Rs.)

	Nature of the Scheme	*No. of Beneficiary*	*Average Income generated per annum*
1.	Calf rearing	1	1500
2.	STW with pump set	1	8060
3.	Carpentry	1	2300
4.	Short term Agriculture	1	3200
5.	Calf rearing + Goatary	1	1700
6.	Bullock cart + Duckary	1	2060

Impact on Income and Employment of the Large Farmer Beneficiary Households

Only three large farmers have restricted their acceptance within the agricultural schemes. Two of them have taken the scheme of shallow tube well with pump set and another one for short-term agricultural loan. Each of the large farmers is found to achieve a high rate of impact on their income. Two beneficiaries of shallow tube well with pump set scheme have generated on an average Rs. 9,300/- per annum. On the other hand from scheme of short-term agriculture the beneficiary has found to generate about Rs. 3,500/- (Table 4.6.8). Though, their utilization pattern of the scheme is same but they are found to generate more income from the scheme than the small farmers or medium farmers also. It is because of the fact that due to higher land account the large farmers are found to take the risk of multiple crops more easily. Now, they do have to spent for an extravagant expense for irrigation purpose or do not have to disturb the stored up crops for procuring higher market price. Thus, they can obtain marketable surplus production.

Table 4.6.8
Income Generation from Different Schemes Among the Large Farmer Beneficiary Households

(In Rs.)

Nature of the Scheme	No. of Beneficiary	Average Income generated per annum
1. STW with pump set	2	9300
2. Short term Agriculture	1	3500

Constraints

From the above schemewise analysis of viability, non-viability and their impact on the income as well as employment generation of the beneficiary households, it reveals that the scheme other than agricultural schemes can not make a remarkable positive impact. Only exceptions are the schemes of rickshaw/rickshaw van. It also reveals that other schemes, those make a positive impact highly on the beneficiaries who have some land and can supplement their schemes. Whereas, in case of the beneficiaries who have no land or very little amount of land can achieve a low impact or sometimes negative impact also. Even where the impact is positive, it has not been so encouraging and significant. It is found that only 20.65 per cent of the beneficiaries below the poverty line can run the scheme viably but their income position has remained constant. On the other hand, 79.35 per cent of the beneficiaries below poverty line have not run their schemes viably and their income position remained below the poverty line (Table 4.6.9). Three beneficiaries of below poverty line are found to take agriculturally related schemes. One has taken for Bullock with cart, one for short-term crop loan and another for calf rearing and short-term crop loan. All of them are found to run the schemes viably but their generated income and employment was not sufficient to uplift them above the poverty line. Performances of the scheme of these below poverty line beneficiaries in case of the animal husbandry sector are same. In case of calf rearing scheme out of eleven below poverty line beneficiaries only in case of three, their schemes were viable and for remaining eight it was non-viable. Out of nine of the heifer-rearing scheme, only one has found to run the scheme viably and for all the remainders the scheme was non-viable. Among nine beneficiaries of below poverty line only two cases the scheme of milch cow is viable but for remaining seven it became non-viable. Out of twenty-seven beneficiaries of calf rearing and goatary scheme, all the beneficiaries were failed to implement the scheme viably. Like this the higher rate of non-viability rather than viability is noticed for every scheme of any sector (Table 4.6.9).

Actually, the landless and the marginal farmers of lower landholdings are always busy to think and solve their deficiency round the year and more or less careless in the maintenance of their assets. In many cases they can not give their animals required quantity and quality of feed and fodder. They keep their animals in unhygienic conditions, which exposes them to different diseases. Sometimes, it is also found that they even sell out their assets not only to fulfil their familial requirements but also for other non-productive purposes such as marriage, death ceremonies, religious festivals, construction of a house or for its repairing etc. Because, they are bound to fulfil some social and cultural obligations to their society at one hand on the other they have to provide

Table 4.6.9

Viability of Schemes among the Beneficiary Households Belonging to below Poverty Line

Sl. No.	*Name of the Scheme*	*No of Beneficiary*	*Viable (No.)*	*Non-Viable (No.)*
1.	Bullock with cart	1	1 (100.00)	-
2.	Calf rearing	11	3 (27.27)	8 (72.73)
3.	Heifer rearing	9	1 (11.11)	8 (88.89)
4.	Piggary	1	-	1 (100.00)
5.	Goatary	1	-	1 (100.00)
6.	Rice processing	3	-	3 (100.00)
7.	Milch cow	9	2 (22.22)	7 (77.78)
8.	Carpentry	1	1 (100.00)	-
9.	Craft	1	-	1 (100.00)
10.	Business	2	-	2 (100.00)
11.	Grocery	5	2 (40.00)	3 (60.00)
12.	Short term Agriculture	1	1 (100.00)	-
13.	Calf rearing + Goatary	27	-	27 (100.00)
14.	Calf rearing + Sheep	3	1 (33.33)	2 (66.67)
15.	Calf rearing + Rice processing	6	2 (33.33)	4 (66.67)
16.	Rickshaw + Rice processing	1	1 (100.00)	-
17.	Veg.Vending + Calf rearing	3	1 (33.33)	2 (66.67)
18.	Calf + Duckary	2	-	2 (100.00)
19.	Calf + Milch cow	1	1 (100.00)	-
20.	Craft + Short term	1	1 (100.00)	-
21.	Grocery + Calf rearing	2	-	2 (100.00)
22.	Craft + Calf rearing	1	1 (100.00)	-
	Total	92	19 (20.65)	73 (79.35)

* Figures in parenthesis indicate percentage of viable/non-viable schemes in number of Beneficiary below poverty line.

all the requirements for their families. Sometimes it is also found that under an agreement with the middlemen they sell their assets at a rate lower than the market price. Therefore, sometimes poverty itself is becoming a very crucial constraint for proper and successful implementation of the schemes.

Lack of awareness among the beneficiaries is another major and important reason for failure in the effective implementation of the developmental schemes. It was found that 60.98 per cent of the total beneficiaries of the study area are illiterate. From the performance analysis of the different schemes received by the illiterate beneficiaries it is found that 41.67 per cent of the total illiterate beneficiaries can effectively implement their schemes. Whereas to 58.39 per cent beneficiaries the schemes were become non-viable (Table 4.6.10). Out of twelve illiterate beneficiaries of shallow tube well with pump set scheme six beneficiaries were failed to maintain it successfully. In case of the schemes of animal husbandry sector, it was noticed that almost in every case rate of non-viability is higher than viability of the schemes. Out of fifteen beneficiaries of calf rearing scheme only one can implement the scheme successfully. On the other hand seven illiterate beneficiaries of milch cow scheme have not implemented their schemes. In case of heifer rearing scheme only two among ten beneficiaries have implemented their schemes viably but remaining eight cases the schemes were non-viable. Like this, in case of goatary, piggery or for other integrated schemes like calf-rearing and goatary, calf-rearing and sheep etc., most of the illiterate beneficiaries have failed to implement their schemes viably. For business and grocery scheme literacy seems to be one of the most essential factor for effective implementation. But it is found that one illiterate tribal has taken the scheme of business and seven have taken the grocery scheme. The only beneficiary of the business scheme and on the other hand six beneficiaries of grocery scheme have failed for an effective implementation of the schemes.

The illiterate beneficiaries have not the required technical and other know-how for maintenance of the assets provided to them. They are not sufficiently awared with regard to the hygienic maintenance of the animals, quantity and quality of their cattle-feed requirements and its economics, seeking veterinary help for animal's etc. This has resulted in some cases in healthy and good breed animals were neglected and weak. Thus, the income

Table 4.6.10

Viability of Schemes Conducting by the Illiterate Beneficiaries

Sl. No.	Name of the Scheme	Total No. of Benefi-ciary	No. of Illiterate Benefi-ciary	Viable (No.)	Non-Viable (No.)
1.	Bullock with cart	34	15	15(100.00)	-
2.	Calf rearing	24	15	1(6.67)	14(93.33)
3.	STW/Pumpset	17	12	6(50.00)	6(50.00)
4.	Milch cow	13	7	-	7(10.00)
5.	Carpentry	6	4	2(50.00)	2(50.00)
6.	Heifer rearing	12	10	2(20.00)	8(80.00)
7.	Rice processing	4	3	-	3(100.00)
8.	Grocery	13	7	1(14.29)	6(85.71)
9.	Rickshaw	3	2	2(100.00)	-
10.	Goatary	2	1	-	1(100.00)
11.	Craft	3	3	-	3(100.00)
12.	Piggery	1	1	-	1(100.00)
13.	Business	4	1	-	1(100.00)
14.	Short term Agriculture	26	16	16(100.00)	-
15.	Calf rearing + Goatary	41	27	4(14.81)	23(85.19)
16.	Calf rearing + Sheep	7	5	-	5(100.00)
17.	Bullock with cart + Duckary	4	2	-	2(100.00)
18.	Calf rearing + Rickshaw	2	1	1(100.00)	-
19.	Calf rearing + Rice Processing	11	10	4(40.00)	6(60.00)
20.	Bullock Cart + Short term	14	7	7(100.00)	-
21.	Rickshaw + Rice Processing	1	1	1(100.00)	-
22.	Veg Vending + Calf Rearing	4	4	1(25.00)	3(75.00)
23.	Calf rearing + Short term Ag.	1	1	1(100.00)	-
24.	Craft + Short term Agriculture	1	1	1(100.00)	-
25.	Grocery + Calf rearing	5	4	1(25.00)	3(75.00)
26.	Calf rearing + Bamboo Work	3	1	1(100.00)	-
	Total		161	67(41.67)	94(58.39)

* Figures in parenthesis indicate percentage of viable/non-viable schemes in number of Illiterate Beneficiary.

generating ability of the assets decreases. The lack of project formulation capabilities of the illiterate beneficiaries is reflected in case of business, grocery, rice-processing, veg. vending schemes.

Besides, the above said reasons there are some other reasons also responsible for the low impact of the schemes was identified. Those are as follows.

Sometimes the existing level of financial assistance was too inadequate to obtain and maintain the assets economically. After the acceptance, all the responsibilities of the scheme are devolved on the beneficiaries. As for example, they have to procure feed and fodder or required basic infrastructure of the animal husbandry schemes, incur expenses for repairing a break down asset like shallow tube well, pump set privately and sometimes at higher prices, which leads to low return through the high maintenance cost. Already, an example is given where a beneficiary of pump set scheme could not continue his scheme after its break down. The technician suggested him to replace an important parts of the pump set. He was unable to incur such expenses.

Here, the example of the basket maker Mahalis should be mentioned specially, as in most of the cases they could not continue their favourite and tradition oriented scheme due to high costs of raw materials. In most of the cases they were failure to supplement the scheme. Sometimes it also frustrated them when they can not able to procure sufficiently and satisfactorily.

Sometimes, the assets provided to them were of sub-standard quality. These assets, under the present system, are acquired through the middlemen. These middlemen, in league with the unscrupulous programme functionaries, acquire sub-standard quality assets, which are supplied to the beneficiaries at an exorbitantly higher price, which would ordinarily fetch for them relatively better quality assets. Thus, the beneficiary got poor quality assets at a higher price. These inferior and defective assets do not generate as much income as would enable the beneficiaries to come above the poverty line. Sometimes, they perforce to sell out their assets to avoid incurring more losses which ultimately make a negative income both for the government finance and for the beneficiary.

For the animal husbandry scheme it was found that the beneficiaries do not have any kind of veterinary service in their village. The only veterinary unit is in Bolpur, situated at a distance. As a result in the absence of any on the door medical service, their animals do not receive proper medi-care particularly when the animals required.

Another crucial reason for low impact of the scheme is inadequate-marketing facilities. Due to this reason, the intermediaries who pay them very low price exploit the beneficiaries. As a result, they don't get a reasonable surplus over the maintenance cost.

Due to lack of follow-up assistance to the beneficiaries to help them in the operation, utilization of the benefit, procurement of the raw materials, maintenance of the assets and the disposal of the final product, the beneficiaries are caught up in the trap of operational difficulties. Thus income and employment generating capacity of the scheme is badly affected.

Wrong identification of beneficiaries is also revealed as an obstacle, which is hindering the proper implementation of the scheme. Proper identification is the basic pre-requisite for achieving the objective of the scheme. In so many cases it was felt that identification are not strictly adhered to be the concerned programme functionaries. There remain some unscrupulous beneficiaries who are chiefly interested in grabbing the assistance rather than running the scheme. To them, the schemes were becoming useless.

Sometimes the wrong inappropriate selection of scheme was also found to be the most important bottleneck in effective implementation of a scheme to create a perceptible impact on the economic status of a beneficiary household.

Selection of scheme should posses a serious and thorough examination about the project formulation capabilities of the applicant, which can be easily visualised as to what technical skills are available with him to conceive a feasible project. Not only that thought should be given to the requirement of basic infrastructure for the successful implementation of the scheme. But in reality it has been largely found that all the needed procedures are exist but all are maintained and ultimately sanctioned in a most superficial manner. It reflects sometimes a deeper and serious deficiency and adversely affected the impact of schemes both on income and employment generation.

Sometimes the procedure of sanctioning financial assistance in favour of beneficiaries is tedious and long. In many cases it becomes very tiresome and discouraging. As a result, the applicant when gets it, found to fed up and lost his interest to give effort for the scheme. Then, the procedural delay became the main obstacle, which badly affects the effective implementation of the scheme.

Impact of the agricultural schemes are however, more impressive than the non-agricultural schemes. Not only that, for all the schemes, whether it is related to agriculture or not, degrees of impact on income and employment of a beneficiary household varied according to the landholding of a beneficiary. In fact, the householder, who have some cultivable land are doing better with their schemes than those who are totally landless. Any landholder could increase his income more easily on the basis of his land. Whereas, a landless have nothing on the basis of which he can increase his income. Here the only exception is the scheme of rickshaw and rickshaw-van. All the landless beneficiaries of these schemes are doing quite well. Actually these beneficiaries have been able to exploit effectively the market of rickshaw-pooling in Bolpur-Santiniketan area, an important tourist spot in the district.

Another important and remarkable feature noticed regarding the impact on income of a scheme on a beneficiary household is that, some beneficiaries are seem to be at ease with their schemes but fail to have increase their average annual income above the poverty line. Though they themselves have a satisfaction that they have been able to earn more than before and can engage themselves more or less round the year.

All the developmental schemes provided to the beneficiaries are for their economic upliftment. But some constraints are hindering for effective implementation of the schemes. Poverty itself and the lack of awareness of the beneficiaries for the proper and updated procedures of implementation of the new variety schemes provided to them are two major and important constraints. In general, it is to be said that constraints involve not only the activities and responsibilities of the beneficiaries but also of the project functionaries.

4.7. The Changing Scenario

The tradition-bound tribal society prior to the independence of India was almost a closed system. In the post-independent period the tribal people became exposed to the forces released by the Community Development movement, urbanization, education and technology - in short the process of modernization. Not only that through the Five Year Plans an attempt has been made for bringing about a comprehensive and integrated change in the social, economic, political and cultural life of the tribal people. The development schemes are thus often a way of bringing about changes, by which the particular community can be absorbed into the larger social organization in a planned manner. Culture of a particular community of specific region changes appreciably due to various factors at work of which development programmes generally bring about in their wake. Such changes are, however, largely influenced by the impact of superior culture of the neighbouring communities and ultimately result into blending of the two. This creates in the process, a new cultural pattern which the backward communities, in general, absorb consciously or unconsciously (Bhowmik, 1992).

In the foregoing discussion an attempt has been made to observe the extent and nature of socio-cultural and socio-economic changes taken place among the tribal beneficiary households by the implementation of various types of development schemes.

To get the nature of changes among the tribal people of the study area some of the major components of their social and economic changes viz, level of living, family, economic structure, educational status, cosmopoliteness etc. have examined and those are depicted at a glance in Table 4.7.1.

Table 4.7.1
Socio-Economic Changes Taken Place in the Study Area

Sl. No.	*Attribute*	*Traditional Practices*	*Changes Taken Place*
1.	Technology	Indigenous	Adopted modern technology like irrigation tubewell, pumpset, thresher, sprayer, farm cart and so on. They are also using HYV seeds, chemical fertilizer, pesticides etc. for better yield.
2.	Agriculture	Subsistence	Commercialisation of Agriculture.
3.	Income generation	Low	High (increase of production, productivity + income from the scheme)
4.	Employment generation	Low	High (increase in cropping intensity)
5.	Occupational differentiation	Low	High
6.	Wealth	Negligible	Worthmentioning
7.	Educational status	Low	High
8.	Consumption Expenditure	Low	High
9.	Family Type	Joint	Nuclear
10.	Health and Hygiene	Using indigenous medicines	More and more hospital orientation and indurated hygienic environment.
11.	Cosmopoliteness	Low	High

Changes in the Economic System

Economic system implies two things : the mode and structure of production and its relations, and the process of distribution existing and operating in a given socio-political set-up. The mode of production implies technique and organization of economic activities relating to production.

Agriculture is the main source of income for the majority of the tribal beneficiaries of the study area. Earlier, they used to practice traditional method for agriculture. Their technology was indigenous. Before the introduction of the developmental schemes they were totally depended on monsoon rainfall. But now they adopted modern technologies like shallow tube wells, pump sets, thresher, sprayer and so on. They are also using HYV seeds, chemical fertilizer, pesticide etc. to achieve better yield. As a result, a remarkable change is noticed in their modes of production. Now, they are cultivating double crops, sometimes multiple-crops also. Those farmers, who do not have pumpsets or STW, they hire it from the owner sources for irrigation purposes and share the benefit. Tribal beneficiary households are also found threshing their crops in the mechanized way. Earlier those were done by manual labour. Though only two beneficiary households have their own thresher and sprayer but majorities of the households were found to use it by hiring in from the owner sources.

The mode of production of the tribal people was styled "familial" or "domestic". In any tribal family, the allocation of labour and production is geared to familial requirements, i.e., they produce what they need. Most of them were subsistence cultivators. The profit motive was totally absent among them. But now commercialization of agriculture is gradually taking place among them. With the introduction of modern agricultural equipment, irrigation facilities, improved seeds, chemical fertilizer, etc., the tribals are also begun to think about the cash crops. Now, they cannot think to keep their land fallow. They are producing various types of crops and better quantity of crops, which is in most of the cases more than their familial requirements. It is already mentioned in this chapter in Table 4.6.3, the production and productivity of major crops of agricultural loan beneficiaries are higher than the non-agricultural loan beneficiaries are. Not only that as they produced various types of crops they are engaged in cultivation almost round the year. It is also already found from the Table 4.6.2 that the cropping intensity of the beneficiary households is higher than the average cropping intensity of the district. As a result they are engaged in cultivation round the year and producing better yield and generating more income from cultivation. So, income and employment generation is taking place more and more.

Other than the agricultural loan beneficiaries specially the landless or some marginal farmers are now engaged in various types of occupations. Now they are not only depending on the income as a agricultural labourers. Besides this income, they are also generating income from their successfully implemented schemes. A remarkable tendency noticed among them to earn more money from any other alternate or subsidiary occupation. Some of the beneficiaries are found to engage as different types of businessman, as shopkeeper, as ricksaw-pooler and service holder also. Besides these they are also found to subsidise their family income working as various types of labour works. They are working as shaw mill worker, rice mill worker, labours in the brick field. So, occupational diversification is taking place more and more. This kind of diversification is quite uncommon in the traditional tribal economy.

With the increasing income and employment generation wealth generation is also increasing which was negligible in the past. Among the tribal people of the study area it was observed that they do not want to spend their generated income lavishly for liquor purposes or any other unnecessary and non-productive wealth generation. They are found to purchase land, the most valuable wealth for them. Sometimes they are also found to purchase either calf, goat etc. or alter their asset like buffalo for a bullock, which is more effective for better production. They are also used to purchase bicycles, wristwatch, torch, radio, etc.

Education and Social Change

Earlier days the tribal people were very conservative in assessing the relevance of present education in their life. After the introduction of so many facilities for the tribal student from the initial stage to the highest level it is observed that the tribal parents are feeling interest to procure the advantages of government facilities for their children. Though it is also not uncommon that one tribal parent treat the rupees for book grant, maintenance cost or scholarship as a source of their family income but a majority of them are conscious about the utility and relevance of education for their children. Almost every parent are trying to impart education to their children by sending them to the school at the age of six years without any discrimination of male or female child. It is also found that parent send their female child to hostel expecting her better and proper education. But, on the other hand, there is a contradiction also playing among them. From their experiences they formed an idea that who got education at the school turned out to be useless. As after the completion of education they became disinterested about any manual work and family lost his or her contribution to its economic activities. In spite of that they are now interested and accepted schooling for their children. It is due to their hope that if their child became educated then they can get some opportunities of service as government reservation policy for them is there. It is already mentioned that among the tribal people of the study area there is a tendency of higher education. There are some tribals are at Madhyamik level, H.S. level and though a very few but there are graduate and post graduates also.

Level of Living

All the economic and social development activities meant for the tribal people has brought about certain economic and social changes and this is truly reflected in their levels of living which is the end product of economic efforts. The term level of living, synonymously indicates the levels of consumption, because the pattern of consumption of a people throws light on their economic well being by bringing our relative importance of various items and groups of items in the total scheme of their consumption (Sengupta and Prasad,1973). To discuss the level of living, expenditure pattern including food consumption, level of use of durable consumer goods, expenditure on education, savings, agricultural investment and the housing condition have been considered.

Expenditure Pattern

Expenditure pattern is the most important indicator to understand the level of living. Food is the basic necessity of all living beings and consists of several components. Average amount of expenditure for food consumption has been calculated among the beneficiary households is Rs. 11,677/-, which is about 63 per cent of the total expenditure (Rs. 18,566/-). During the course of the field investigation it has been observed that the amount of money spent is proportionately lesser on grains and more on oils and fats, vegetables and as well as meat, fish and eggs. They buy fish and meat regularly from the hawkers who are visiting their villages in the morning. A habit of drinking tea in the morning with *muri* or bread is also noticed among them.

After the satisfaction of demand for food, clothing and housing are the needs for which human being make efforts to fulfil them. Among the four communities of Santal, Mahali, Kora and the Sardars, Santals specially the Santal woman are always keeping themselves neat and clean and fond of decorating their body with ornaments, flowers and *ulki* but only a few of them are found to have more than one pair of garments. It is same for the other communities also. Most of them are found to wear blouse and *sari* and female childs are found to wear frok. The men of all the communities usually use a small piece of *dhoti* or *lungi* as loincloth. Normally they do not use any upper garments but they are found to use banians and shirts when they go out side the village. But it is remarkable that almost every young man possesses pant and shirts and they are fond of decorating themselves with the modern dresses. In most of the cases only one time in a year and in some cases two times in a year they buy new cloths for all the members of a family. Mostly they prefer to buy it after the harvesting period and enjoying their most important annual festival. But in case of the Sardars there is an exception. They prefer to wear the new cloths at the time of Durga Puja or Kali Puja the most important Hindu festival. It is because of the fact that they are found to celebrate the Kali Puja in their own village. Average amount of expenditure for clothing is calculated Rs.184/-, which is about 3 per cent of the total expenditure per household.

After the expenditure for food and cloth the most important expenditure is the investment for agriculture purpose. All the male and female members of a household engaged themselves in agricultural activities. In very few cases they are found to invest money for hiring labour. They don't have to invest money for the natural manure like cow-dung or ashes. Those who have no cattle of their own, take it from the neighbour of their own village or from the neighbouring Hindu caste people. They are found to spend money for chemical fertilizer, HYV seeds and pesticides for the better yield. Next major and most important investment is for irrigation purpose. Few tribals have their own shallow tube well with pump set. In other cases they take water from the neighbouring caste or tribal people. It costs Rs. 30/- to Rs. 35/- per hour in case of pump set and Rs. 550/- to Rs. 600/- per season for the submersible pump. The tribal beneficiary households are also found to use thresher. Two beneficiary households have their own thresher. The other households take it from the owner of their own village or from the caste people by Rs. 60/- per day. By this way they do not cultivate only paddy they also cultivate wheat, potato, mustard, various types of cereals as well as various types of vegetables. It is calculated that on an average Rs. 5554/-, which is about 30 per cent of the total expenditure is invested for agricultural purposes. Thus, it is to be said that after the introduction of irrigation facilities and other modern agricultural equipment through the Integrated Tribal Development Projects the tribal people of the study area become more conscious and try to invest more for agriculture purpose for better yield.

After the satisfaction of demand of food and clothing and the major investment for agricultural purposes they are found to invest money for other necessities like health, education, ceremony, liquor and maintenance of house. Not only that a tendency of savings is also noticed among the beneficiary households. The tribal people of the study area are conscious about their health. Now, they are not totally depending on their traditional medicine man *ojhas* or *jangurus*. They try to take guidance from the modern medical practioners and use medicine for their treatment. It was calculated that on an average Rs. 48/-(0.26 per cent) they spent for medicine and treatment.

Another remarkable purpose of expenditure is for education. Though the calculated average percentage of expenditure for the purpose of education is not remarkable but their changing attitude about the utility and essentiality of education for their children is noticeable. It is important to note here that the illiterate parents, who are comparatively in better economic conditions, try to invest money besides the financial help of Government for giving the guidance of private tutor to their children.

The different phases of the productive activities of each of the tribal communities of the study area are always found to accompany by some rituals and ceremonies those are held communally at the village level and then at the household level. For communal festivals subscriptions in cash/kind are raised from every households. Besides their traditional festivals they are also found to celebrate some Hindu festivals like Saraswati Puja, Kali Puja, Manasa Puja, Dharam Puja and so on. In these cases also they collect subscription from every household. Besides these religious festivals they have to perpetuate some social ceremonies like marriage, obsequal ceremonies and so on. At the time of marriage for each of the tribal community there is a custom of paying bride price. The amount of bride price and the bride wealth is same for all irrespective of their socio-economic condition but it varies from tribe to tribe. In case of the Santal it is Rs. 11/- and 5 tins of paddy whereas in case of the Sardars it is Rs. 22/-. Among the Sardars a growing tendency of taking dowry of a heavy amount like the neighbouring caste people is remarkably noticed. During the field investigation one marriage ceremony was observed where the rate of dowry was Rs. 4000/- in cash and 7 brass metal utensils. At the time of marriage hosts have to entertain all the kins and the villagers with meat curry, rice and of course with a lot of rice beer. These kinds of entertainment continue upto 3-4 days. Not only that, in case of the Mahalis a custom is noticed that the parents of a bride or of a groom when invite their villagers, have to give some amount of rice with *bakor* (locally manufactured yeast, used in brewing) for the preparation of rice beer for the day of marriage.

At the time of obsequial ceremonies also they have to sacrifice some animals (Pig, Hen, Goat) and entertain all the members of the village and their kins with country liquor. However a good amount of money they have to spend at the time of various religious festivals and some ceremonial purposes for the fulfilment of their social obligations. It is accounted that on an average, a tribal household spends Rs. 295/- (1.59 per cent) for the ceremonial purposes in a year.

Generally, it is found that almost all the tribal people are very fond of drinking country liquor rice beer. They take it almost round the year specially during summer days and on festive occasions. At the time of any festive occasion it is very common to the tribal men to remain entirely on drink of rice beer for two to three days at a stretch. But now, it is found that the tribal people are reluctant to take it like this. Expenditure for liquor is gradually decreasing in some cases. But unfortunately side by side it is also noticed that some young people are becoming habituated

Table 4.7.2
Expenditure Pattern of Beneficiary Households

(In Rs.)

Food	Cloth	Medical Treat-ment	Education	Ceremony	Liquor	Agri-cult-ural Invest-ment	Maint--enance of House	Savings	Others	Total
11677	484	48	35	295	175	5554	80	54	164	18566
(62.89)	(2.61)	(0.26)	(0.19)	(1.59)	(0.94)	(29.91)	(0.43)	(0.29)	(0.88)	(100.00)

(Figures in parenthesis indicate the percentage)

Table 4.7.3
Housing Condition of the Beneficiaries

Kuncha			Pucca			Mixed		
Tatal No.	%	Average Value	Total No.	%	Average Value	Total No.	%	Average Value
261	98.86	13212	-	-	-	3	1.14	22045

to drink distilled liquor from outside, which is sold at everywhere through the distilleries. This liquor is high in alcohol content than their country liquor. This drink is expensive but these tribal people are prepared to spend their earning for it as they have fallen into the habit of taking a strong drink. On an average Rs. 175/- is their expenditure for liquor purposes, which is 1 per cent of the total expenditure (Table 4.7.2).

There is an another important issue of expenditure is for the maintenance of house. Most of the tribals of the study area live in mud-built houses, which require some maintenance at least one time in a year. After the harvesting period the tribals turn their attention for the repairing of their houses or built up of new huts. At this time all the members engaged themselves for this work. If any householder need any additional labour, he seeks the help of the other members of their village. Those neighbours extend their labour are not paid in cash or in kind. They are entertained with rice beer and puffed rice (*khichuri*). But an exception is also observed during the course of the study in the Sardar village, Dholtikuri. Here, one Sardar householder thatched his hut with new straw and got additional labour from two Sardar neighbours of his own village by paying Rs. 60/- per head per day. Generally, the necessary straw they get from their own field but the landless have to collect it from their landowners as a loan. It costs around five hundred rupees per *Kahan*, which varies according to the season. Bamboo is needed for the erection of their hut, which may be of their own or buy it from the market or collect from the neighbours. It is also found that they substituted it by the stem of the date palm or palm tree or any other trees those were collected and gathered during the storm from their locality. Sometimes, it is found that the beneficiary households replace their straw thatched roof by corrugated iron sheets, cementing their floors and made walls with bricks. These kinds of houses are called mixed type houses. In the study area it was observed that 98.86 per cent households live in *kancha* houses and average value is Rs. 13212/-. There are three households live in mixed type houses and their average value is Rs. 22045/- (Table 4.7.3). From Table 4.7.4 it is also found that a remarkable percentage (24.24 per cent) of beneficiary households have separate kitchen and separate cattle shed (28.79 per cent). Thus, it is clear here that with the increasing income of beneficiary households they are trying to spend their income for a better, safe and more hygienic condition.

Table 4.7.4
Distribution of Households of the Beneficiaries by Separate Kitchen, Separate Cattle Shed and Separate Latrine

	No.	%
Separate Kitchen	64	24.24
Separate Cattle shed	76	28.79
Separate Latrine	-	-

Lastly, the most important point is to be noted here that there is a tendency of savings is grown among them. They are found to make fixed deposit in the commercial bank and even found to save money by purchasing certificate of Life Insurance Corporation. Though the average amount (Rs. 50/-) and its percentage (0.29 per cent) to the total expenditure is negligible but tendency of thinking for their old age and also for their next generation is remarkable because generally they are always subsistence in nature and indifferent for the future.

Some percentage of money they spent for other purposes like maintenance of their cattles, and the other assets like radio, torch etc. as well as for some luxury goods. All these expenditures are accounted Rs. 164/- (0.88 per cent) and mentioned as others in the Table 4.7.1. Thus, from the above discussion it is clear that conspicuous consumption expenditure is increasing with income augmentation among the beneficiary households.

Health and Hygiene

During the field investigation, the general health condition of young generation and their sense of hygiene make an impression that they are far better than the old-aged people. Malnutrition and unhygienic habits have made the tribal people victim of several diseases. Their general complains was about their anaemic condition and tuberculosis. During the rainy season they generally suffer from ulcers, eye-ache and stomach-ache. Malaria is also rampant during this season. Both male and female suffer from these diseases. Earlier they seek the remedy from the tribal quakes or *ojhas* or *jangurus* and totally depending on the indigenous medicines. But now it is observed that their awareness regarding health and hygiene is increasing. Now, their income has increased and they are taking better foods. They are not only depending on their traditional medicines of traditional medicine man. They are now going to the hospital and take guidance from the modern medical practitioners and use medicines for treatment and some percentage of money spent for medical care. Tribal people were generally used their open air courtyard for cooking purposes and in the rainy season used one portion of enclosed veranda as a kitchen and another side as a cattle-shed. But now it is noticed specially who are above the subsistence level, have a separate kitchen and cattle-shed. They are found to sleep on the cots and use the mosquito nets regularly.

Cosmopoliteness

The Santal, the Mahali, the Kora and the Sardars each have a long tradition of managing their village affairs through Panchayats of their own. In the olden days, the traditional Panchayats were the only means through which disputes were settled and justice dispensed in the tribal areas. Through the introduction of Panchayati Raj the traditional Panchayats have suffered a setback. Government Panchayats have entered into the tribal's social organization. Though a compromise between the traditional Panchayats and statutory Panchayats has taken place, but it was felt during the field investigation that the power of traditional village system has weakened considerably. A large number of tribal people are found to go to the Government Panchayats at first to solve any kind of disputes like theft, assault, dispute about property, land disputes etc. Another group of people is found to go first time to their traditional Panchayat. If they are dissatisfied with their decisions they take the help of the statutory Panchayat. Thus, it may be said that the tribal solidarity is gradually weakening and the tribal village leaders do not command the implicit obedience of all the young and enlightened people. In the past, traditional Panchayat was all in all to settle any kind of disputes and enjoyed ample powers of punishment. But today the functions of the traditional Panchayat are mainly social and religious. They traditionally regulate all ceremonies and matters relating to birth, marriage and death even now. Besides this, some other minor village disputes falling within the jurisdiction of the traditional Panchayat are, breach of promise of marriage, restoration of bride, adultery, family quarrels relating to partition and succession of property and sometimes breach of village morality. After all types of breaches of the rules of clan exogamy and tribal endogamy are referred to the village Panchayats.

Today the tribals are in the sphere of modern democratic experiments. The periodical elections to elect representatives for Parliament and State Legislatures and village Panchayats have created a new awareness among the tribal voters regarding their political rights, power, alignments and functional roles of the leaders. Not only that they also take part actively in the Gram Panchayat elections. Women are also taking part in the process. The statutory Panchayat meeting is attended by at least one member of every household.

From the opinion, expression and attitude of tribals towards the administrators, Panchayat members explicit the change of their universe of thought and discourse and awareness about the present statutory Panchayat system. During the field investigations it was found that some tribal people have some complaints against the administrators regarding the allotment and distribution of developmental schemes of ITDP. These are as follows:

(i) Complain of breach of promises.

(ii) Complain about the administrator's partiality to some individuals as well as to some areas.

(iii) Complain against the administrators that they do not keep in touch with them except at the time of election.

(iv) Complain of corruption against the Panchayat members and bankers. They make an idea that these people take a bride from the whole-sellers and purchase the bad quality of units in low price. But the officially recorded project cost is higher than that price of purchase.

(v) Some tribals were noticed who make an idea that government Panchayat members and the Bankers should have some interest of getting concessions by giving them the facilities of loans and this system of giving loans is nothing but a business of the Government.

One Mahali young man expressed his doubt that though one elected Panchayat member do not get any remuneration but how he can spent his days at the Panchayat Office. He also complained against the Panchayat of squandering away of money of government those were scheduled for the upliftment of the tribals. He said that he makes the idea from the dissimilarity between the allotment he had heard from the radio broadcasting and their real experiences. In spite of so many complains against them in reality it is found that they influence the majority of the tribal people of the study area. Sometimes, many tribal people expressed their unwillingness to attend the political meetings or keeping regular contract with the Panchayat members or political leaders. But, in spite of that they have to do this from their interest to get government facilities specially to get the ITDP loans. Almost 100 per cent of them are found to make a regular contract with the members of Panchayat, Panchayat Pradhan, Secretary / Job assistant of Panchayat, Bank Officer, Local ruling Party leaders. Not only that it

Table 4.7.5

Distribution of Households According to the Extent of their Contact with Different Extension Personnel

Sl. No.	Source	Frequency of Meeting/Contact			Total No. of Beneficiary
		Frequently	Sometimes	Rarely	
1.	Members of Panchayat	257	7	-	264(100.00)
2.	Panchayat Pradhan	248	16	-	264(100.00)
3.	Secretary/Job Assistant of Panchayat	182	82	-	264(100.00)
4.	Inspector of ITDP	14	27	46	87(32.95)
5.	BDO	-	21	63	84(31.82)
6.	Bank officer	-	45	219	264(100.00)
7.	Members of Co-operative Society	26	62	12	100(37.88)
8.	Fellow Progressive Persons	35	42	109	186(70.45)
9.	Members of Social Organisation	-	8	26	34(12.88)
10.	Local Ruling Party Leaders	241	23	-	264(100.00)

(Figures in parenthesis indicate the percentage)

was also noticed they are used to contact with the inspector of ITDP, members of co-operative society, BDO, Bank Officers, fellow progressive persons or members of social organizations (Table 4.7.5) from their interest to avail the government facilities and suggestions also.

Thus, now the political life of the tribals is an admixture of the traditional and modern political set-up. The traditional village Panchayat is still exists and active in their social life whereas the statutory Panchayat is approached mainly for judicial matters. Political parties are actively creating for themselves a favourable atmosphere among the tribals, which has been able to create sometimes a political ambition in their mind and a sense of self-reliance.

4.8. Policy Recommendations

A number of development programmes taken up by the government for the socio-economic development of the tribal people in order to bring these backward people at par with the mainstream of the society. But from the overall discussion it reveals that in spite of these ameliorative measures the result has been far from satisfactory. On the basis of the identified constraints, which are hindering the successful implementation of the programme, following policy measures have been recommended to revitalize the schemes to set its fullest potential.

Policy Recommendation for Agricultural Development

(i) The land of the tribals should be brought under assured irrigation facilities to cultivate their land throughout the year.

(ii) There should be an arrangement of field demonstration, which will encourage the tribals to assimilate the techniques of modernization in agriculture and can easily accept the new varieties of crops and new methods of cultivation.

(iii) Cooperative Society should be started by which tribal people can get assistance from different sources pertaining to agriculture and allied activities.

(iv) Collection and proper distribution of products and inputs should be organised through regulated markets and marketing cooperations at the Block level.

(v) Short-term agricultural loan should be more available specially for the small and marginal farmers to make their land double and multiple cropping.

(vi) Training should be imparted for adoption of new agricultural technologies. It should be arranged irrespective of sex, as all the members of a tribal family participate in farm activities.

Policy Recommendations for Animal Husbandry Sector

(i) Quality of units of animal husbandry schemes like goat, sheep, calf etc. should be better and properly checked by the veterinary doctors and should be given some essential scientific advice for proper rearing.

(ii) When hybrid varieties of birds, goats and cows are supplied to the tribals then there should be an assurance of regular feed and medical aid.

(iii) Proper health measures are to be taken to cheque the epidemic of such birds and animals.

(iv) Veterinary services should be strengthened and designed in such a manner that the loanees can use the service upto their fullest capacity.

(v) Proper marketing facilities should be arranged for the animal husbandry schemes through co-operative society which can be effectively stop the exploitation of the middle-men.

Policy Recommendations for Basket Making Scheme of Mahalis

(i) Some special measures should be taken for the basket maker tribal community, the Mahalis.

There should be enough provision for supplying raw materials in low costs to encourage them to develop their own skill and industry.

(ii) There should be an arrangement of training to utilize their skill and originality to make modern equipment. Side by side marketing facilities should be arranged in such a manner that the tribal people without the help of any middle man can sell their wares in a profitable price.

Policy Recommendations in the Aspect of Tribal Education

(i) In case of education importance should be given to minimize the dropout students in order to utilize the maximum possible extent.

(ii) To encourage the tribal people more job-oriented education should be introduced.

Policy Recommendations for Extension of Credit, Basic Infrastructure Facilities and Formulation of Schemes

(i) Before implementing any scheme, technical feasibilities and other possible infrastructural facilities should be examined.

(ii) For each of the scheme a periodical/mid-term evaluation and thorough scrutiny for the assessment of its performance must be done by which lapses can be detected and may be remedied.

(iii) Along with agricultural loan or other family benefit schemes a special fund should be raised at Panchayet level and maintained as buffer for providing consumption loan to the poor tribal farmers at the lean period as well as for their immediate contingencies. All the responsibilities to look after and to keep it alive should be given to the tribal themselves. It will involve their self and thus, it is expected they will take proper care of the buffer and avoid misuse of it.

(iv) Those tribals who are at the lower rungs of the economic ladder should be given top priority. But, there should be a careful selection of the schemes for them, which will be in tune with their interest and absorptive capacity.

(v) Government loan should be given in proper time by minimizing the level of official formalities, which sometimes make the tribal people disinterested.

(vi) Tribals should aware about the usefulness/ necessity of repayment of government loan, which encouraging them for regular repayment.

(vii) Before execution of the work of any minor irrigation project, a proper technical survey is very much necessary. Regarding selection of sites the opinion of the local tribal people should be taken into consideration.

(viii) Preparation of the list of target group should be unbiased. Unnecessary political interference during implementation and selection of beneficiary should be avoided. Consultation may be done with the traditional institution at the village level and with the veteran persons.

(ix) It is essential to make them understand that the financial assistance of the government agencies is not for grabbing the assistance only as a recipient but for assist them to stand on their own feet to compete with the stronger brethren and participate as the equals with the larger society. It should help the tribal people to be self-reliant and self-confidant to avail the benefits under the Integrated Tribal Development Programme.

From the entire study it was felt that after a long run of development programmes among the tribal people of the study area two categories of people are emerged. One category consists of the people having lack of confidence about themselves regarding the implementation of developmental activities and never feel themselves as the integral part of the larger society. The other category consists of the people who actively participate in political activities and also involved themselves in monitoring the developmental activities. But after a certain period people feel alienated from the mass of their own society and also feel incongruent within the broad frame of administration and activities. However, policy should have the provision of ensured participation of tribal people. Their should be a policy to bridge up the gaps between the tribal people and the administrators.

In spite of so many changes occurred among the tribal people, cooperative feelings among them still exist. Now there should be some policies to make them duty conscious. Then the combination of cooperative fillings and duty consciousness will be helpful in implementing the programmes successfully.

Present policies are unidirectional. Concentration should be given on regional needs of the local people. Human relational dimension should be stated specifically in the policies. It may give the solutions to understand and to overcome the bad view of the tribal people about the administrators. In the policies it should reflect how to monitor the human relationship to analyse the peoples' thinking about the implementors and monitors.

5
Summary and Conclusion

Tribals are an integral part of Indian civilization. Though, in the context of aboriginality of the Indian tribes different views have been expressed by different authorities, yet they are popularly known as *adivasi,* i.e., the indigenous peoples. In the early historical period of India, which coincides with the Hindu period, the tribals either compromised with the Hindu neighbours or went in the deep forests. In this period tribals had more or less good relations with Hindu neighbours and find themselves assimilated to an extent with Hindu culture. The tribals enjoyed autonomy until the beginning of the Medieval period. By the end of 16th century they were harassed by the Mohammedan rulers and gradually lost their status.

During the British period the tribals had to face many conflicting situations. These people were approached in quite a different way. The policies, adopted by the British rulers, were primarily intended to isolate these people from the purview of the normal administration. The policy of isolation by the British Government was largely effected by their deliberate efforts not to develop communication in the tribal areas and as a result, the tribals remained cut off from the rest of the population and the mainstream of the economic and political life of the British India.

After independence, the Government of India thought of and planned for the upliftment of the tribal peoples. The Constitution of India contains many provisions for the protection and welfare of the tribal population. To sustain the constitutional safeguards given to them, Government also adopted many programmes through the plan periods.

During the First Five Year Plan Period Community Development Programme was launched. This programme along with other backward communities covered the tribal peoples. It was found that only 1 per cent of the total outlay was allotted for the tribal peoples. But soon it was felt that the tribal groups needed special treatment as the most of the tribal people lived in the hilly and forest regions, with poor communication and little institutional infrastructure.

To solve the problem of tribal regions/areas during Second Five Year Plan Period Multipurpose Tribal Development Project was launched as a part of Community Development Project. It covered 5.37 per cent tribal population of the country but the percentage of the total outlay for tribal development was decreased from 1 per cent to 0.9 per cent.

In the year 1961, the Commission under the chairmanship of U.N. Dhebar submitted the report by evaluating the actual position of planned development of the tribal community during the last two decades. The Commission observed that the development programmes lacked an integrated planned approach and recommended that the tribals and the concern for their welfare should be treated separately.

Special Tribal Development Block was renamed as Tribal Development Block in the Third Five Year Plan. These Blocks were multiplied except in case of West Bengal and Karnataka for their dispersed tribal population. During this plan period percentage of tribal population covered, increased to 32.50 per cent but it was significantly noticed that percentage of total outlay decreased to 0.6 per cent. It was also noticed that the programme did not have the desired impact and felt that the gains so far required to be consolidated.

The Community Development approach during the First Five Year Plan Period and Tribal Development Block approach of the Second and Third Five Year Plan, were essentially multisectoral in nature; hence the projects formulated and launched during these periods could do only a little for tribal welfare.

In the Fourth Five Year Plan Government decided to set up a Special Tribal Development Agencies in certain States like Andhra Pradesh, Bihar, Madhya Pradesh and Orissa for massive investment.

Up to this plan period the areas with more than two-thirds of tribal population only were identified for the implementation of the development programmes. As a result the areas with dispersed tribal population could not be covered.

On the eve of the Fifth Five Year Plan, in the year 1972, the Planning Commission constituted a working group for the tribal areas under the chairmanship of Sri H.N. Haldipur. The experiences and insights of the working group enabled the planners and policymakers to think in terms of formulating an integrated tribal development strategy with intimate linkages with national strategy. As a result, in the Fifth Five Year Plan a new strategy of Tribal Sub Plan was adopted within the broad frame-work of the country's development both at the State and national level. Tribal Sub Plan was adopted for the States and Union Territories having dispersed Tribal population by paying special attention to patches of tribal concentration.

Three categories of Projects were adopted for the Tribal Sub-Plan areas of which, Integrated Tribal Development Projects (ITDP) was for the areas having 50 per cent or more tribal population.

For the preparation of the Tribal Sub Plans, the Planning Commission issued a set of guidelines to the States. The guidelines laid down the criteria for the identification of Tribal Sub-Plan areas, the approach and strategy for their development and also the pattern of funding and formulation of programme in these areas. The guidelines further notes that each of the Sub-Plan areas in each State should comprise a number of viable projects. The unit of planning for an Integrated Tribal Development Project (ITDP) in a State comprised an aggregate of Development Blocks. The lowest unit identified in the programme is the development Block. It has a development team with the Block Development Officer as its leader. Programmes have to be planned for an ITDP in the shape of a Sub-Plan for the tribal region of the State. Guidelines laid down that the planning should be based on the needs of the area and the people, and hence, the process has to be commenced at the grass-root level, i.e., the development block and funneled upwards to the ITDP, State and National level.

Integrated Tribal Development Project was initiated as an area development approach. During the Sixth Plan emphasis was placed more on target group where individual families/households were the units. The families were selected on the basis of their economic status, the poorest being given the first preference. Any tribal householder of an ITDP Mouza, whose age is not below 18 years and income does not exceed Rs. 11,000/- per annum may take loans from the family benefit schemes.

In Birbhum district ITDP was launched in the year 1983, and various kinds of family benefit schemes were introduced in this area.

In the present study the researcher is intrigued to study empirically the extent and nature of adoption of the schemes by the tribal people of the study area and subsequently its impact on the lifestyle of the people. The study is also intended to evaluate the implementation of ITDP and to note the extent to which the programme has succeeded in improving economic and social status of the tribal beneficiaries in the area. An attempt has also been made to delineate the level of awareness of the people as well as their organizational capabilities in the context of the existing development programmes.

It was observed in the study area that in spite of financial assistance from ITDP; the tribal people have been exploiting private sources for loans and occasional monetary assistance. These are standing between the development agencies and the beneficiarics as an alternative. In the present study, an attempt has therefore been made to find out the contexts in which the tribal people are compelled to take loans from these alternative sources.

Four tribal groups are present in the study area. They are the Santal, the Mahali, the Kora and the Oraon, locally called Sardar. Numerically the Santal holds third position of all the tribal communities in India and in West Bengal they constitute the single largest tribal group. Primarily the Santal is known as an agriculturist tribe. The Mahali is primarily known as an artisan tribe having close affinity with the Mundary speaking peoples. The Koras are a little known community of the state of West Bengal. The term Kora seems to be a generic one, signifying the occupation of earth digging. In the present day they earn their livelihood primarily as cultivators and agricultural labourers in addition to their traditional occupation of digging tanks, wells etc. The Oraons form a community of settled agriculturists and best known in many parts of India as 'Dhangors', which may mean any hillman.

Each of the four tribal groups is largely controlled by the social cultural norms of the ethnic group at the village level. Every household of a tribal village is in fact, embedded within the larger social and cultural matrix of the village. It is reflected in every sphere of their life; their economic decisions, production, consumption, and distribution, ritual process, behaviour pattern during different village festivals etc.

Each of these tribal societies is a kin-based society. In their day to day interaction the relationship based on descent or affinity or proximal relationship are given more importance than their individual gain, benefit or wealth formation. They are characterized by a strong in-group sentiment.

Concluding Observations

Total 264 tribal households have been identified as beneficiary households. Of which 223 households are Santals, 18 households are Mahalis, 18 households are Sardars and only 5 households are the Koras.

The most important asset of the rural tribal people is their land. Most of the beneficiaries of the study area are marginal farmers. Next among the beneficiary households are small farmers. Then there are some landless beneficiaries. A few among the beneficiaries are medium farmers and large farmers. The average operational holding of land is higher among the Sardar beneficiaries. Generally all these tribal people leased in land from the neighbouring Hindu caste people and known as *bhagchasi,* i.e., the sharecroppers. The other category is the *kishan* who have neither land nor plough, mostly work as annual contract labourers in the land of landowner. Most of the sharecropper beneficiaries share the production with their landlord in the ratio of 75 : 25. In these cases all the inputted costs of cultivation are for the sharecroppers. When inputted costs of cultivation is equally shared by the sharecropper and the landlord then the ratio of sharing is 50 : 50. Some sharecropper beneficiaries are also there who shared the production during rainy season in the ratio 75 : 25, while during summer season they shared by 50 : 50 or 60 : 40. It depends on the sharing of inputted costs. The ratio of sharing between landlord and the *kishan* is 60 : 40.

Cultivation is the main occupation of majority of tribal beneficiaries in the study area. Besides, they are found to work as agricultural labourers. The important point was felt regarding the occupational pattern of the beneficiary households is that in so many cases each member of a household engaged in different types of occupations to earn more for their livelihood. This kind of diversification is prominent in case of the Santal households. Besides cultivator or agricultural labourers they are found to engage as rickshaw pooler, business man, service holders or various type of labourers like shaw mill or rice mill worker, mason or mason helper, labour in brick field and so on. Exceptions are noticed in a few cases among the traditional basket maker, the Mahalis. They try to continue their traditional occupation and are also found as service holder and as a mason.

Though the tribal individuals of the beneficiary households are found to engage in different types of occupations but it was noticed for every community that the major source of income is cultivation and then from agricultural labour. Beneficiary households have taken different types of schemes but income level of them are directly proportionate with their land size. Most of the landless beneficiaries and a good number of marginal farmers (63 out of 153) are still below the poverty line. On the other hand, the small farmers, medium farmers or large farmers are lying in the higher income level.

Among the beneficiaries, literacy rate is very poor. Most of them are illiterate. In case of literacy rate of beneficiary households for each of the category male literacy rate is higher than females.

It was however, observed that almost every parents are trying to impart education to their children by sending them to the school at the age of 6 years without any discrimination between male and female child. They are conscious about the utility of education for their children and interested to obtain all the financial support of government. But a contradiction also plays among them when one tribal family, the production unit of their economy faces a loss of their male or female child's contribution to its economic activities. As a result, educational levels of the beneficiary households show a high rate of dropout.

Educational level of a tribal household is directly proportionate to the economic condition of the household. This is because of the fact that the people who are at the lower rungs of the economic ladder are compelled to engage themselves earlier for earning to support their family income.

So many family benefit schemes are running under the Integrated Tribal Development Project in this project area of Birbhum. These schemes are designed for their economic protection and economic upliftment. Inputs of various sectors are intensified and channalized through these schemes among the tribal famillies. Five different categories of schemes are distributed among the beneficiary households. Those are: (i) Agriculturally related schemes (crop loan, bullock with cart and shallow tubewell with pump set); (ii) Animal husbandry and poultry bird schemes (calf rearing, goatary, duckary etc.); (iii) Schemes for trade and commerce (grocery, vegetable vending etc.); (iv) Some employment generating schemes (rickshaw, rickshaw van etc.) and (v) for bamboo work (specially for the traditional basket maker Mahalis). In terms of time duration all these schemes are two types. Only the crop loan is the short-term loan; given for only six months. Other than short-term crop loan all the schemes are medium term loans given for five years.

All the schemes are financed partly by subsidy and partly by bank loans. For the crop loan scheme no subsidy is given except for the tribals whose land size is upto one acre. Medium term loans are consisting of 50 per cent subsidy, 30 per cent bank loan and remaining 20 per cent margin money of the total project cost of a scheme. Bank loan and margin money should be returned with interest of 12 per cent and 4 per cent respectively within the due period of five years.

For getting a financial support from government one tribal individual has to go through a long-term official procedures like Panchayat, Block, Bank, Scheduled Caste and Scheduled Tribe Corporation etc. and take time of atleast one to two years.

For the landless households, two categories of schemes are there. One involves animal husbandry and the other involves trading like grocery, vegetable vending or other kinds of business. But from the acceptance pattern it appears that the scheme of animal husbandry is preferable to them than that of trading. All the tribal groups in this region have some knowledge of rearing animals, and the scheme of animal husbandry is thus within their capability. Trading involves not only risk but also more time and energy. The tribal people think that if they go for business, they would not get time to work in lands as labourer or sharecropper. Moreover, there is little capacity that this would be able to flourish in business since they have hardly any knowledge in it. Many of the landless tribals therefore, were not willing to accept the schemes of trading for fear of losing there masters confidence in them as labourer.

The marginal farmers have accepted almost all types of schemes of the economic sector but their most preference is animal husbandry sector. Side by side they are also found to lean for the schemes of agricultural sector like bullock with cart, Shallow Tube well with pump set and crop loan. These are most essential to them but they could never invest themselves. Due to small land holding and low productivity the marginal farmers are lacking surplus production. It results a scarcity of cash money among them.

The small, medium and large farmers obviously prefer the schemes of agriculturally related schemes. But it was significantly noticed that the small farmers have needed support for more or less every part of cultivating lands. Whereas, the large farmers, having a considerable land, accepted only the scheme of irrigation sector for increasing the capability for better and more yield.

Utilization nature of the accepted schemes is not so impressive. To a noteworthy percentage of beneficiaries the schemes were misutilized. Nature of misutilization for different types of schemes are different. According to their common nature seven different types of misutilization nature were identified. These are; consumption, ceremonies, religious festivals, midway breakup of the unit, savings, and purchase of asset and exclusively for liquor purposes. Though savings and purchase of assets are not misutilization, but here it has been considered as misutilization. Because the objectives of the schemes are to generate continuous employment vis-a-vis income with the help of the schemes. But the utilization nature of some beneficiaries did not fulfill such objectives. Most of the schemes were misutilized for midway break up (39.83 per cent) then for consumption purposes (35.59 per cent). Some factors are responsible for the midway breakup of a scheme like; loss of units, break down of assets, family breakage, death of beneficiary etc. It was significantly noticed that to a remarkable number of beneficiaries of animal husbandry schemes, the schemes were misutilized due to the quality of units. Either the units were very poor or their lack of adequacy for rearing new variety of birds and animals. Here, lack of awareness among the beneficiaries, lack of proper periodical veterinary service, guidance and suggestions for the recovery of units are also the reasons for the loss of units.

Other two noticeable natures of misutilizations are for ceremonies and for religious festivals, which is the integral part of their social and cultural life. The tribal village, as a community always trying to persist its solidarity and its distinct socio-cultural pattern. Every tribal household is, in fact, embedded within the larger social and cultural matrix of their own village. This is highly reflected during their various types of religious festivals round the year. All these festivals they perform communally and then at the household level of their own. For both the cases they have to sacrifice some animals like goat, hen, pig, duck etc. It is not surprising that a tribal individual use the accepted unit like, pig, hen, duck or goat for sacrifice or sell it to fulfill their social obligations to perpetuate their own identity. At that time it becomes more important to them than the importance of the scheme for making some profit for their future.

The short-term crop loan and the schemes those are directly related to agriculture utilized more properly by the beneficiaries than the schemes of animal husbandry sector, business sector or the sector of small scale industries. This is because of the fact that the beneficiaries who have some land, cultivation is their first and foremost source of income. They also earn by working as agricultural labourers or any other kinds of daily labourers. From this scheme the landholders can increase their income more easily by utilizing the agricultural equipment. Whereas to a landless beneficiary a scheme of animal husbandry sector can not give an immediate increase in income or can not be a continuous source of income. They get an asset from which they can earn some amount after a certain period of at least two years. By this time they have to face so many immediate contingencies or have to meet the social obligations during the ceremonies or rituals and various types of religious festivals those are the most integral part of their social life. For the fulfillment of this kind of unavoidable requirements they obviously use the readily available assets procured from the scheme.

Mobility and success of any developmental scheme is reflected in terms of repayment behaviour of the beneficiaries. In case of landless and marginal farmer beneficiaries it was largely found that the land of a beneficiary and his repayment performance is indissoluble with each other. But overall performance does not reveal that the land size of beneficiaries is the only major factor for their good repayment performance. It is quite obvious because of the fact that among the landless and in few cases of marginal farmers, whose major source of income is agricultural labour, deficiency exists round the year. All the income they generated from the scheme are being spent for consumption purposes and the loan remain unpaid.

A considerable number of beneficiaries are found to pay partly. Here also, round the year deficiency among the landless and marginal farmer households are responsible in majority of cases for partly payment of loans. After paying two or three instalments if any one miss the next instalment due to any contingency purpose Bank noticed him to pay the instalments by calculating the present amount of instalment with the last unpaid instalment with interest and the amounts become more. As a result, in this time he is not able to repay the full payment after meeting all the familial requirements. By this way if the due time of five years is over rate of interest of marginal money of his project cost is increased from 4 per cent to 10 per cent and the amount of instalment is increased more and more. By this time after a long period of repayment the beneficiaries were becoming frustrated about the complicated and long term system of cash repayment and stopped to repay the loan.

Best repayment performance of the beneficiaries is found in case of crop loan (82.62 per cent fully paid), which is the only scheme given for a short-term basis. To a landholder, crop loan is essential as it gives them HYV seeds, chemical fertilizer, minikit etc. Repayment of this loan is comparatively easy, as its amount is not so high and can repay their loan after harvesting. Realization regarding the facilities of this scheme from the previous experiences makes them interested to procure it again and again. They feel an urge of repayment as the no-dues certificate is needed when they will apply to obtain a crop loan for the next time. On the other hand, the amount of any medium term loan is comparatively high. They can not get any immediate action from the scheme and have to continue repayment for minimum five years and repayment must be in cash. Sometimes, these characteristics are becoming the factors for discontinuation of the repayment.

Twelve different reasons have identified for non-payment of loan on the basis of peoples' perception. These are:

(i) income was not generated from the schemes;
(ii) income generated from the scheme was spent on family consumption;

(iii) break down of assets;
(iv) used in purchase of alternative assets;
(v) incomplete unit was given;
(vi) death of beneficiary;
(vii) family breakage;
(viii) bad quality of units;
(ix) form an idea that loan is remitted;
(x) breach of promise of political leaders;
(xi) never noticed; and
(xii) willing defaulter.

Among these, the most common factor working behind the non-payment of loans are-generated income from the scheme totally spent for family consumption and then for bad quality of units or break down of assets or loss of units. For the first factor the social and economic aspects of the beneficiaries and for the second and third factor lacuna in the scheme itself are responsible for non-payment.

There are some other cases of default in which the beneficiaries are often reluctant to pay back the loans owing their power linkage to the local statutory bodies entrusted to look after the implementation and monitoring of the programmes. These people did not pay back their loans and took undue advantage of their positions in the local body.

The other beneficiaries expressed their attitude regarding the repayment of Government loans something differently. Sometimes their attitude reflect their value orientation, morality and liability to the Government and also to their own society. These are as follows:

(i) Some beneficiaries feel grateful to the government for the loans extended to them and think that repayment in time is their moral duty.
(ii) Another group of beneficiaries is interested to repay the loan only to get it again.
(iii) Some beneficiaries' attitude about repayment is not so spontaneous specially due to lack of success in implementation of the schemes and hence

benefits accrued have been partial or nothing.

(iv) Some people opined that if they fail to repay the loan, they will not only be going against the customary rules of their own community but also be lowering down the prestige of the other community members including those of their own family to the eyes of the administrators and welfare workers. There are, however, a few beneficiaries who nourish a fear of punishment from the Government if they fail to repay the loan.

After proper utilization, better repayment performance of the schemes of agriculture and irrigation sector, it is found that the schemes of these sector also get success in *performance* of implementation. On an average ninety-one per cent cases the agricultural associated schemes are running viably. This kind of successful implementation is obviously reflected on the cropping pattern, cropping intensity, production and productivity of major crops cultivated by the beneficiary households.

It was found that after the introduction of modern agricultural equipment and irrigation facilities they are not depending on the monsoon only. They are now cultivating various types of crops round the year and hence, their cropping intensity is increasing. District Birbhum is a mono-cropped area and average cropping intensity of the district is 110 per cent. Whereas for each of the category of the beneficiary households average cropping intensity is more than the average cropping intensity of the district. As a result, they are engaged in cultivation almost round the year.

An endeavour has been made to measure the impact of agricultural schemes on the production and productivity of major crops of the beneficiary households it was found that the productivity is better for the beneficiaries who have taken agriculturally associated schemes. The schemes of agriculture and irrigation sectors have thus made a positive impact on the income and employment of the beneficiary households.

The impact of the schemes other than agriculture or irrigation sector is however not so impressive. The schemes of animal husbandry have adopted by some beneficiaries. In all the cases, it was observed that the householders who have some cultivable land are doing better with their schemes than those who are totally landless. It may, however be noted in this connection that only the landless beneficiaries who have taken loans for rickshaw and rickshaw-van are doing quite well. These beneficiaries have been able to effectively exploit the market of rickshaw pulling in Bolpur-Santiniketan area, an important tourist spot in the district Birbhum.

Here, it reveals that the schemes have made a positive impact highly on the beneficiaries who have some land and can supplement their scheme from the income of cultivation. Whereas, in case of beneficiaries who have no land or a very small land, have made a low impact or sometimes negative impact. There are some beneficiaries who seem to be at ease with their schemes though they fail to have raised their average annual income above the poverty line. They have, however, been able to earn more than before. Not only that they also have a satisfaction as they can engage themselves more or less round the year.

Lack of awareness among the tribal beneficiaries is found to be another major and important reason for non-viability of a scheme. Majority of the beneficiaries is illiterate. The illiterate beneficiaries have no required technical awareness and other know how for maintenance of the assets provided to them. They are not sufficiently aware regarding the hygienic maintenance of new variety animals, quantity and quality of their feed requirements and its economics, etc. Lack of project formulation capabilities of the illiterate beneficiaries is reflected in case of the business, grocery, rice processing or vegetable vending schemes.

Besides these two major constraints, some other obstacles were identified those are hindering successful implementation of the schemes. These are as follows:-

1. Wrong identification of beneficiary.
2. Wrong selection of scheme.
3. Inadequate financial assistance.
4. Provided sub-standard quality assets.
5. Poor veterinary service.
6. Inadequate marketing facilities.
7. Lack of follow up assistance.
8. Lack of co-ordination.
9. Lack of project formulation capabilities of the beneficiaries.
10. Lack of training among the beneficiaries.
11. Chief interest of some beneficiaries in grabbing the assistance rather than running a scheme viably.

The schemes, however, could not make similar impact on the beneficiary households. Impact of the schemes whether it is positive or negative, and its constraints for proper implementation are involves activities and responsibilities both of the project functionaries and the beneficiaries themselves.

These are also reflected in the attitude and perception of the beneficiaries. Here again the land account of a beneficiary standing as a major factor in respect of his willingness or unwillingness for further acceptance of ITDP loans. Majority of the marginal farmers are unwilling about further acceptance. Reasons behind their unwillingness are:-

(i) afraid about the repayment in cash;

(ii) bad experience of inadequacy in financial assistance;

(iii) bad experience of substandard quality;

(iv) frustration about the long-term official process and formalities;

(v) long-term repayment procedure;

(vi) don't feel necessary of further assistance.

From the nature of willing schemes of the willing beneficiaries for further acceptance it is revealed that the landless and considerable numbers of marginal farmers prefer the animal husbandry schemes. Another good number of marginal farmers and most of the small farmers have preferred the short-term agricultural schemes, which will help them for a better yield but the schemes will be more easily accessible and more easy to repay. Their next preference is the medium term scheme of irrigation sector. Whereas, the large farmers have the only preference for medium term scheme of irrigation. They don't bother about the heavy amount project cost or about the long-term system of repayment.

The facilities of family benefit schemes are quite large but this kind of institutional credit covers only a part of the huge canvas of needs of the poor tribal people. The most important limitation of the institutional credit system of developmental project is that it never gives support when the poor tribals required a financial assistance purely for consumption and contingent activities. To solve this problem the tribal people are depending upon some private sources for borrowing money. And an alternative collateral system of informal credit exists with the institutional credit system.

Sources of the informal credit system are private moneylenders, *aratdar* (local assemblers), the landowners, friends or relatives and from other sources. Among these sources the most preferable source is the landowners. The landowners are generally the neighbouring Hindu Caste people in whose land most of the landless tribals are working as agricultural labourers round the year and the sharecroppers sharing lands with them and also working as agricultural labourers in their land.

It was found that the intention of taking loan from private sources by the landless and a major part of the marginal farmers are always to meet their round the year deficiency and immediate contingencies. Whereas, the small, medium or large farmer beneficiaries are always used to borrow money with an intention to improve their production as well as their level of income. Hence, it is to be said that though the government financial assistance is more relevant to the landless and the marginal farmers but in reality, as they are, the poorest of the poor remained at the same situation. Because, Government financial assistance never fulfill the real needs of these tribal people. Still they have to think about their own salvation from round the year deficiency and immediate contingencies, which were also the major problems before acceptance of a Government scheme. They therefore, try to get rid of the crucial situations and turn back to their age-old practice of taking loans from their landowners.

Three different categories of lenders were identified according to the pattern of interest taken from the borrowers. One category lends their money with interest (professional moneylenders, *aratders*) another category lends money without interest (landowners, friends, relatives, shaw mill or rice mill owners) and only a few lend on contractual basis. Majority of the borrowers borrowed money from the second category, i.e., without interest. Almost all of these borrowers have taken loans from their landowners. During the lean period when they have to confront an unavoidable deficiency or at the time of any other unavoidable immediate contingencies, they borrow money either in cash or in kind from their landowners. They never pay off their borrowed money in cash but by giving their labour at the season time without any remuneration. Here, the most significant feature is that their wage rate is counted not according to the wage rate of the season time but according to the wage rate when the landowners lend their money and the wage rate was very low. In case of a sharecropper, his pay-off money or crops are counted according to the market price of paddy of borrowing time not according to the price of the time of repayment. The sharecroppers are obliged to repay their loans just after harvesting and it was found that they are compelled to sell their paddy in low market price. Thus, an implicit interest is existing in this informal system of money lending. The tribal beneficiaries are not however, unaware of this kind of implicit interest. Yet they take it consciously but sometimes helplessly. Their perception is that they have no scope to get any financial help of government during their crucial time whereas the landowners are always with them as their reclaimers. Not only that, through this long-term practice, sometimes generation after generation they feel obliged to their reclaimers.

The long-term tenant-cultivator relationship and the superb minute adjustments in the entire range of terms and condition of this informal credit system seems to stand as complementary to these poor section of tribal beneficiaries rather than a substitute of the formal credit system. The matter of fact is that neither institutional nor non-institutional sources can fully meet the needs of the poor tribal borrowers.

The informal credit has its capabilities to supply loans as well as to receive repayments in a variety of forms and without any specific schedule of payment and repayment. Whereas, the institutional sources have some limitations on these aspects. Institutional loans are not easily available and go through a long term official procedures and a contractual obligations, which may be called enforceable but through a codified legal system.

The developmental schemes are often a way of bringing about changes, by which the particular community can be absorbed into the larger social organization in a planned manner. From the entire study, some observation have been noticed regarding the tribal peoples' extent and nature of socio-cultural and socio-economic changes after a long run of existing planned development for their upliftment in the study area.

Agriculture is the main source of income for the majority of the tribal beneficiaries of the study area. Earlier they used to practice traditional method for agriculture. Their technology was indigenous. But now they are adopting modern technologies like shallow tubewell with pump sets, thresher, sprayer and so on. They are also using HYV seeds, chemical fertilizer, pesticides etc. As a result a remarkable change in their modes of production is noticed.

The mode of production of the tribal people was styled "familial" or "domestic". They produced what they needed primarily for their subsistence. But now commercialization of agriculture is gradually taking place among them. With the introduction of modern agricultural facilities they have also began to think about the cash crops. Now, they cannot think to keep their land fallow. They are now producing various types of crops, and engaged in cultivation round the year. As a result the cropping intensity is increasing and therefore, employment generation is increasing. Use of improved seeds, chemical fertilizer, pesticides has increased their production and productivity and thereby, acquires some surplus productions besides their familial requirements. Hence, their capacity of income generation is increasing.

The landless beneficiaries are not only depending on agricultural labour-work; but also found to engage themselves in different types of business, shopkeeping, rickshaw pooling and service. A remarkable tendency to earn more money from any other alternative or subsidiary occupation is noticed among them. It results in an occupational diversification, among the people with perceptible economic motive, which was quite uncommon in the traditional tribal economy.

With the increasing income and employment generation, wealth generation is also increasing which was negligible in the past. They are now disinterested to spend their income lavishly for liquor purposes or any other unnecessary non-productive affairs. Their tendency is now to purchase land, the most valuable wealth for them.

The tribal people are now diversifying their expenditure pattern into several spheres. Earlier, they were used to expend most of their incomes on food. But due to increase in income and awareness they are now spending money for other durable consumer goods and also on education, health care etc. It is significantly noticed that a tendency of savings has also been developed. They also allot a remarkable amount for agriculture purposes to achieve better yield.

Earlier, the tribal people were very conservative in assessing the relevance of education in their life. After the introduction of so many facilities for the tribal student from the initial stage to the highest level, it is observed that the tribal parents are showing interest to procure the advantages of government facilities. Majorities of them are conscious about the utility and relevance of education for their children. Almost all parents are trying to impart education to their children by sending them to the school at the age of 6 years without any discrimination of male and female child. They are also aware about the reservation policy of government and hope that if their children are educated they can avail the opportunity of getting service in Government Offices/Institutions.

The general health condition of young generation and their sense of hygiene make an impression that they are far better than the old aged people. Now, their income has increased and they are taking better food; they seem to have overcome the very old problem of malnutrition. Now they are depending not only on their traditional medicines and traditional medicine man; they are also going to the hospital and taking guidance from the modern medical practitioners.

In the olden days, the traditional panchayats were the only means through which disputes were settled and justice dispensed within the tribal areas. But now the power of traditional village panchayat system has weakened considerably with the introduction of Panchayati Raj. The Traditional Panchayat was all in all to settle any kind of disputes and enjoyed ample power for punishment. But today their power and function is restricted within social and religious performances.

Today the tribals are in the sphere of modern democratic experiments. The periodical elections and regular connection with administrators, bankers and other personalities regarding the acceptance of government loans have awared them about their political rights, power, alignments and functional roles of the leaders in one side and on the other, a change have noticed in their universe of thought and discourse and created sometimes a political ambition in their mind and a sense of self reliance. Not only that they are also taking active role in the statutory Gram Panchayat elections.

In general, however, the process of upliftment/ modernization through the operation of developmental schemes is bringing about some significant impact as well as changes among the tribals but the rate of impact is evidently different from one individual to another in terms of degree. This unevenness of impact and change has been owing to the differential preparedness of the respective tribal individual to accept and use the opportunities available to them at one side and on the other side his existing economic status on the basis of landholding. The predetermined goals or objectives of development strategy also contradict with their broad canvas of needs.

Upliftment of the tribals from the poverty line and their integration to the mainstream is considered as the major objective of the developmental project. It is no doubt that the tribals are now close to the outside world. But do they feel integrated with the mainstream? If it is so, then till now the donor-recipient relationship between the management of development programme and its beneficiaries do not exist. Majority of them remain at the receiving end from where they only accept whatever is given to them by the delivery agencies and it automatically projects one superior to another.

The tribals are, however, passing through an accelerated phase of transformation. They are consciously or unconsciously maintaining equilibrium between the tribal solidarity, morality and ultimately social obligations to the traditional society with the growing sense of ownership, privatization of modernization and a contradiction between them. They are now running through a phase of admixture of these three. Whatever it may be it is to be said that the tribal development programmes have definitely broken the stagnation of tribal society and accelerated transformation.

Bibliography

Adhikary, Ashim Kumar; 1981 : "Development Programme and the Tribals : A Case Study of the Birhor : A Nomadic Hunting and Gathering Community of Orissa" in *The Profiles of the Marginal and Pre-farming Tribes of Central-Eastern India*, ed. by L.P. Vidhyarthi, Special Series No. 26, Bulletin of the Cultural Research Institute, Scheduled Castes and Tribes Welfare Department, Calcutta.

Adhikary, Ashim Kumar; 1985 : *Social and Cultural Organisation of Subsistence Activities : A Preliminary Appraisal of the Santals of West Bengal*, Palli Charcha Kendra (Centre for Rural Studies) Sriniketan, Visva-Bharati.

Aiyappan, A; 1960 : "Tribes in the South", *Seminar*, 14 October, 1960.

Bailey, F. G.; 1971 : "The Peasant View of Bad Life", in *Peasants and Peasant Societies*, ed. by Shanin, Penguin Mode in Sociology Readings.

Bailey, F. G.; 1960 : *Tribe, Caste and Nation*, Oxford University Press.

Baine, Sir A.; 1891 : *Census of India*, 1891, Report.

Bapuji, M.; 1993 : *Tribal Development Administration*, Kanishka Publishing House.

Belshaw, C. S.; 1972 : "Development : The Contribution of Anthropology", *International Social Science Journal*, 24 : 83 – 94.

Bhatt, Anil; 1990 : *Poverty, Tribals and Development : A Rehabilitation Approach*, Manohar Publications, New Delhi.

Bhowmik, K.L.; 1986 : *Tribal India : A Profile in Indian Ethnology*, The World Press Private Limited, Calcutta.

Bhowmik, Pradip Kumar; 1993 : *Dynamics of Tribal Development*, Inter India Publications, D – 17, Raja Garden, New Delhi.

Bhowmik, P.K.; 1982 : "Approach to Tribal Welfare", in *Tribal Development in India Problems and Prospects*, ed. by Buddhadev Choudhury, Inter India Publication, Delhi.

Bhowmik, P.K.; 1987 : "Development and Anthropology : Rebuilding Rural and Tribal Economy", in *Anthropology, Development and Nation Building*, ed. by A. K. Kalla and K.S. Singh, Concept Publishing Company, New Delhi.

Bhowmik, P.K.; 1996 : "Reconsidering Tribal Studies in India - Historicity, Development and Quality of life", *Everyman's Science*, Vol. XXXI, No. 1, April-May, 1996.

Bose, Nirmal Kumar; 1929 : *Cultural Anthropology and Essays*, Calcutta.

Bose, Nirmal Kumar; 1941 : "Hindu Method of Tribal Absorption", *Proceedings of the Indian Science Congress*, reprinted in Cultural Anthropology, Calcutta (first published in 1928).

Bradley-Birt, F. B.; 1903 : *Story of an Indian Upland, Chhotanagpur: A Little known Province of the Empire*, London, Smith Elder & Co.

Brahmachari, Mohan Kumar; 1991 : *Agrarian Development, Myth and Reality*, Manak Publication (P) Ltd.

Choudhury, Buddhadev; Choudhury, Sumita; 1982 : "On Some Tribal Problems", in *Tribal Development in India, Problems and Prospects*, ed. by Buddhadev Choudhury, Inter India Publication, Delhi.

Choudhury, M.K.; 1996 : "Impact of Tribal Planning in India with Special Emphasis on West Bengal" in *Socio-Economic Transformation in India*, ed. by Biswanath Ray, Kanishka Publishers, Distributors, New Delhi.

Clifton, James A; 1968 : *Introduction to Cultural Anthropology*, Houghton Mifflin Company, Boston.

Dalton, E.T.; 1982 : *Descriptive Ethnology of Bengal*, Bengal Government Press.

Dar, S.U.;1992 : *Impact of Integrated Rural Development Programme*, Anmol Publications, New Delhi.

Das, A.K.; Raha, M.K.; De, S.K.; 1990 : *Tribal Situation in West Bengal*, Firma KLM Private Ltd., Calcutta.

Das, A.K.; Raha, Manis Kumar; 1963 : *The Oraons of Sunderban*, Bulletin of the Cultural Research Institute, Special series No. 3, Tribal Welfare Department, Government of West Bengal.

Das, A.K.; Choudhuri, M.K.; Basu, S.K.; Saha, R.N.; Khan, N.C.; 1978 : *Scheduled Tribes and Scheduled Castes of West Bengal : Programmes Facts and Figures*, Cultural Research Institute, Scheduled Castes and Tribes Welfare Department, Government of West Bengal, Calcutta.

Das, B.; 1986 : "Development of the Tribal Economy : A Spatial Approach", *Kurukshetra* , Vol. XXXIV, No. 4, January, 1986.

Dasgupta, S.; Dhar, R.; 1975 : "An Approach to Development of Santal Pargana Tribal Area", *Integrated Tribal Development Planning*, Papers and Proceedings of Seminar held at NICD, Hyderabad May 2-4 1975, National Institute of Community Development, Hyderabad.

Datta, Samar Kumar; 1997 : *Changing Perspective on Rural Credit between Mid-80s and Mid 90s - Experiences of Two West Bengal Villages*, Working Paper, W.P. No. 1391, Indian Institute of Management Ahmedabad, India.

Deogaonkar, S.G.; 1994 : *Tribal Administration and Development*, Concept Publishing Company, New Delhi.

Deshai, A.R.; 1977 : *Tribe, Caste and Religion in India*, Ramesh Thapar (ed.), Macmillan Company of India Ltd., Delhi.

Dube, S.C.; 1960 : *Manav aur Sanskriti*, Delhi, Rajkamal Prakashan, (2nd edition 1969).

Dube, S.C.; 1998 : "Tribal Education" in *Antiquity to Modernity in Tribal India*, Vol. I, ed. by S.C. Dube, Inter-India Publications, D - 17 Raja Garden, New Delhi.

Dube, S.C.; 1998 : "Development Designs and Tribal People" in *Antiquity to Modernity in Tribal India*, Vol. I, ed. by S.C. Dube, Inter-India Publications, D - 17 Raja Gaden, New Delhi.

Dutta, S.K.; 1991 : *Cooperative Societies and Rural Development*, Mittal Publications, New Delhi.

Dutta, Sujit K; Ghosh, Dilip K.; 1994 : "Peoples Participation in Rural Development : Need and Scope", *Participation and Governance* Vol. 1, No. 2, November 1994.

Elwin, Verrier; 1942 : *The Loss of the Nerves : A Comparative Study of the Contact of People in the Aboriginal Areas of Bastul State, Central Province of India.*

Elwin, Verrier; 1944 : *The Aboriginals*, Oxford University Press, London, Revised Edition.

Elwin, Verrier; 1959 : *A Philosophy for NEFA*, Shillong, The Advisor to Governor of Assam.

Elwin Verrier; 1960 : *Committee on Special Multipurpose Tribal Development Blocks 1959 - Report*, Delhi, Manager of Publication.

Furer - Haimendorf, Christoph Von ; 1960 : *Seminar* 14, October, 1960.

Geertz, Clifford; 1993 : *The Interpretation of Cultures*, Fontana Press, An imprint at Harper Collins Publishers, 77-85 Fulham Palace Road, Hammersmith, London, W 6, 8JB.

Ghouse, Ghulam; 1975 : "Preparation of Integrated Tribal Development Project - Approach and Methodology", *Integrated Tribal Development Planning*, Papers and Proceedings of Seminar Held at the NICD Hyderabad, May 2-4, 1975.

Ghurye, G.S.; 1959 : *The Scheduled Tribes*, Bombay Popular Prakashan (3rd ed.; 1963).

Godelier, Maurice; 1977 : *Perspective in Marxist Anthropology*, Cambridge University Press.

Grierson ; 1931 : *Linguistic Survey of India*, Vol. IV.

Guha, B.S.; 1951 : *The Tribes of India*, 2 Vols., (ed.) New Delhi, Bharatiya Adimjati Sevak Sangh.

Guha, B.S.; 1955 : "Indian Aborigines and who they are", *Adivasi*, Delhi Publication Division (Revised 1960).

Hazra, Amit Kumar; Paul, Sujit Kumar; Mitra, Kakali; 1997 : "Santal Rituals and Agroecosystem", *Bulletin*, Cultural

Research Institute, Vol. XIX, No. 1, Backward Classes Welfare Department, Government of West Bengal.

Kalappa, A.; 1971 : "Tribal Development in Mysore", *Kurukshetra*, Vol. 15, May 1, 1971.

Mahalingam, S.; 1992 : *Tribal Cooperative System*, Rawal Publications, Jaipur.

Mahalingam, S.; 1988 : "Tribal Development Programmes : A Review", *Kurukshetra*, Vol. XXXVI, No. 4, January, 1988.

Majumdar, D.N.; 1950 : *The Affairs of a Tribe*, Universal Publishers, The Mall, Lucknow.

Majumdar, D.N.; Dutta Ray, B.; 1984 : *Tribal Occupational Mobility*, Research India Publications, Calcutta for North-East India, Council for Social Science Research, Shillong.

Mathur, Indu; 1987 : *Change in Agrarian Society*, Printwell Publishers, Jaipur.

Mathur, K.S.; 1972 : "Tribe in India : A Problem of Identification", *Tribal Situation in India*, Kumar Suresh Singh (ed.), Indian Institute of Advanced Study.

Mehta, Sushma; 1981 : "Problems of Tribal Development in India", *Vanyajati*, Vol. XXIX, No. 4, October, 1981.

Nongbri, T.; 1989 : "Some Reflections on Culture and Development Among the Tribes", *Vanyajati*, Vol. XXVII, No. 4, October, 1989.

O' Malley, L.S.; 1906 - 25 : *Bengal District Gazetteers*, Calcutta, Bengal Secretariat Book Depot., 38 Vols.

Pachauri, S.K.; 1984 : *Dynamics of Rural Development in Tribal Areas*, Concept Publishing Company, New Delhi.

Patel, M.L.; 1992 : "Economic Constraints of Tribal Development" in *Socio-Economic and Ecological Development*, ed. by Buddhadev Choudhury, Inter-India Publications. D-17, Raja Garden, New Delhi.

Patel, M.L.; 1994 : *Tribal Development without Tears*, Inter-India Publications, D-17 Raja Garden, New Delhi.

Patnaik, N.; 1972 : *Tribes and Their Development - A Study of Two Tribal Development Blocks in Orissa*, National Institute of Community Development, Hyderabad.

Pathy, Jaganath; 1984 : *Tribal Peasantry - Dynamics of Development, Inter India Publication*, New Delhi – 110015.

Pradip, Prabhu; 1993 : "Sustainable Tribal Development," *Indian Journal of Public Administration*, Vol. XXXIX, July-September, 1993, No. 3.

Prashad, L.M.; 1995 : "Ethics in Tribal Administration", *The Indian Journal of Public Administration*, July - September 1995, Vol. XII, No. 3.

Ragozin, Zianide A.;1961 : *Vedic India*, (2nd ed.), Munshiram Manoharlal, Delhi.

Ramaiah, P.; 1981 : *Tribal Economy of India*, Light and Life Publishers, New Delhi.

Ramaiah, P.; 1988 : *Issues in Tribal Development*, Chugh Publications, Allahabad (India).

Ramamani, V.S.; 1988 : *Tribal Economy, Problems and Prospects*, Chugh Publications, Allahabad.

Rao, P. Venkata; 1982 : "Tribal Development : Some Observations", Vanyajati, Vol. XXX, No. 4, October, 1982.

Rathnaiah, E.V.; 1977 : *Structural Constraints in Tribal Education*, Sterling Publishers Pvt. Ltd., AB/9 Safdarjang Enclave, New Delhi.

Report of the Commission for Scheduled Castes and Scheduled Tribes, April 1985 - March 1986, Eighth Report, ed. by Virendra Singh, Concept Publishing Company, New Delhi.

Report of the Commission for Scheduled Castes and Scheduled Tribes, 1983 - 84.

Risley, H.H.; 1891 : *The Tribes and Castes of Bengal*, Vol. I & II, Calcutta, Bengal Secretarial Press.

Roy Burman, B. K.; 1979 : "Challenges and Responses in Tribal India", in *Social Movements in India*, ed. by M.S.A. Rao, Manohar, New Delhi.

Roy Burman, B.K.; Harit, H.L.; 1991 : *A Preliminary Appraisal of the Scheduled Tribes of India*, New Delhi, Office of the Registrar-General, India.

Roy Burman, B.K.; 1995 : *Tribal Situation and Approach to Tribal Problems in India : A Preliminary Appraisal*, Rajiv Gandhi Institute for Contemporary Studies.

Roy, S.C.; 1915 : *The Oraons of Chhotanagpur*, Ranchi.

Roy, U.K.; Das, A. K.; Choudhury, M.K.; Basu, S.K.; 1980 : *A Look at Institutional Support for Development of Areas and People of West Bengal*, Special Series No. 25, Bulletin of the Cultural Research Institute, Scheduled Castes and Scheduled Tribes Welfare Department, Calcutta.

Sachapera, I.; 1956 : *Government and Politics in Tribal Societies*, Watts, 40 Dury Lane, London WC_2.

Sachchidananda; 1988 : *Social Change in Village India, Munda and Oraon*, Bookland Private Limited, Calcutta.

Sachchidananda; 1964 : *Culture Change in Tribal India, Munda and Oraon*, Bookland Private Limited, Calcutta.

Sanders, Irwin T.; 1985 : "Theories of Community Development", *Rural Sociology*.

Schneider, Harold K.; 1975 : "Economic Development and Anthropology", in *Annual Review of Anthropology*, B.J. Siegel, et. al. (ed.).

Sengupta, Sunil; Prasad, R.N.; 1973 : *Santal Rural Economy*, Agro-Economic Research Centre, Visva-Bharati, Santiniketan.

Sharma, B.D.; 1977 : "Administration for Tribal Development", *Indian Journal of Public Administration*, Vol. 23, No. 3.

Sharma, B.D.; 1986 : "New Education Policy and the Tribal People", *Indian Journal of Public Administration*, Vol. XXXII, July - September, 1986, No. 3.

Sharma, B.D.; 1993 : "Basic Issues in Tribal Development", in *Sparks from Bidisa*, Volume-one, Tribal Development, ed. by S.N. Ratha, Institute of Social Research and Applied Anthropology.

Shoobert ; 1931 : *Census of India 1931*, C.P. and Berar Report.

Singh, Bhupindar; 1985 : "Tribal Administration : A Critique", *Indian Journal of Public Administration*, Vol. XXXI, July - September, 1985, No. 3.

Singh, Bhupindar; 1990 : *Roll of Co-operative Organisations in Developing Economy*, Mittal Publications, New Delhi.

Singh, Bhupindar; 1998 : "The Tribal Sub-Plan : A Critique" in *Antiquity to Modernity in Tribal India*, Vol. I, ed. by S. C. Dube, Inter India Publication, New Delhi.

Singh, B.D.; 1992 : *Planning for Rural Development and Poverty Alleviation*, Mittal Publication, New Delhi.

Singh, K.S.; 1994 : *The Scheduled Tribes*, National Series, Vol. III, Anthropological Survey of India, Oxford University Press.

Singh, Sakendra Prasad; 1983 : "Development Programmes for the Tribals : Need for New Approach", *Indian Journal of Public Administration*, Vol. XXIX, October-December, 1983, No. 4.

Sinha, A.K.; 1992 : "Changing Dimensions of Tribal Economy in Chhotanagpur with Special Reference to their Problems among the Korwa Tribe" in *Socio-Economic and Ecological Development*, ed. by Buddhadev Choudhury, Inter India Publication, D - 17, Raja Garden, New Delhi.

Sinha, Surajit; 1981 : *Tribes and Indian Civilization, Structure and Transformation*, N.K. Bose Memorial Foundation, Varanasi.

Sparkman, Hohn J; 1961 : "Economic, Social and Political Implications of Community Development", *Community Development Review*, 6, 1-9, 1961.

Srichandan, G.K.; 1993 : Tribal Development and Welfare Legislation in Orissa, Prativa Prakashan, Delhi.

Tribal Sub-Plan, Annual Plan, 1994-95 : Development of Scheduled Castes and Tribal Welfare, Government of India.

Tripathi, Premendra; 1985 : "Administration for Tribal Development – an Analytical Review", *The Indian Journal of Public Administration.*

Trivedi, Hari Ballabh; 1988 : *Economic Development of Tribes in India*, Himanshu Publication, Delhi.

Verma, M.M.; 1996 : *Tribal Development in India : Problems and Perspective,* Mittal Publications, New Delhi.

Varma, R.B.S.; 1995 : "Development Administration and Integrated Rural Development Programme", *Contemporary Social Work,* Vol. XII, April 1995.

Vidyarthi, L.P.; 1963 : *The Maler : A Study in Nature Man-Spirit Complex of a Hill Tribe,* Calcutta Book Land Pvt. Ltd.

Vidyarthi, L.P.; 1966 : "Cultural Tribes in Tribal India with Special Reference to Tribal Bihar", *Proceeding of the Summer School of Anthropology,* Darjeeling, ed. by N.C. Choudhury, Calcutta, Anthropological Survey of India.

Vidyarthi, L.P.; 1981 : Forward, *The Profiles of the Marginal and Pre-farming Tribes of Central Eastern India,* ed. by L.P. Vidyarthi, Special series No. 26, Bulletin of the Cultural Research Institute, Scheduled Castes and Scheduled Tribe Welfare Department, Calcutta.

Vidyarthi, L.P.; Rai, B.K.; 1985 : *The Tribal Culture of India,* Concept Publishing Company, New Delhi.

Vyas, S.N.; 1967 : *India in the Ramayan Age,* Delhi, Atma Ram and Sons.

Zaheer, M.; 1975 : "Policy for the Planning of Development in Tribal Areas", *Integrated Tribal Development Planning,* Papers and Proceedings of Seminar held at the NICD, Hyderabad, May 2-4, 1975, National Institute of Community Development.

Index

M

N

O

P